MW01129034

ANGELS
AND
DEMONS

Agents of God & Satan. . . A Biblical Study

ANGELS AND DEMONS

Agents of God & Satan. . . A Biblical Study

VICTOR KNOWLES

COLLEGE PRESS
PUBLISHING COMPANY
Joplin, Missouri

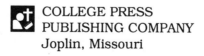

Second printing 1995

Library of Congress Catalog Card Number 94-071485
International Standard Book Number 0-89900-675-2

For My Father
Dale V. Knowles
Parent, Preacher, Poet

WMCA
NEW YORK • 570AM

I thank our Sovereign, Heavenly Father for using you so mightily on September 26th, when you were featured as a guest on WMCA Christian Radio's live, call-in talk show, "ANDY ANDERSEN LIVE," to discuss your book *ANGELS AND DEMONS*! It was so refreshing to hear your well-balanced, thoroughly biblical approach to this fascinating subject, which, sadly, is usually used as an opportunity for sensationalism and ear-tickling, or which is neglected or avoided altogether.

I am reading your book myself and have been tremendously edified and educated through your vast research and exhaustive study on this valuable topic. As I absorb the wealth of information you have deposited within the pages of this excellent work of yours, I am constantly reminded of the love and Fatherly protection that our Lord provides for His children, through the agency of His ministering angels. The Holy Spirit has filled me with an extra measure of peace, warmth and joy as a result of your book, which has helped me to become more sensitive and aware of the strong arms of Christ Jesus, securely wrapped around me in a loving embrace. How I marvel at the thought of His embracing me, when the only thing I truly deserve is to be crushed by His powerful arms and cast into Hell.

Your outstanding treatise has also reminded me of the nightmare I lived in, prior to my salvation, being inescapably trapped in the clutches of Satan's demonic host. I can never thank our merciful and gracious Redeemer enough for setting me free from the devil's grip, and for protecting me from ever being conquered and controlled by him again! My heart is grieved for my friends and loved ones who shun Christ, and in doing so, remain prey for Lucifer's ravenous wolves. I pray that our Sovereign Lord uses *ANGELS AND DEMONS* to open the eyes of many lost and wandering souls groping hopelessly in the darkness, so they can plainly see their only escape from the devil's dungeon . . . our Rescuer, Christ Jesus!

Brother Victor, may God always use your pen in powerful ways to strengthen the faith of true disciples, and to draw the lost into the light of Christ!

A station of
Salem Communications Corporation

Christopher J. Arnzen · P.O. Box 805 · Amityville, NY 11701

CONTENTS

INTRODUCTION

Angels are all the rage. According to *Publisher's Weekly*, five of the ten best-selling religious paperbacks are about angels. Secular bookstores like Waldenbooks and B. Dalton have devoted entire sections to such books as *A Book of Angels, Angel Letters, Touched by Angels, Where Angels Walk, Angels Watching Over Me,* and *Guardians of Hope and Messengers of Light.* The aforementioned *Angel Letters*, by Sophy Burnham, has sold 500,000 copies and has gone into its eighteenth printing. Religious bookstores, not to be outdone (certainly not to be outsold), have countered with two blockbuster sellers by novelist Frank Peretti, *This Present Darkness* and *Piercing the Darkness.*

The rage for angels seems to know no bounds – angel newsletters, angel seminars, even angels-only boutiques where you can buy angel figurines, angel sweaters, and angel jewelry. *Time* magazine reported that the nation's first lady, Hillary Rodham Clinton, wears a pair of gold angel's wings on days she needs a little extra help.

Television and movies have capitalized on the rage for angels. The late Michael Landon played the part of Jonathan Smith, an angel whose mission was to help people love each other, in the popular TV series *Highway to Heaven.* Jimmy Stewart was saved by the guardian angel Clarence, a lovable fellow who was trying to "earn his wings," in the holiday classic *It's a Wonderful Life. Wings of Desire* is a German movie about angels in the skies over the former West Berlin. Angels help big league baseball players catch fly balls in *Angels in the Outfield.* A Pulitzer-prize-winning Broadway play, *Angels in America*, features an angel ministering to a man afflicted with AIDS.

An angel even made the cover of *Time* magazine on December 27, 1993, "The New Age of Angels." The feature story, "Angels Among Us," reported that 69 percent of Americans believe in the existence of angels; 55 percent believe angels are "higher spiritual beings created by God with special powers to act as his agents on earth," while only 18 percent believe angels were "an important religious idea but merely symbolic." Thirty-two percent of those surveyed believe they have "personally felt an angelic presence in their life."

Some observers believe we are in the "third wave" of angel interest today. The first wave, of course, would be the biblical era. Angels are mentioned approximately three hundred times in Scripture. The second wave of interest in angels was generated during the Middle Ages, especially in the arts. Dante's *Divine Comedy* is replete with angel imagery. Milton's *Paradise Lost* and *Paradise Regained* (superbly illustrated by the English mystic William Blake) delve into the wonder of fallen angels. Renaissance artists like Angelico (appropriately named!), Raphael, and Michaelangelo (there it is again!) soared to new heights in painting angels. Handel is said to have had a profound angelic encounter while composing *Messiah*.

Much of today's fascination with angels, alas, seems to be more New Age than New Testament. Modern angelologists tell us that angels are positive thoughts, dreams, or ideas, whereas in biblical times angels were "ministering spirits" (Heb. 1:14) who appeared to God's people in the form of men (cf. Gen. 18:1,2; 19:1,2). One writer suggests we picture an angel above us with a vacuum hose, pulling all our negative, bad thoughts out of us. Such trivialization of angels leaves me feeling a bit empty!

The appearance of angels, according to the New Age angelologists, are accompanied by brilliant colors – especially blue and green. They are supposed to trail certain fragrances which have different meanings. The sudden scent of roses, for example, may indicate an angel has just passed by. The smell of a pine forest is supposed to signify an angel on a healing mission; the fragrance of sandalwood indicates the arrival of angels with an inspirational or instructional message.

One writer details how you can draw to yourself "designer angels" – assigning angels to oversee your painting, writing, music, teaching, business, etc. She believes we can even adopt our own angels and give them names. (Only two angels are named in Scripture, Michael and Gabriel.) Communication with angels and praying to angels is common among the New Age crowd. Such fascination borders on the worship of angels, forbidden in Scripture (Col. 2:18). In fact, angels can become a substitute savior if one is not careful. Always remember, as wrote John Francis Wade, in his great hymn, "O Come, All Ye Faithful," that Christ was "born the King of angels." Christ's superiority over angels is documented in Hebrews 1:5-14.

Should the current "third wave" rage over angels or the abuses of the New Age angelologists deter us from a healthy interest in these agents of God who have been divinely "sent forth to minister for those who will inherit salvation," i.e., you and me? Certainly not. Angels are still with us. God has not "recalled" them, as GM or Ford does with defective automobiles. If angels no longer exist or intervene in the affairs of men, how do we account for the many experiences believers have had in being providentially protected from injury or even divinely delivered from death? "The angel of the LORD encamps around those who fear him, and he delivers them" (Psa. 34:7). Angels continue their ministry of guiding, guarding, preserving, protecting, delivering, and even destroying.

Angels also continue their watch over the church (1 Cor. 11:10). Every day we are a "spectacle to angels" (1 Cor. 4:9). Angels are with us from here to eternity. The fact that most Christians never see angels does not negate their presence or work. The writer of Hebrews reminds us that many of God's people have "entertained angels unawares" (Heb.

13:2). We would sense their presence more if we would be more sensitive to their presence.

Angels are all around us. They minister to us. Some day God will signal them to bring us to heaven. Let's get acquainted with them *now* so we can thank them *then!*

—Victor Knowles

Part One:

ANGELS

1 WHY STUDY ANGELS?

"Why study about angels?" That is a perfectly legitimate question to ask. There is so much in the Bible to study. Even during a lifetime of studying we will never exhaust the Bible's vast storehouse of worthwhile subjects. This is not to suggest that the subject of angels (angelology) is not worthy of our consideration. To the contrary, there are several valid reasons why we should involve ourselves in a study of angels.

ANGELS: A BIBLICAL TOPIC

The Bible is the inspired Word of God. Any mention of anything is therefore of genuine significance. God has revealed His mind to us in His Word. What the Bible says about angels is what God wants us to know about these marvelous beings. This inspired teaching will be profitable to us. "All Scripture is God-breathed and is useful for teaching, rebuking, correcting and training in righteousness, so that the man of God may be thoroughly equipped for every good work" (2 Tim. 3:16,17). We should study angels, therefore, because it is a biblical topic and a helpful topic. To neglect the subject of angels is to rob ourselves of a great blessing. Billy Graham has testified that when he first decided to preach a sermon on angels, he found practically nothing in his library on the subject. Many teachers and preachers have found themselves in the same boat. Graham also stated that he had never heard anyone preach a sermon on angels (*Angels: God's Secret Agents*, pp. 7, 30).

NUMEROUS MENTION DEMANDS "EQUAL TIME"

We should also turn our attention to the angels of God because of the sheer number of times they are mentioned in the Bible. While numbers alone is not the main reason why a subject should be explored (consider how many times the words "a" and "the" appear in a book), yet the amazing number of times angels are mentioned in Scripture surely merits our attention. Think of how much column space is devoted in religious literature to the "rapture," a topic never mentioned at all in the Bible! Whole books have been devoted to the topic. Yet angels are mentioned about 300 times! Don't they demand "equal time"?

ANGELS ARE INTERESTED IN US

A third reason we should show an interest in angels is because they are extremely interested in us. In the parables of the lost sheep and the lost coin, Jesus declared that angels rejoice in the presence of God over the repentance of a sinner on earth (Luke 15:7, 10). Since all have sinned (Rom. 3:23), angels are interested in all of us. And if they are that interested in us, we should show some interest in them. Furthermore, the Bible teaches that angels watch over the church (1 Cor. 4:9; 11:10; 1 Tim. 5:21). Anyone who is that concerned about us should stimulate a like concern on our part. Angels desire to know more about the salvation we enjoy as blood-bought members of the church (1 Pet. 1:12). We should desire to know more about them.

WE SHALL BE LIKE THEM

Fourth, we should learn more about the angels because we shall be like them some day. Our Lord taught that in the resurrection we will neither marry nor die for we shall be "like the angels" (Luke 20:36). It seems reasonable that if we believe in heaven and our future existence, it will be both sensible and commendable to learn what we will be like before we get there. After all, we are going to be there a long, long time! It's nice to know now what it will be like. To get involved in this study of angels will sharpen our desire and whet our appetite to be with Jesus and the holy angels in heaven.

ANGELS MINISTER TO US

Still another reason to study angels is to increase our awareness of and enhance our appreciation for what angels do on our behalf. Angels have received a special commission from a loving Father in heaven to minister to those who will inherit eternal salvation (Heb. 1:14). That's you. That's me. Standing in the need of care – the daily ministry of caring angels. How foolish we would be not to understand or appreciate this fact. If we don't know how angels operate, how can we cooperate?

ENTERTAINING ANGELS UNAWARE

We should learn everything we can about angels because some of God's people have actually "entertained angels unaware" (Heb. 13:2). One example is godly Abraham who entertained angels without realizing who his guests actually were (Gen. 18:1-16; 19:1).

ANGELS PROVIDE "RAPID TRANSIT" TO HEAVEN

A seventh reason is because the Bible teaches that angels are our source of transport from this world to heaven. When a Christian dies, angels carry his spirit into the presence of God (Luke 16:22; Eccl. 12:7). Christians who are alive at the second coming of our Lord Jesus Christ will be gathered together by the angels and transported to their homes in heaven (Matt. 25:31; Luke 9:26). Talk about "rapid transit!" In life and in death we are constantly in the loving watchcare of the angels of God. It is for these reasons (and more could undoubtedly be added) that we undertake this noble study of these noble creatures.

2 ARE ANGELS FOR REAL?

Before we begin this study of what the Bible says about angels, one thing needs to be made clear: angels are for real. We are not talking about some imaginary, fanciful or make-believe creatures. Angels really do exist. Their continued existence today is not to be denied. This may be difficult for some today to accept. We live in a skeptical, cynical world. If men do not believe in the existence of God, why should they believe in the existence of angels? Nevertheless, God-fearing, Bible-believing, born-again Christians will believe in the presence and ministry of angels. The skeptical reader may be asking, "Why?" Why would any reasoning, rational person believe in angels? There are at least three good reasons for believing in the reality of angelic beings.

THE TESTIMONY OF SCRIPTURE

About 300 times in Scripture we find references to the heavenly messengers and ministers of God. A person's view of Scripture will largely determine whether or not he believes in angels. God's Word is true (John 17:17). It is impossible for God to lie (Titus 1:2). If God has declared in His Holy Word that angels exist, who is man to argue or resist? The apostle Paul wrote, "What if some did not have faith? Will their lack of faith nullify God's faithfulness? Not at all! Let God be true, and every man a liar" (Rom. 3:3,4). That is the Christian response to critics on any Biblical topic. The Christian believes that all Scripture is inspired of God (2 Tim. 3:16,17). If God speaks of angels in His Word (and He does, about 300 times), then it is simply a matter of our taking God at His word.

Our faith comes from hearing the Word of God (Rom. 10:17). Belief in angels, then is a matter of faith. Not blind faith either. Believing faith. Speaking personally, I have never (to my knowledge) seen an angel. Does that bother me? Not in the least. The Christian walks by faith, not sight (2 Cor. 5:7). Faith, Biblically defined, is the conviction of things not seen (Heb. 11:1). Most of us have never seen an angel but that does not mean we do not believe in their existence, presence and ministry. Our faith is solidly grounded in Scripture, and the Scriptures, time and time again, call witness to angels.

THE WITNESS OF JESUS

Angels must be real because Jesus Christ spoke of them as real beings. Jesus was truth personified. He declared, "I am the way and the truth and the life" (John 14:6). He did not just speak truth; He was truth. No guile or deceit ever passed His lips (1 Pet. 2:22). Everything that Jesus spoke was truth, including His many references to the angels. Henry H. Halley, in commenting on Jesus' teaching on the angels, wrote: "Jesus Himself said these things. His statements about angels are so specific, so varied, and so abundant that to explain them on the theory that Jesus was merely accommodating Himself to current beliefs would undermine the validity of any of Jesus' words as truth" (*Halley's Bible Handbook*, Abridged Edition, p. 336). Angels are for real because the Lord Jesus Christ spoke of them as such.

Concerning the testimony of the Old Testament to the reality of angels, C. Fred Dickason, author of *Angels: Elect and Evil*, writes,

> The Old Testament presents angels as genuine personal beings who serve as messengers and ministers of God. Their character, position, power, and activity are revealed in some

> detail. These creatures of God are either good or evil, depending on whether they serve God or Satan. They are so essentially bound in the narrative that to rip them from the record would do violence to the cause and continuity of many significant historical events and would destroy the concept of a moral battle that involves and yet transcends the human race (*Angels: Elect and Evil*, p. 19).

Summarizing the New Testament record of angels, Dickason continues:

> If there are no such beings as angels, then we must doubt some direct revelations and key attestations of truth presented as coming through angels in the New Testament. We must then also doubt the miraculous deliverances and interventions by angels in Acts and consider that the epistles are pure imagination or accommodation to ignorance when they speak of Christ's superiority to and victory over angels. We must ignore any reference to supernatural enemies and spiritual warfare in the Christian life. We must also regard the book of Revelation as either a fictional masterpiece of deception or a figurative mass of incoherent revelation. Furthermore, the more highly developed doctrine of Satan, his angels, their system and influence found in the New Testament revelation is complete speculation without any real correspondence in experience. And this is probably what Satan would desire to have us believe. But the New Testament gives abundant evidence of the existence of angels (*Ibid.*, p. 21).

PERSONAL EXPERIENCES

While personal experience should never take precedence over Scripture, the fact remains that many people have been ministered to by angels. This personal experience is actually based on what the Bible says about the work of angels. Angels, according to Hebrews 1:14, are ministering servants whom God has sent to help those who will inherit salvation. All who are saved and will enjoy eternal life have been – and are being – ministered to by the angels of God. If children are attended to by the angels (Matt. 18:10), then what of the children of God in the spiritual sense? Every grown person must look back on his life and admit that there were times when protection from injury or death could only be attributed to angelic intervention. The testimony of hundreds of thousands could be called on at this point. Perhaps they never saw the angel but they were certainly aware of some divinely sent presence that spared or protected them.

This reason is placed last because some will say it is pure subjectivism. Left to itself it could be considered as such. But the very fact that God says that angels exist to minister to us makes it subjective experience that is based on objective truth, i.e., the Word of God and the testimony of Jesus.

Again we cite Dickason:

> The combined witness of the Scriptures, the Old and New Testaments, and of the Saviour, assure us that there is a world of intelligent, powerful, invisible creatures about us and above us that warrants our prayerful and careful study and challenges us to expand our categories of thought and to change our conduct of life in accord with God's truth (*Angels: Elect and Evil*, p. 23).

Do you believe in the reality of angels? If you are not sure or somewhat reserved, it is hoped that this study will help you to appreciate more the ministry of angels. If you are already certain that angels are for real, may this study build an even greater faith in the God who, time and time again, has proved His love and faithfulness by sending His angels to minister to man.

3 WHAT IS AN ANGEL?

The Holy Spirit uses a variety of terms for angels in Scripture. This should not surprise us. Consider the different names and titles that we find for Jesus in the Bible: Alpha and Omega, Ancient of Days, the Anointed One, Branch of Righteousness, Bright and Morning Star, Captain, Christ, Consolation of Israel, Counselor, Emmanuel, Everlasting Father, Holy One, Messiah, Prince of Peace, Root of David, Seed of Abraham, Son of God, Son of Man, etc. It has been suggested by some that there are more than 200 different names and titles for Jesus in the Bible! There are so many different terms and titles for the other members of the Godhead, God and the Holy Spirit. Each of the names is significant and has special meaning. So it is with the angels.

DEFINITION OF "ANGEL"

The Hebrew word for angel, occurring some 100 times in the Old Testament, is *malak*. The word means to dispatch as a deputy or messenger, especially a messenger of God. The Greek word for angel, *angelos*, occurs some 165 times in the New Testament and also means a messenger.

W.E. Vine points out that "angels are always spoken of in the masculine gender, the feminine form of the word does not occur."

Herbert Lockyer says, "The word is chiefly used in the Bible to represent those superhuman beings whose abode is heaven and who function as the unseen agents in the execution of the will of God" (*Everything Jesus Taught*, p. 437).

Martin Luther defined an angel as "a spiritual creature without a body created by God for the service of Christendom and the church" (*Angels: God's Secret Agents*, p.8).

Smith's Bible Dictionary reads, "By the word 'angels' (i.e. 'messengers' of God) we ordinarily understand a race of spiritual beings of a nature exalted far above that of man, although infinitely removed from that of God – whose office is 'to do him service in heaven, and by his appointment to succor and defend men on earth.'"

John Calvin, in Volume I of his *Institutes of the Christian Religion* said, "Angels are the dispensers and administrators of the divine beneficence toward us. They regard our safety, undertake our defense, direct our ways, and exercise a constant solicitude that no evil befall us" (*Angels: God's Secret Agents*, pp.7, 8).

Charles Erdman has this to say about angels:

> What then are angels? Are they mere creatures of fancy, as fairies and gnomes and elfs? Is the word only a figure of speech which personifies the forces of nature and denotes winds or fire or storm? Or does the term describe the spirits of those who have survived death and constituted the inhabitants of the unseen world?
>
> Possibly no more helpful answer can be given than that of the author of Hebrews: "Are they not all ministering spirits sent forth to do service for the sake of them that shall inherit salvation?" Accordingly it must be concluded that they are actual beings, of surpassing power and intelligence, whose special task it is to serve God by their ministry to the people of God. Thus they are not divine. They are not to be worshiped. They are distinct from human beings who are living on earth or in heaven. Such seems to be the representation of Scripture. Men have been created "a little lower than the angels," yet in the world to come the redeemed are to "judge the angels."
>
> ...Aside from the statement of Scripture nothing is known of these mysterious beings. It is unwise to reject these statements as embodying ancient superstitions, and equally unwise to allow the fancy to play upon them with too great

freedom (*The Epistle to the Hebrews: An Exposition*, pp. 30, 31).

SEVENFOLD USE OF "ANGEL" IN SCRIPTURE

In her book *Angels and Demons*, Mrs. George C. Needham writes that the word angel is used in seven different senses in Scripture.

1. For human messengers. "And David sent messengers unto the men of Jabesh-gilead, and said unto them, Blessed be ye of the Lord, that ye have showed this kindness unto your lord, even unto Saul, and have buried him" (II Sam. 2:5). "And when the messengers of John were departed, he began to speak unto the people concerning John, What went ye out into the wilderness for to see? A reed shaken with the wind?" (Luke 7:24).

2. For human messengers bearing a divine message. "Then spake Haggai the Lord's messenger in the Lord's message unto the people, saying, I am with you, saith the Lord" (Hag. 1:13). "And my temptation which was in my flesh ye despised not, nor rejected; but received me as an angel of God, even as Jesus Christ" (Gal. 4:14).

3. For impersonal providences. "And lest I should be exalted above measure through the abundance of the revelations, there was given to me a thorn in the flesh, the messenger of Satan to buffet me, lest I should be exalted above measure" (II Cor. 12:7).

4. For bishops or pastors. "Unto the angel of the church of Ephesus write . . . Unto the angel of the church of the Laodiceans write . . ." (Rev. 2:1; 3:14).

5. For demons without bodies, who roam the air in partial bondage and take possession of men. These are called the Devil's angels, he being stated to be their prince (Matt. 12:24; 25:41).

6. For heavenly beings, such as guarded Jacob. "Jacob went on his way, and the angels of God met him. And when Jacob saw them, he said, This is God's host; and he

called the name of that place Mahanaim" (Gen. 32:1,2).

7. For one of pre-eminent excellency, named distinctively The angel of the Lord (Exod. 3:2). (*Angels and Demons*, pp. 16,17).

Of these seven different uses of the word angel in Scripture, we will be looking at numbers six and seven in particular in this book. Needham's belief that demons are fallen angels will be covered in Part II of this book, *Angels and Demons*.

BIBLICAL TITLES GIVEN TO ANGELS

In his work *The Ruin and Redemption of Man*, Burton W. Barber sees five different titles of angels, all of them ascribing a holy character to angels.

1. Angels are called "holy ones," "I saw in the visions . . . a watcher and an holy one came down from heaven" (Dan. 4:13). "The king saw a watcher and an holy one coming down from heaven, and saying, Hew the tree down and destroy it" (Dan. 4:23).

2. Angels are called "saints." "The Lord came from Sinai . . . he with ten thousands of saints: from his right hand went a fiery law for them" (Deut. 33:2).

"Then I heard one saint speaking, and another saint said unto that certain saint which spake, How long shall be the vision concerning the daily sacrifice? . . ." (Dan. 8:13).

3. Angels are called "sons of God," and "sons of the Mighty." "There was a day when the sons of God came to present themselves before the Lord, and Satan came also among them" (Job 1:6; 2:1).

"When the morning stars sang together, and all the sons of God shouted for joy?" (Job 38:7).

4. Angels are called "ministers" (of God). "Ye his angels . . . Bless ye the Lord, all ye his hosts; ye ministers of his, that do his pleasure" (Psa. 103:21).

"And of the angels he saith, Who maketh his angels spirits, and his ministers a flame of fire" (Heb. 1:7).

"Are they not all ministering spirits, sent forth to minister for them who shall be heirs of salvation?" (Heb. 1:14).

5. Angels are called "watchers" (of God's interests). "I saw in the visions . . . and, behold, a watcher and an holy one came down from heaven" (Dan. 4:13).

> This matter is by the decree of the watchers, and the demand by the word of the holy ones; to the intent that the living may know that the most high ruleth in the kingdom of men, and giveth it to whomsoever he will, and setteth up over it the basest of men (Dan. 4:23). (*The Ruin and Redemption of Man*, pp. 90,91).

Barber proceeds to show how all five titles are interconnected with holiness:

> (1) The title "holy ones" clearly attributes holiness to angels. (2) The title "saints" means substantially the same as "holy ones." Both "holy" and "saints" come from the same root word. Anything used of God is holy – such as an animal, a mountain, an altar, or a human being. But "saint" is used only to indicate a holy being or personality. (3) The titles "sons of God" and "sons of the Mighty" indicate a holy nature in that God is altogether holy, and therefore all of His "offspring" will be holy, too. Unless, and until, any offspring of God corrupts itself, it would be partaker of His holiness. (4) The title "ministers" indicates a holy nature inasmuch as God never uses any unholy servant to carry out his will. "Ministers" means "servants." And while he may coerce some unholy power or person to play a part in His divine program, yet that power or person is not willingly carrying out that divine will. Such would not be a servant of God, but a momentary slave. (5) The title "watchers" indicates the guardianship of God's divine program, kingdom, and will. They are trusted servants to see that God's will is carried out, and as such, they must be in full sympathy with His program (*The Ruin and Redemption of Man*, p. 91).

SUMMARY

What is an angel? Although they have a number of terms and titles in Scripture, we will content ourselves with this description: angels are holy messengers sent from God to minister to the needs of God's people, wherever they are, whatever their need.

4 THE ORIGIN OF ANGELS

Where did angels come from? Have they always existed? If not, how did they get here? We have already stated that angels are for real. The Bible, the inspired Word of God, mentions their existence time and time again. We believe the Bible. God said it, we believe it, that settles it. But the inquiring mind still asks, "Where did angels come from? When? Why?"

NOT PRE-EXISTENT

First of all, the Bible states that angels have not always existed. If they had, they would be on a par with the Godhead itself. God, Jesus and the Holy Spirit are self-existent and pre-existent. The word for God in Genesis 1:1 is plural. God said, "Let us make man in our image . . ." (Gen. 1:26). The entire Godhead cooperated in the creation of the world and man. The Godhead has always existed; not so with the angels.

Angels are servants of God. He sent them to serve those who would inherit salvation (Heb. 1:14). Jesus is superior to them (Heb. 1:4). "For to which of the angels did God ever say, 'You are my son; today I have become your Father'?" (Heb. 1:5).

CREATED BEINGS

The Bible clearly teaches that angels are created beings. In this sense they differ from Jesus, the Son of God, who–in spite of what Jehovah's Witnesses and other cults teach – was not a created being. The prophet Isaiah declared, "For to us a child is born, to us a son is given" (Isa. 9:6). As a child of Mary, Jesus was born; as the son of God, Jesus was given. The pre-existence of Jesus is taught in such Scriptures as Micah 5:2; John 1:1,2; 8:58; 17:5; Colossians 1:17; and Revelation 22:13. The angels of God were created by the Son of God, Jesus Christ. From Colossians 1:15-17 we learn the following:

1. Jesus created all things. "For by him all things were created . . . ." All things would of course include angels.

2. Jesus created the things in heaven. "Things in heaven and on earth . . . ." The angels dwell in heaven with God.

3. Jesus created all things, both seen and unseen. "Visible and invisible. . . ." Angels are invisible beings who can take on visible form.

4. Jesus created the various orders of angels. "Whether thrones or powers or rulers or authorities. . . ." These terms are generally understood to be talking about the rank and organization that exists among angels (see Eph. 6:12; Rom. 8:38).

5. Jesus created all things for Himself. "All things were created by him and for him." Angels ministered to Christ and continue to do His bidding.

WHY WERE ANGELS CREATED?

Have you ever wondered why angels were created? What was God's purpose and intent when He created the angels? C. Fred Dickason offers these thoughts:

> The primary purpose for the creation of angels was that they might glorify God and His Christ, for they were created 'for him' (Col. 1:16) . . . . In their intricate natures, angels reflect the creative wisdom and power of God (cf. Ezek. 28:12-15). In their activities they worship and serve God in the administration of His will (Heb. 1:7). They execute His commands with swift obedience and delight (*Angels: Elect*

and Evil, pp. 25,26).

Angels, therefore, were created to glorify God and to minister to mankind.

PROOF FROM THE OLD TESTAMENT

The Old Testament also teaches that the angels were created. The Psalmist states that angels should praise the Lord because they were created at His command. "Praise him, all his angels, praise him, all his heavenly hosts . . . . Let them praise the name of the Lord, for he commanded and they were created" (Psa. 148: 2,5).

The Levites praised God for creating all things, including the "hosts of heaven" (a term for angels) in Nehemiah 9:6.

God Himself, in questioning the patriarch Job, declared that the angels were present at the creation of the world and rejoiced in it. This means they must have been created before the creation of the world, "Where were you when I laid the earth's foundation? . . . while the morning stars sang together and all the angels shouted for joy?" (Job 38:4,7).

Angels, then, were created by Christ to do His bidding. This creation took place sometime before the creation of the world itself. When? C.C. Crawford wisely observes, "How long it was between the creation of angels and the creation of man we have no means of knowing, for the simple reason that eternity cannot be measured by our human concepts" (*Survey Course in Christian Doctrine*, Vol. I, p. 117).

CHRIST IS SUPERIOR TO ANGELS

The Book of Hebrews clearly teaches the superiority of Christ to the angels. The angels were a magnificent addition to the world, no doubt about it. But the coming of Jesus was a far greater addition as far as God's scheme of redemption was concerned. The first two chapters of Hebrews underscore this truth. Edward Fudge comments,

> In chapter one our author seems to have two points in mind. First, by showing Christ's superior position to angels, he sets forth also the superiority of the new covenant to the old covenant which was mediated by angels. Second, he prepares the way for chapter two, in which he explains how and why the Son became lower than the angels for a brief period of time (*Our Man in Heaven*, p. 15).

Charles Erdman adds,

> In the mind of the writer angels were venerated because of their part in the giving of the Law to Israel (Acts 7:53; Gal. 3:19). For this reason he begins his argument by proving the superiority of Christ to angels. Such proof might seem superfluous. If Christ was divine, why need he be compared with any created beings? It is because the writer is concerned with the work of mediating between God and men. Even a divine mediator might not be a perfect mediator. Yet one who was both divine and human would thus be perfect. For this reason the writer proceeds to show that Christ is superior to the greatest of all mediators, namely, the angels. He is superior because, as the Son of God, he is the supreme manifestation of God.
>
> The writer of the epistle proves this superiority by the quotation of seven Old Testament passages. Six of these are from the Psalms and one is from the Second Book of Samuel. By the way of contrast with the angels, Christ is declared to be a Son while they are servants; he is Sovereign while they are subjects; he is Creator while they are creatures; he is Heir of all things while they are ministers to those who are to inherit his salvation and to share his glory (*The Epistle to the Hebrews: An Exposition*, p. 31).

The writer of Hebrews begins his book by stating that Christ is superior to the angels.

> The Son is the radiance of God's glory and the exact representation of his being, sustaining all things by his

> powerful word. After he had provided purification for sins, he sat down at the right hand of the Majesty in heaven. So he became as much superior to the angels as the name he has inherited is superior to theirs (Heb. 1:3, 4).

Why is Jesus superior to the angels? For at least three reasons:

1. Jesus Is the Son: Angels Are Servants

"For which of the angels did God ever say, 'You are my Son; today I have become your Father'? Or again, 'I will be his Father, and he will be my Son'?" (Heb. 1:5). The first quotation is from Psalm 2:7; the second from 2 Samuel 7:14. Were any of they angels ever promised Sonship? No. What place do the angels have, then, in the government of God? They are servants. "And again, when God brings his first-born into the world, he says, 'Let all God's angels worship him.' In speaking of the angels he says, 'He makes his angels winds, and his servants flames of fire'" (Heb. 1:6,7). The first quotation is from Deuteronomy 32:43 (LXX) and Psalm 97:7; the second is from Psalm 104:4. The fact that angels worship Christ points to His superiority over these servants of God.

2. Jesus Is Sovereign; Angels Are Subjects

"But about the Son he says, 'Your throne, O God, will last for ever and ever, and righteousness will be the scepter of your kingdom. You have loved righteousness and hated wickedness; therefore God, your God, has set you above your companions by anointing you with the oil of joy" (Heb. 1:8,9). This is a quotation from Psalm 45:6,7 and shows how the Son of God was promised Sovereignty. The writer then asks, "To which of the angels did God ever say, 'Sit at my right hand until I make your enemies a footstool for your feet'?" (Heb. 1:13). The Psalmist is again being quoted (Psa. 110:1) to show that Jesus is Sovereign and angels are subject to Him. The writer continues, "Are not all angels ministering spirits sent to serve those who will inherit salvation?" (Heb. 1:14). Angels are willing subjects of King Jesus who minister to us who will inherit eternal salvation.

3. Jesus Is the Savior; Angels Minister to the Saved

> It is not to angels that he has subjected the world to come, about which we are speaking. But there is a place where someone has testified, "What is man that you are mindful of him, the son of man that you care for him? You made him a little lower than the angels; you crowned him with glory and honor and put everything under his feet" (Heb. 2:5-8).

The Hebrew writer here quotes from Psalm 8:4-6 showing that Christ was made a little lower than the angels. What does this mean? Isn't it a contradiction of what the writer has been saying? How can Jesus be superior to the angels and yet be made lower than the angels? Hear Erdman:

> . . . the fact that Christ for a time was made "a little lower than the angels" is no evidence against his being superior to the angels, for by incarnation and suffering and death he was qualified to render for man a ministry even higher than that assigned to angels. He became able to sympathize and to save, and is destined to be, as the Representative of man, the universal Sovereign in "the world to come" (*The Epistle to the Hebrews*: *An Exposition*, p. 42).

Christ, for a brief period of time, became a man in order to atone for man's sins. "But we see Jesus, who was made a little lower than the angels, now crowned with glory and honor because he suffered death, so that by the grace of God he might taste death for everyone" (Heb. 2:9). Our Lord was made lower than the angels only so He could suffer and die in the flesh for man's sin. In so doing, He became the Savior of man so that the angels could serve the saved. "Since the children have flesh and blood, he too shared in their humanity so that by his death he might destroy him who holds the power of death – that is, the devil – and free those who all their lives were held in slavery by their fear of death. For surely it is not angels he helps, but Abraham's descendants" (Heb. 2:14-16). Jesus did not die for angels. He died for men. Angels, as servants, minister to those for whom Christ died (Heb. 1:14).

SUMMARY

Angels, the created beings of God, know their place. Jesus Christ is the Son of God; they are the servants of God. He is Sovereign; they are humble and loyal subjects. Jesus is the Savior of the world; they are "ministering spirits sent to serve those who will inherit salvation."

5 THE NATURE OF ANGELS

What kind of nature do the angels have? Man, in the flesh, is a sinner (Eph. 2:3). Is this true of the angels as well? Man is tri-dimensional, having spirit, soul and body (1 Thess. 5:23). Are angels different from man in this respect? What is the nature of an angel?

SPIRIT BEINGS

Angels, essentially, are spirit beings. The Hebrew writer calls them "ministering spirits" (Heb. 1:14). What do we mean by "spirit" beings? We mean that angels, like God, are pure spirit in nature. God is spirit (John 4:24). Jesus taught that a spirit does not have flesh and bones (Luke 24:39). It should be noted, however, that angels – like God Himself – had the capability to "put on flesh" and, like God in the incarnation, did so when the situation merited such material manifestations.

Billy Graham said, "Our eyes are not constructed to see them ordinarily any more than we can see the dimensions of a nuclear field, the structure of atoms, or the electricity that flows through copper wiring. Our ability to sense reality is limited . . . . So why should we think it strange if men fail to perceive the evidences of angelic presence?" (*Angels: God's Secret Agents*, pp. 37, 38)

God is spirit, yet He was "manifested in the flesh" (1 Tim. 3:16). He did this when He came to earth in the person of His Son, Jesus Christ (John 1:1,14). Angels, although essentially spirit beings, also took on flesh to perform their God-directed duties on behalf of mankind.

For example, Genesis 18:2 says that three men appeared to Abraham by the oaks of Mamre. One of these three men was the Lord Himself (cf. vs. 1, 13). After being royally entertained by Abraham and his wife, two of the men departed for Sodom but Abraham "remained standing before the Lord" (Gen. 18:22). In Genesis 19:1 the two men, making their arrival in wicked Sodom, are now called "angels."

These spirit beings, angels, could and did make their appearance to men as men. Perhaps the Hebrew writer had Abraham in mind when he wrote that men should show hospitality to strangers since in so doing "some people have entertained angels without knowing it" (Heb. 13:2).

A New Testament example is Luke 24:4 where the women at the empty tomb of Jesus encountered two men clothed in shining garments. The men are later identified as angels in the chapter (Luke 24:23). John's account of this incident calls the two men "angels" (John 20:12).

According to Biblical evidence, angels are spirit beings who reside in heaven. When commissioned to go to earth to minister in some way to man, they generally appeared in human form.

HOLY BEINGS

Angels are also holy in nature. In the previous chapter we have seen how holiness in character is attributed to angels in their titles. In nature they are holy as well. Jesus often referred to "the holy angels" (Matt. 25:31; Mark 8:38; Luke 9:26, et al). Sometimes angels are called "the holy ones" (Dan. 4:17, et al). To be holy is to be like God. We are told to be holy because God is holy (1 Pet. 1:16.) To be holy is to be separated from sin. It is to live above sin. The angels choose to be holy. Those that chose to sin suffered terrible consequences (2 Pet. 2:4). When we say that angels are holy in nature we do not mean that they are completely sinless. Jesus Christ was the only person to ever live a totally sinless life (1 Pet. 2:22). The angels of God have a holy nature although they can sin if they choose to (Jude 6). Sins of a greater magnitude – such as the rebellion in heaven – seem to merit greater punishment.

As to nature, angels are both spiritual and holy.

6 CHARACTERISTICS OF ANGELS

We have seen that the Bible says that angels are both spiritual and holy in nature. Now let us consider several interesting characteristics of the angels of God.

MASCULINE

Jesus said that in the resurrection men would neither marry nor be given in marriage but would be "like the angels in heaven" (Matt. 22:30). Angels do not marry for the simple reason that they are all masculine. There is no support in Scripture for the idea that angels are sexless beings. The word for "angels" in Scripture always appears in the masculine form, never in the feminine or neuter. God is always referred to in the masculine gender and so are His angels. One can see how the artists have been influenced more by sentiment and superstition than the Scriptures in their beautiful but somewhat fanciful artistic conceptions of angels with feminine features. Concerning this, C.C. Crawford writes,

> It is obvious that pictorial representations of angels which have come down to us from medieval art, in which they are represented as creatures with wings, are unscriptural. Angels are invariably referred to in scripture in the masculine; furthermore, ethereal beings would have no need for wings. We must distinguish between scripture teaching and human tradition on all such subjects as this (*Survey Course in Christian Doctrine*, Vol. I, p. 119).

INNUMERABLE

The Bible also says that angels are innumerable. Obviously, since angels do not marry, there is no procreation, no "baby cherubs" that adorn so many beautiful Christmas cards. The number of angels today – whether good or bad – is the same number that has existed since creation. What is that number? Who can say? The Bible just calls them "innumerable" (Heb. 12:22 KJV). The New International Version reads, "You have come to thousands upon thousands of angels in joyful assembly."

Ten thousands of angels descended upon Mt. Sinai when Moses received the Law (Deut. 33:2). The New International Version says "myriads," a great but indefinite number. David mentioned 20,000, even thousands of angels at Mt. Sinai (Psa. 68:17). John the Revelator heard the voice of "many" angels around the throne of the Lord. How many? "Ten thousand times ten thousand, and thousands of thousands" (Rev. 5:11). An incredible number!

Daniel saw a magnificent vision of countless angels ministering to the white-robed, white-haired Ancient of Days who sat on a flaming throne. How many did Daniel see? "Thousands upon thousands, ten thousand times ten thousand" (Dan. 7:10). There is no word for "million" in Hebrew. A thousand thousands stood for a million, so 10,000 times 10,000 would be 100 million!

When well-meaning Peter came to Jesus' defense with a sword in Gethsemane, the Lord rebuked him with these words: "Do you think I cannot call on my Father, and he will at once put at my disposal more than twelve legions of angels?" (Matt. 26:53). A Roman legion consisted of 6,000 soldiers. Twelve legions would be 72,000 angels! Just a prayer from Jesus would have unleashed this great avenging horde!

SWIFT

Yet another characteristic of the angels is their swiftness with which they perform their God-ordained assignments. In the Lord's Prayer Jesus prayed, "Thy will be done on earth, as it is in heaven" (Matt. 6:10). How is the Lord's will done in heaven? It is done *instantly*, without hesitation or argumentation. The obedient angels serve as a wonderful example for us who dwell on earth. We should obey God with all haste as the angels in heaven do.

Angels can travel faster than the speed of light. In Biblical accounts, they appeared, disappeared and reappeared with amazing rapidity. "Faster than a speeding bullet" could truly be said of these super beings.

Abraham looked up one day and three men stood before him (Gen. 18:2). Their appearance was sudden, unexpected, unannounced. An angel suddenly blocked the road that Balaam was traveling. His donkey saw him right away but Balaam, for awhile, was not even aware of the angel's presence (Num. 22:22-35). Gideon looked up from threshing wheat to behold an angel sitting under an oak tree. When Gideon placed a meal on a nearby rock for the angel, fire flared from the rock and the angel instantly disappeared (Judges 6:11-21). An angel made a sudden appearance to Samson's mother and announced that she would have a son (Judges 13:3-9). Shepherds near Bethlehem were nearly scared out of their wits when a great number of angels "suddenly" joined the announcing angel (Luke 2:13).

Hungry lions, about to devour poor Daniel, suddenly had their mouths shut by an angel (Dan. 6:22). The angel Gabriel came to Daniel in "swift flight" with an important message (Dan. 9:21). Deep in the middle of a midnight sleep an angel awakened Peter and led him out of prison to safety (Acts 12:7). Proud Herod was smitten "immediately" by an angel (Acts 12:23).

Traversing space in the twinkling of an eye, the angels move from heaven to earth, from one place on earth to another, and back to heaven. Talk about a "space shuttle!"

Yet, because they are not omnipotent, their travels are sometimes delayed. A heavenly messenger was once detained for three weeks in his efforts to carry an important message to Daniel (Dan. 10:10-15). Only through the aid of Michael the archangel was the original messenger able to get by the prince of Persia (an apparent reference to Satan) and deliver his long-awaited message.

POWERFUL

A fourth unique characteristic of angels is their awesome power. These heavenly creatures are endowed with superhuman powers. Peter testified that angels are "greater in power and might" than men (2 Pet. 2:11). Peter could speak with authority, having been miraculously released from an inner prison by an angel (Acts 12:7-11). The Psalmist declares that angels "excel in strength" (Psa. 103:20). The Apostle Paul calls them "mighty" in 2 Thessalonians 1:7. The word he used for "mighty" is *dunamis*. We get "dynamite" from that word. Dynamite packs a powerful punch; so do the angels of God.

For example, an angel appeared in the center of a white-hot furnace to protect Shadrach, Meshach and Abednego. The raging fire had no power over him or the three Hebrews. This outstanding miracle caused a pagan king to marvel (Dan. 3:24-28). Fierce lions were about to mangle Daniel when an angel appeared in their midst and forced their slavering jaws shut (Dan. 6:22). Not a mark could be found on Daniel when he was taken up out of the den. The hovering death angel killed 185,000 Assyrian soldiers in one night (2 Kings 19:35). An angel rolled away a very great stone at the tomb of Jesus – a stone so large that the combined strength of several people could not budge it (Matt. 28:3; Mark 16:5).

In spite of their tremendous strength, angels are not all-powerful. God alone is omnipotent. As we mentioned earlier, Satan detained an angel from delivering an important message. Angels do not have authority to rebuke Satan. That power, too, belongs only to God (Jude 9). Angels are more powerful than men but not as powerful as God.

INTELLIGENT

Fifth, angels are known for their wisdom and intelligence. They are not just powerful creatures with no mind of their own. The wise woman of Tekoah, an intelligent lady herself, declared that David had wisdom "like that of an angel of God" (2 Sam. 14:20). Since they were able to view the creation of the world they have knowledge of that momentous event that no man enjoys. Having been sent on far-flung missions for God, they enjoy a vast reservoir of wisdom from their varied experiences. Vast and wide as their knowledge is, angels are not omniscient, all-knowing. Omniscience, like omnipotence, belongs exclusively to God.

For example, although angels will be favored by announcing the second coming of Christ, they do not know the day nor the hour of His coming (Matt. 24:36). Truly, fools rush in where angels fear to tread! The presumptuous date-setters claim to know what angels don't!

Angels take a great interest in the affairs of the church (Luke 15:7; 1 Cor 4:9; 11:10; 1 Tim 5:21). Yet, the church remains a great mystery to them. They long to know and understand the full meaning of the gospel story (1 Pet. 1:10-12).

Angels are not immune to making mistakes. They can err in judgment. Job 4:18 says God "charges his angels with error." The gravest error angels ever made was to join the Satanic rebellion in heaven whereby they were forced to leave their first estate (2 Pet. 2:4; Jude 6).

AGELESS

The last characteristic of angels we will consider is their agelessness. It appears that angels do not age, become ill or die. Jesus told the Sadducees (who did not believe in the resurrection) that in the resurrection, men and women would not die anymore but would be like the angels (Luke 20:27-36). The angels of God are not subject to the aging process, sickness or death. No wonder heaven will be so wonderful!

SUMMARY

In summary, we have seen that angels have several unique characteristics. Being masculine in gender they are innumerable, swift, strong, wise, and they never die. What a wonder these heavenly beings are! And to think that God has sent them to minister on our behalf (Heb. 1:14). How undeserving we are of such special and loving attention.

7 AUTHORITY AMONG ANGELS

The angels of God are not some loose-knit organization, some going off here and there at random, others criss-crossing their paths in wasted energy. Man, unfortunately, is like that (Isa. 53:6). It is not in man to direct his own steps – even though he tries and fails. It is not for angels to "do their own thing" either. A detailed sense of order exists among the countless colonies of angels. God is not the author of confusion (1 Cor. 14:33). In the Bible we see a very definite structure of order among the angels.

UNDER GOD AND JESUS CHRIST

The Bible teaches that the entire organization of holy angels is under the authority of God the Father and His Son, the Lord Jesus Christ. When our Lord ascended into heaven and took His rightful place at the right hand of God, "angels and authorities and powers" were made "subject unto him" (1 Pet. 3:22). Jesus is their "commander in-chief." In the garden of Gethsemane Jesus stated that He could have called for more than 12 legions of angels who could have prevented His impending capture (Matt. 26:53). Angels respond to Christ's command. Christ is the head of the angels. God is the head of Christ (1 Cor. 11:3). All the holy angels are in submission to God and Jesus Christ.

BY RIGHT OF CREATION

The angels are under divine control by virtue of creation. "For by him all things were created: things in heaven and on earth, visible and invisible, whether thrones or powers or rulers or authorities; all things were created by him and for him" (Col. 1:16). The "things in heaven," the "invisible" things, are undoubtedly a reference to angels. The expression "thrones or powers or rulers or authorities" may well be referring to angelic personalities as well, for in Ephesians 3:10 we discover that these rulers and authorities are in "the heavenly realms." By comparing 1 Peter 3:22 with Ephesians 1:21 it appears that these rulers, authorities, powers and dominions are indeed a part of the angelic structure that worship and serve God and Christ.

GRADED RANKS AMONG ANGELS

There are a number of Scriptures that imply organization and rank among the angels, both holy and unholy. Various levels in the angelic superstructure are seen in such titles as Thrones, Dominions, Principalities, Powers, Rulers, Authorities, Spiritual Hosts of Wickedness, etc. Some have attempted to grade and number these ranks but there does not seem to be enough hard evidence in Scripture to make such an organizational chart. That various ranks are implied is not to be doubted (see Rom. 8:38; 1 Cor. 15:24; Eph. 1:21; 3:10; 6:12; Col. 1:16; 2:10,15). By examining these passages we can gain some semblance of idea regarding angelic ranks. Consider the following comparison of translations on these passages on the next page.

W.E. Vine, compiler of *Vine's Expository Dictionary of Old and New Testament Words*, defines these words as follows:

1. Thrones (*thronos*). Metonymy for angelic powers.
2. Dominions (*kuriotes*). Lordship (*kurios*, a lord). A grade in the angelic orders, in which it stands second.
3. Principalities (*arche*). A supramundane being who exercises rule, both holy angels (Eph. 3:10) and evil angels (Col. 2:15).

King James Version	American Standard Version	New International Version
Ephesians 1:21		
principality	principality	rule
power	power	authority
might	might	power
dominion	dominion	dominion
Ephesians 3:10		
principalities	principalities	rulers
powers	powers	authorities
Ephesians 6:12		
principalities	principalities	rulers
powers	powers	authorities
rulers of the darkness of this world	rulers of the darkness of this world	powers of this dark world
spiritual wickedness in high places	spiritual wickedness in high places	spiritual forces of evil in the heavenly realms
Colossians 1:16		
thrones	thrones	thrones
dominions	dominions	powers
principalities	principalities	rulers
powers	powers	authorities
Colossians 2:10		
principality	principality	power
power	power	authority
Colossians 2:15		
principalities	principalities	powers
powers	powers	authorities

4. Powers (*dunamis, exousia*). Angelic beings.

5. Rulers (*kosmokrator*). Spirit powers, who, under the permissive will of God, and in consequence of human sin, exercise Satanic and therefore antagonistic authority over the world in its present condition of spiritual darkness and alienation from God.

6. Authorities (*exousia*). A spiritual potentate.

7. Spiritual Hosts of Wickedness (*pneumatikos*). Angelic hosts.

While we do not want to be dogmatic in assigning graded ranks to the angels, we should at least recognize that there appear to be several ranks among the angels, both bad and good.

MICHAEL THE ARCHANGEL

The Bible also indicates that above all the angels (but beneath God and Christ), is one special angel known as the "archangel." The word never appears in the plural, only in the singular. There are many angels; there is only one archangel. The prefix "arch" indicates a chief or principal angel. In Scripture we find this archangel's name to be Michael (Jude 9). "Michael" means "who is like unto the Lord." If we were putting together a simplified "flow chart" for the angelic organization, it would look like this:

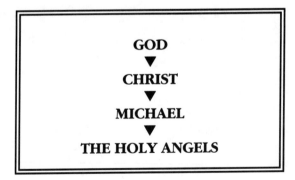

GOD
▼
CHRIST
▼
MICHAEL
▼
THE HOLY ANGELS

Michael plays a very important role in Scripture. He is associated with at least five major events in history. Let's look briefly at each of them.

1. Michael and his angels fought against the devil and his angels (Rev. 12:7-9). Some place this titanic struggle at the beginning of time and others choose to place it at the end of time. It would seem more fitting to place it at the very beginning of time since Michael and Satan are lifelong enemies in Scripture. In any event, a great war took place in heaven (Rev. 12:7). Satan and the angels that joined his rebellion were not strong enough to defeat Michael and his angels (Rev. 12:8). The devil and his angels were cast out of heaven and hurled to earth (Rev. 12:9).

2. Michael disputed with Satan over the body of Moses (Jude 9). The archangel is the archenemy of Satan! Why were they disputing over Moses' body? No one can say for sure. We do know that the Lord Himself buried Moses. The Bible says, "No one knows where his grave is" (Deut. 34:6). Perhaps Satan, devious spirit that he is, was trying to find the burial ground of Moses and turn it into a shrine in an attempt to get men to worship Moses instead of God. Or perhaps he was trying to wrest the spirit of Moses from the angels. Angels have charge of the dead and carry their departed spirits to God (Luke 16:22; Eccl. 12:7). Perhaps neither of these guesses is worth anything. In any event, the battle between Michael and Satan continues.

3. Michael came to the assistance of an angel that had been sent by God to Daniel but had been detained for 21 days by the prince of Persia (perhaps a reference to Satan). This account is found in Daniel 10:1-14. For three successive weeks the angel had tried to get a message to Daniel. Satan hindered him. Michael intervened and the original angel was able to deliver the message after all.

4. Michael will fight for God's people in the perilous times preceding the second coming of Jesus Christ (Dan. 12:1). He will protect the people of God and fight against his ancient nemesis once more. God's people will be delivered through the ministry of Michael.

5. Michael will co-announce the return of Jesus Christ (1 Thess. 4:16). Christ Himself will give a shout. The voice of Michael will be heard as well – "the voice of the archangel." Both voices will be joined by the trumpet call of God. At the same time, angels will gather people from the four corners of the earth for the final judgment (Matt. 13:41, 42; Mark 13:27). One other angel of note in Scripture is Gabriel, the announcing angel. We will give more detail to him in the chapter highlighting the various ministries of angels.

SUMMARY

In summary, the righteous angels of God are not left to themselves. They are under divine authority. Michael, the archangel, has been commissioned by the Creator to coordinate their work and service. All angels, Michael included, do the will of God and Jesus Christ.

8 CHERUBIM AND SERAPHIM

One of the first songs I remember singing in church as a small boy is Reginald Heber's *Holy, Holy, Holy*. The second stanza included a phrase that intrigued me: "Cherubim and seraphim falling down before Thee." What in the world is a cherubim? Or a seraphim?

This chapter will tell you who the cherubim and seraphim, mentioned several times in scripture, are. The following is taken from Burton W. Barber's book, *The Ruin and Redempion of Man* (P/R Publications, San Juan, Puerto Rico), and is reproduced here with author's kind permission.

THE CHERUBIM OF GOD'S GOVERNMENT

Ezekiel gives the only two lengthy references to cherubim in the Bible. These are to be found in chapter one and chapters nine and ten. The angelic creatures are not called cherubim in the first reference, but they are in the second and are identified as the same creatures. The first references introduces us to them thus: "It came to pass . . . as I was among the captives by the river Chebar, that the heavens were opened and I saw visions of God . . . . I looked and behold, a whirlwind came out of the north, a great cloud, and a fire engulfing itself, and a brightness was about it, and out of the midst thereof as the colour of amber, out of the midst of the fire. Also out of the midst thereof came the likeness of four living creatures" (Eze. 1:1-4). The second reference identifies these as cherubim: "This is the living creature that I saw by the river of Chebar . . . and I knew that they were the cherubims" (Eze. 10:15, 20).

In the Hebrew, the singular form is cherub and the plural form is indicated by the suffix "im" making the word "cherubim," although an "s" is sometimes used – "cherubims."

1. There are four cherubim: "Out of the midst thereof came the likeness of four living creatures" (Eze. 1:5).

2. Each cherub appeared to Ezekiel with the form of four faces: "Every one had four faces apiece . . . and the likeness of their faces was the same faces which I saw by the river of Chebar" (Eze. 10:21, 22).

3. Each face symbolized a distinct characteristic of cherubim: "As for the likeness of their faces, they four had the face of a man, and the face of a lion on the right side: and they four had the face of an ox on the left side: they four also had the face of an eagle" (Eze. 1:10). "Every one had four faces: the first face was the face of a cherub, and the second face was the face of a man, and the third the face of a lion, and the fourth the face of an eagle" (Eze. 10:14).

Since the two accounts represent the same creatures, the apparent difference of one of the faces ("ox" in 1:10 and "cherub" in 10:14) need not disturb us. Suffice it to say that "ox" is the best rendering if for no other reason than it is in keeping with the other figures which are of the "animal" kingdom. Thus, the four faces are: man, lion, ox, and eagle. The evident characteristics of each of these must surely denote kindred characteristics of cherubim. As a man is predominately intelligent, so are cherubim. As a lion is outstandingly courageous and fierce, so are cherubim. As an ox is patiently industrious, so are cherubim. As an eagle possesses a far-sighted view and speed for the execution of its objectives, so do cherubim.

4. These four characteristics are set forth in the prophet's visions of them.

(1) As a man is predominately an intelligent, responsive being, so are cherubim. These facts are evident from the first narrative: "This was their appearance; they had the likeness of a man . . . they had the hands of a man under their wings on their four sides . . . they four had the face of a man . . . whither the spirit was to go, they went" (Eze. 1:5, 8, 10, 12). These facts are evident in the second narrative: "When he (God) had commanded the man clothed with linen, saying, Take fire from between the wheels, from between the cherubims, then he went in and stood beside the wheels. And one cherub stretched forth his hand from between the cherubims unto the fire that was between the

cherubims, and took thereof, and put it into the hands of him that was clothed with linen: who took it, and went out" (Eze. 10:6-7).

(2) As an eagle possesses far-sighted vision and speed to execute its objectives, so do cherubim. Their perception is keen and their performance immediate.

First cherubim possess far-sighted vision: "Their wings were full of eyes round about them four" (1:18). "Their whole body, and their backs, and their hands, and their wings, and the wheels, were full of eyes round about them four" (1:18). "Their whole body, and their hands, and their wings, and the wheels, were full of eyes round about" (10:12).

Second, cherubim possess speed to execute their objectives. It seems significant that it was pointed out to Ezekiel several times that when they took flight, they need not turn around, but went straight forward: "They turned not when the went; they went every one straight forward . . . whither the spirit was to go, they went, and they turned not as they went" (10:11), also verse 22. This fact is stated at least six times, which apparently was to indicate speed of departure. But their speed of action is plainly stated: "The living creatures ran and returned as the appearance of a flash of lightning" (1:14).

(3) As an oxen is patiently industrious, so are the cherubim. They wait for the orders and then proceed to execute them. "The sole of their feet was like the sole of a calf's (ox's) foot . . . they four had the face of an ox" (1:7, 10). They appear to be pictured as an ox drawing a cart or wagon. Instead of being hitched to the wagon, however, they are seen attached to the wheels themselves. As will be seen later, these seem to be the wheels of the throne of the Almighty. Their connection with the wheels is as follows: "I beheld the living creatures, behold one wheel upon the earth by the living creatures . . . and when the living creatures went, the four wheels went by them: and when the living creatures were lifted up from the earth the wheels were lifted up. Whithersoever the spirit was to go, they went, thither was their spirit to go; and the wheels were lifted up over against them; for the spirit of the living creature was in the wheels. When those went, these went; and when those stood, these stood; and when those were lifted

up from the earth, the wheels were lifted up over against them: for the spirit of the living creature was in the wheels" (1:15-21). "(The cherubim's) whole body, and their backs, and their hands, and their wings, and the wheels, were full of eyes round about, even the wheels that they four had . . . and when the cherubims went, the wheels went by them: and when the cherubims lifted up their wings to mount up from the earth, the same wheels also turned not from beside them. When they stood, these stood; and when they were lifted up, these lifted up themselves also: for the spirit of the living creature was in them . . . and the cherubims lifted up their wings, and mounted up from the earth in my sight: when they went out, the wheels also were beside them" (10:12, 16, 17, 19).

Note the inseperableness of the cherubim and the wheels: "When the living creature went, the four wheels went by them: and when the living creatures were lifted up from the earth, the wheels were lifted up. Whithersoever the spirit was to go, they went, thither was their spirit to go . . . .for the spirit of the living creature was in the wheels. . . when those were lifted up from the earth, the wheels were lifted up over against them . . . when they went out, the wheels also were beside them." The cherubim appear to be in charge of one of the four wheels, so that having the same mind, the wheels carry about the throne of God.

(4) As a lion is outstandingly courageous and fierce so are the cherubim. Between the wheels resides the fierceness of God's wrath. "I looked, and, behold, a whirlwind came out of the north, a great cloud, and a fire enfolding itself, and a brightness was about it, and out of the midst thereof as the colour of amber, out of the midst of the fire. Also out of the midst thereof came the likeness of four living creatures . . . as for the likeness of the living creatures, their appearance was like burning coals of fire, and like the appearance of lamps; it went up and down among the living creatures; and the fire was bright, and out of the fire went forth lightning" (1:4, 5, 13). "Then I looked, and, behold, in the firmament that was above the head of the cherubims there appeared over them as it were a sapphire stone, as the appearance of the likeness of a throne. And he spake unto the man clothed with linen, and said, Go in between the wheels, even under the cherub, and fill thine hand with coals of fire from between the cherubims, and scatter them over the city . . . And it came to pass, that when he had commanded the man

clothed with linen, saying, Take fire from between the wheels, from between the cherubims; then he went in, and stood beside the wheels. And one cherub stretched forth his hand from between the cherubims unto the fire that was between the cherubims, and took thereof, and put it into the hands of him that was clothed with linen: who took it, and went out" (10:1, 2, 6, 7).

5. The cherubim escort the throne of God wherever He wishes to go: "When the living creatures went, the wheels went by them: and when the living creatures were lifted up from the earth, the wheels were lifted up . . . and when they went, I heard the noise of the wings, like the noise of great waters, as the voice of the Almighty, the voice of speech, as the noise of an host: when they stood, they let down their wings. There was a voice from the firmament (above) that was over their heads: when they stood, they let down their wings. And above the firmament that was over their heads was the likeness of a throne, as the appearance of a sapphire stone: and upon the likeness of the throne was the likeness as the appearance of a man above upon it . . . This was the appearance of the likeness of the glory of the Lord. And when I saw it, I fell upon my face, and I heard a voice of one that spake" (1:19, 24-28). "And the glory of the God of Israel was gone up from the cherub, whereupon he was . . . Then I looked, and, behold, in the firmament that was above the head of the cherubims there appeared over them as it were a sapphire stone, as the appearance of the likeness of a throne . . . Then the glory of the Lord went up from the cherub, and stood over the threshold of the house . . . and the cherubims lifted up their wings, and mounted up from the earth in my sight: when they went out, the wheels also were beside them, and every one stood at the door of the east gate of the Lord's house; and the glory of the God of Israel was over them above" (9:3; 10:1, 4, 19).

6. The following are fair conclusions which can be drawn from the Scriptures regarding the work of cherubim. Cherubim are beings of action. As has been noticed, they are pictured to us as possessing the dominant characteristics of a man, a lion, an ox, an eagle. They intelligently, courageously, patiently, industriously, swiftly see and execute their duties. They are said to perceive and act so speedily that no time appears to elapse between the giving of a commandment and its execution.

THE SERAPHIM OF GOD'S GOVERNMENT

1. *Seraphim are described by Isaiah.* "In the year that king Uzziah died I saw also the Lord sitting upon a throne, high and lifted up, and his train filled the temple. Above it stood the seraphims: each one had six wings; with twain he covered his face, and with twain he covered his feet, and with twain he did fly. And one cried unto another, and said, Holy, holy, holy, is the Lord of hosts: the whole earth is full of his glory. And the posts of the door moved at the voice of him that cried, and the house was filled with smoke. Then said I, Woe is me! for I am undone; because I am a man of unclean lips, and I dwell in the midst of a people of unclean lips: for mine eyes have seen the King, the Lord of hosts. Then flew one of the seraphims unto me, having a live coal in his hand, which he had taken with the tongs from off of the altar: and he laid it upon my mouth, and said, Lo, this hath touched thy lips; and thine iniquity is taken away, and thy sin purged. Also I heard the voice of the Lord, saying, Whom shall I send, and who will go for us? Then said I, Here am I; send me" (Isa. 6:1-8).

In the Hebrew, the singular form is "seraph" and the plural form is indicated by the suffix "im" making the word "seraphim," although an "s" is sometimes used – "seraphims."

Seraphim differ from cherubim in several respects. Though they both have similar appearance, having faces, feet, and wings, and both are in some way related to the righteous judgment of God, yet considerable differences are to be noted.

(1) They differ in appearance.

First, cherubim have four faces each: "Every one had four faces apiece" (Eze. 10:21), whereas seraphim have but one each: "Each one had six wings; with twain he covered his *face*" (Isa. 6:2).

Second, cherubim have four wings each: "Every one had four wings" (Eze. 1:6), whereas seraphim have six wings each: "Each one had six wings; with twain he covered his face, and with twain he covered his feet, and with twain he did fly" (Isa. 1:2).

(2) They differ in work.

Cherubim escort the throne of God, and the almighty speaks for Himself: "There was a voice from the firmament that was over their heads, when they stood, and had let down their wings. And above the firmament that was over their heads was the likeness of the throne . . . and upon the likeness of the throne was the likeness as the appearance of a man above upon it . . . This was the appearance of the likeness of the glory of the Lord. And when I saw it I fell upon my face, and I heard a voice of the one that spake" (Eze. 1:25-28). "The glory of the God of Israel was gone up from the cherub . . . then the glory of the Lord went up from the cherub . . . and the glory of the God of Israel was over them above" (Eze. 9:3; 10:1, 4, 19). Seraphim, however, speak in behalf of God: "One cried unto another, and said, Holy, holy, holy, is the Lord of hosts: the whole earth is full of his glory. And the posts of the door moved at the voice of him that cried . . . Then flew one of the seraphims unto me, having a live coal in his hand, which he had taken with the tongs from off the altar: and he laid it upon it upon my mouth, and said, Lo, this hath touched thy lips; and thine iniquity is taken away, and thy sin purged" (Isa. 6:3-7). "Seraphim" comes from "seraph" that means "brightness" or "burning."

2. *Seraphim as described by Christ.* "Before the throne there was a sea of glass like unto crystal: and in the midst of the throne, and round about the throne, were four beasts (living creatures) full of eyes before and behind. And the first beast was like a lion, and the second beast like a calf, and the third beast had the face of a man, and the fourth beast was like a flying eagle. And the four beasts had each of them six wings about him; and they were full of eyes within: and they rest not day and night, saying, Holy, holy, holy, Lord God Almighty, which was, and is, and is to come" (Rev. 4:6-8).

These creatures, called "beasts," but better translate to "living creatures," are commonly thought to be cherubim. The writer thinks otherwise.

(1) Some favor the cherubim. Like cherubim, they have four faces characteristics of a man, an eagle, an ox, and a lion. Also, they are said to be "full of eyes," just as the cherubim are.

(2) Some things favor the seraphim. Like the seraphim, they have six wings, not four, and speak, which seems not to be a characteristic of cherubim, but of seraphim. They say the thing that the seraphim of Isaiah do; namely, "Holy, holy, holy, Lord God Almighty."

It is possible that if Isaiah had given us a full description of the seraphim, they would have appeared more like the cherubim as Ezekiel's account represents them. In other words, it may be that they have four faces instead of one (though Isaiah mentions only one). And it may that each face resembles a man, an eagle, an ox, and a lion. Also it may be that they are full of eyes without and within. It is easier to believe that this may be so than it is to harmonize the number of wings (cherubim having four and seraphim having six), to say nothing of the position and use of them. And an important, though simple fact, is to remember that the creatures of Rev. 4 are heard saying the same thing that the creatures of Isa. 6, and we know the latter to be seraphim. While the cherubim, as Ezekiel pictures them, had an abundance of opportunities to speak, they said nothing.

Noteworthy Reflections:

(1) Comparative rank of cherubim and seraphim is unknown and is of little or no importance. But, it is evident that they are among the highest ranking creatures in God's Kingdom. They appear to be personal "aids" to Jehovah. Michael and Gabriel seem to be generals, for they are among the "chief" of angels. We noticed that Michael was particularly God's warring angel. Even so, cherubim are personal escorts of God's judgment throne. We also noticed that Gabriel was particularly God's announcing angel. Likewise, the seraphim are those creatures who ceaselessly praise God, and speak for God. They appear to be leaders of praise, because the passage in Revelation pictures the twenty-four elders and the hosts of angels falling before God to praise Him just as the seraphim did (Rev. 4:8-11; 5:8-12).

(2) Complete subjection to God is characteristic of all angelic beings, but particularly evident in the brief work of cherubim and seraphim. We cannot be otherwise than impressed with the unfaltering, unhesitating response of the cherubim to God's orders. We are no less impressed with the endless, tireless praise of the seraphim. If we are prone to wonder at, and be amazed by these creatures, we should

know that God is Wonderful. These creatures merely *know* it. Jehovah, not these angelic beings, are to receive our admiration.

(3) As was noticed relative to Michael and Gabriel, so we repeat concerning cherubim and seraphim that each would be as willing to mete out God's judgment as to speak the pleasing message of hope, and each would be as willing to praise God as to condemn man. For them to act, God needs only to speak. They act as all creatures should act. They praise God as all creatures should praise God. What we learn about them is not to stir in us appreciation for *them*, but to exemplify for us the praise and obedience for Jehovah that ought to be instant, and consistent.

9 SATAN IS AN ANGEL

Strange as it may seem, the devil himself is an angel. So far in this study we have been considering angels primarily in a good light. But the Bible also teaches that evil angels exist. These are angels who were created holy but chose to sin (2 Pet. 2:4; Jude 6). Satan was one of these.

The holy angels of God have a leader, Michael the archangel. The angels that have sinned have a leader, too. His name is Satan. Scripture refers to "the devil and his angels" (Matt. 25:41).

SATAN WAS ONCE A HOLY ANGEL

It is difficult for us to think of the devil being an angel. Our minds envision angels as being holy beings. And, for the most part, they are. Satan and his angels are the exceptions to this rule. Satan, at one time, was good. God made all things (Neh. 9:6; Isa. 44:24; Eph. 3:8, 9; Col. 1:16; Rev. 4:11). After God had created every living creature He declared that His work was good (Gen. 1:24, 25). Before creation of the world He created the angels, for they observed the creative process and rejoiced over it (Psa. 148:2, 5).

Jesus taught that Satan did not remain in good state: "He was a murderer from the beginning, not holding to the truth, for there is no truth in him" (John 8:44). The King James Version says "he abode not in the truth." You have to be *in* the truth before you can depart from it. Satan was once good and abode in truth.

THE UNHOLY TRINITY: PRIDE, JEALOUSY, AMBITION

Apparently, Satan corrupted himself, for we certainly cannot put the blame on God. Our heavenly Father does not attempt to tempt anyone – Satan included – with evil. "Each one is tempted, when, by his own evil desire, he is dragged away and enticed" (Jas. 1:14). This is how it must have been with Satan. He sinned by choice, just as Adam and Eve did in the garden.

The Bible seems to indicate that pride was the downfall of the devil. The apostle Paul says that pride was the condemnation of the devil (1 Tim. 3:6), and warns would-be leaders in God's Church about the same danger. Perhaps Satan became proud of his position as an angel and reached out, wanting more power and authority. What else would there be in heaven to battle for? It is possible that he may have harbored bitter envy and selfish ambition in his heart, for James says that such "wisdom" is "of the devil" (Jas. 3:14, 15).

C. C. Crawford states that pride, jealousy and ambition were the devil's undoing:

> (1) This is intimated in 1 Tim. 3:6 – "not a novice, lest being puffed up he fall into the condemnation of the devil." Here the apostle Paul admonishes Timothy not to appoint a new convert to the responsible position of an elder in a local church, lest being puffed up with pride, he should fall into the condemnation of the devil; that is lest he should fall, as Satan himself fell, by becoming inordinately proud and ambitious. (2) Isa. 14:13-15, "For thou hast said in thine heart, I will ascend into heaven. I will exalt my throne above the stars of God, I will be like the Most High. Yet thou shalt be brought down to hell, to the sides of the pit" (A. V.). Ezek. 28:15-17, "Thou wast perfect in thy ways from the day that thou wast created, till iniquity was found in thee . . . . Thine heart was lifted up because of thy beauty; thou hast corrupted thy wisdom by reason of thy brightness" (A. V.). These references could scarcely have been made with reference to earthly monarchs. It seems evident that orthodox Christian Scholarship is right in interpreting them as allud-

ing to the rebellion and fall of Lucifer. (3) It seems that the archangel's fall was due to pride, jealousy and false ambition; and that his appeal to his fellow creatures was the specious plea of "personal liberty" – a plea which has damned more souls than any other single lie. It is quite possible that he influenced other angels with false charges and lying accusations against God, as, for example that the Creator was tyrannical and unjust in imposing His will upon free creatures, etc.; and that he exhorted them to follow him in breaking away from all divine restraint and in setting up a rival government somewhere in the heavens. Many of the angels evidently listened to his lies and followed him into open rebellion; but by far the greater number rejected his appeal and remained loyal to the divine government (*Survey in Christian Doctrine,* Vol. I, p. 130).

Robert Milligan adds,

How pride got possession of Satan's heart it may be difficult for us to conceive. But it seems probable, from the statement of Paul in Timothy, that it was in some way owing to his elevation above those around him. He may have once been the Archangel, superior even to Michael. But in his evil hour his eye was turned from his Creator to himself as the highest, the most gifted, and the most influential of all creatures of God. His heart swelled with pride; ambition took possession of his soul; and rebellion was then seen in Heaven.

"But justice and judgment are the dwelling-place of God's throne" Psalm 89:14. He reigns in the midst of the most perfect righteousness, and no sin can be tolerated for a moment in his presence. And hence he had but to speak the word, and Satan, with all his rebel hosts that kept not their first estate, were instantly cast out of Heaven and bound in "eternal chains under darkness to the judgment of the Great Day" Jude 5, 6 (*An Exposition and Defense of the Scheme of Redemption,* pp. 4, 5).

EZEKIEL 28: SATAN'S RISE AND FALL

There are many students of the Bible who believe that

two chapters in the Old Testament have much to say about Satan. One of those passages in Ezekiel 28:12-17. While the context itself indicates it is a prophecy against the king of Tyre (v. 12), there are enough statements made about this king that are typical of Satan's origin and career to make us believe that the king of Tyre was acting very much like another who once sought power and position – the devil himself. Consider the following comparisons.

1. God said of the king of Tyre, "You were the model of perfection, full of wisdom and perfect in beauty" (Ezek. 28:12). Satan was once holy and abode in truth. (John 8:44).

2. God said the king of Tyre, "You were in Eden, the garden of God . . ." (Ezek. 28:13). Satan, in the form of the serpent, certainly was in Eden (Gen. 3:1).

3. God reminded the king of Tyre, "You were anointed as a guardian cherub, for so I ordained you" (Ezek. 28:14). Satan apparently had been appointed to a very important position by God himself.

4. God said to the king of Tyre, "You were blameless in your ways from the day you were created till wickedness was found in you" (Ezek. 28:15). Since God created Satan, he was holy. Satan *chose* to sin. As we have suggested, pride, bitter envy and selfish ambition must have crept into his life.

5. God charged the king of Tyre with violence and sin. "Through your widespread trade you were filled with violence, and you sinned" (Ezek. 28:16a). Satan was a murderer from the beginning (John 8:44). He inspired Cain to commit the world's first murder (Gen. 4:7, 8; 1 John 3:12).

6. God told the king of Tyre that he would be banished in disgrace. "So I drove you in disgrace from the mount of God, and I expelled you, O guardian cherub from among the fiery stones" (Ezek. 28:16b). The curse of this devil is found in Genesis 3:14, 15.

7. God accused the king of Tyre of pride. "Your heart became proud on account of your beauty, and you corrupted your wisdom because of your splendor" (Ezek.

28:17a). Paul says that pride was the signal sin of Satan (1 Tim. 3:6). Satan must have been striking physical specimen. His physical beauty created spiritual pride within. Angels must be very pleasing to look at. Stephen's face was described as looking "like the face of an angel" when brought before the Sanhedrin (Acts 6:15).

8. God made a spectacle of the king of Tyre, throwing him to the earth. "So I threw you to the earth; I made a spectacle of you before kings" (Ezek. 28:17b). Satan and his rebel angels were "hurled to the earth" (Rev. 12:9). Jesus said that He saw this occur (Luke 10:18).

9. God punished the king of Tyre with all severity. "By your many sins and dishonest trade you have desecrated your sanctuaries. So I made a fire come out of you, and it consumed you, and I reduced you to ashes on the ground in the sight of all who were watching. All the nations who knew you are appalled at you; you have come to a horrible end and will be no more" (Ezek. 28:18, 19). The awful fate of Satan is vividly described in such passages as Matthew 25:41 and Revelation 20:10.

It is hard to understand how some can rule out any reference to Satan at all in this passage, Ezekiel 28:12-19. The passage fairly reeks with Satanic overtones. True, not everything that is said about the wicked king of Tyre can be paralleled with Satan. But enough is said to lead us to believe that the many accusations God made against the king of Tyre are also made against Satan. This man was so evil in his deeds that Scripture uses him as a personification of evil, or, more properly, the evil one – Satan. The wicked king of Tyre helps us to understand how evil this once-holy angel, Satan, really is.

ISAIAH 14: SATAN'S RISE AND FALL

Another passage that likens an evil man to Satan, thus giving us additional insight into the evil nature of the devil, is Isaiah 14:12-14. This prophecy was directed against the king of Babylon (v. 4). Yet, there is striking similarity in the accusations that God makes against the king of Babylon with Satan. Consider a few of them.

1. God told the king of Babylon that he had fallen, had been cast down. "How you have fallen from heaven, O morning star, son of the dawn! You have been cast down to the earth, you who once laid low the nations! (Isa. 14:12). The meteoric rise and fall of this king is likened to the rise and fall of the angel, Satan (Rev. 12:9).

2. God reminded the king of Babylon of his grasping ambition. "You said in your heart, 'I will ascend to heaven; I will raise my throne above the stars of God; I will sit enthroned on the mount of assembly, on the utmost heights of the sacred mountain. I will ascend above the tops of the clouds; I will make myself like the Most High'" (Isa. 14:13, 14). The king, like Satan, was very proud, very self-willed and assertive (notice the five "I wills" in vs. 13, 14). Satan wants to be God (2 Thess. 2:4) and wants all to worship him, even Jesus Christ (Matt. 4:9).

3. God predicted the demise of the king of Babylon. "But you are brought down to the grave, to the depths of the pit" (Isa. 14:15). The devil be thrown into the bottomless pit (Rev. 20:1-3).

This portion of Scripture, like the Ezekiel passage, was directed against a human king who was so evil that God compared him to the devil himself. Both kings exhibited attitudes, ambitions and actions that are characteristic of Satan. Hence we are able to learn more about the evil nature of the once-holy angel, Satan.

WAR IN HEAVEN

Whatever motivated Satan to sin, war was the result. His ungodly pride, bitter envy and selfish ambition led him to lead a revolt against the established authority in heaven. Other angels, influenced by his brash and overt behavior, accepted him as their king and joined the Satanic rebellion (Rev. 9:11). Marshalling these forces who were in sympathy with his push for power, Satan and his rebel forces went to war. It was a lost cause from the beginning. Michael, the archangel, gathered the holy angels and defeated the devil and his angels. The apostle John records the results: "They lost their place in heaven" (Rev. 12:8). The devil and his angels were cast out, hurled to the earth. Jesus said that he beheld the fall of Satan, "like lightning from heaven" (Luke 10:18). His fall was as swift as the battle must have been short. God is always greater than Satan (1 John 4:4).

THE WORLD TODAY IS UNDER SATANIC DOMINATION

John said that Satan was "hurled to the earth." The earth has never been the same. Satan, now appearing to man in the form of a serpent, induced Adam and Eve to rebel against God's authority (Gen. 3:1-7). They, in turn, were cast out of the beautiful garden (Gen. 3:22-24), just as Satan had been cast out of heaven (Rev. 12:8). The devil has not let up since. He roams the earth (Job 1:7), seeking whom he may devour (1 Pet. 5:8). So successful has been his wicked campaign that the apostle John wrote that "the whole world is under the control of the evil one" (1 John 5:19). He will not be victorious forever, for when Jesus returns the devil and his angels will be cast into hell (Matt. 25:41) where he and his helpers will be tormented day and night forever (Rev. 20:10).

Today Satan masquerades as an "angel of light (2 Cor. 11:14). What a devious cover! He accomplishes his evil work through men who masquerade as "servants of righteousness" (2 Cor. 11:14). This should not come as any big surprise to us. It has always been his method to get individuals, angelic beings or human beings, to do his will. Let us not be deceived by his cunning cover. Beware of this masquerading angel!

10 "THE ANGELS THAT SINNED"

Man was given power of choice. Like Adam and Eve in the garden, we can choose to obey or disobey God. That is the way God chose to make us. He did not want robot-like service. He wants us to serve Him because we love Him. He does not force His will on us. The angels were made like that, too. They could choose to sin or not to sin. Unhappily, both for them and us, some angels chose to sin.

LED ASTRAY BY SATAN

As we learned in the previous chapter, an angel named Satan was the first to sin. Because of his beauty and wisdom, pride crept in. Envy and ambition took over. This noteworthy angel wanted to usurp the throne of God Himself (Isa. 14:13, 14).

Sin seldom stays at home. It often affects others. The rebellious and ambitious nature of Satan undoubtedly began to influence other angels. "One bad apple can spoil them all." One sinning angel caused many to sin. Although the angels had been created by God to serve Him, some chose to serve Satan.

THE ANGELIC REBELLION

The angels who were adversely influenced by Satan's behavior joined him in rebellion against God. The Bible says that Michael, the archangel, along with other holy angels who wanted to serve God, went to war with Satan and his rebellious forces (Rev. 12:7). How the battle must have raged! In the end, the forces of the faithful angels under Michael prevailed. Satan and his angels were cast out of heaven and hurled to the earth (Rev. 12:9). How they must have gnashed their teeth in rage and despair. No wonder they work with such ferocity today!

It is important to remember that the angels chose to sin. The Bible says "they abandoned their own home" (Jude 6). They could have remained in heaven, worshiping and serving God as before. But they made a choice, and it was a bad one – to hail Satan as their king (Rev. 9:11). Not only was it a bad choice, it was a sad choice. When he fell, they fell. When he lost all, they lost all. Even angels must reap what they sow.

SOME FALLEN ANGELS ARE BOUND

What happened to the angels that sinned? Were they killed in the angelic conflict in heaven? Were they fatally injured in the fall to earth? The answer to these last two questions must be "no," for angels, even evil ones, are not subject to death. Jesus taught that angels do not die (Luke 20:36). Where are these angels then? Are they like Satan, alive and well on planet earth?

The answer is found in 2 Peter 2:4 and Jude 6. The apostle Peter says that God did not spare the angels that sinned, but cast them down to "hell," confining them in gloomy dungeons to await the judgment. The word for "hell" here is the Greek word *tartarus*. Tartarus is separated from the heaven-like compartment, Paradise, by a great gulf (Luke 16:26). It is a dreadful place marked by torment, thirst and remorse.

In addition to this, Jude writes that the angels who sinned are kept bound in darkness, bound with everlasting chains for the Judgment (Jude 6). Sin does not pay! How these angels must have regretted their decision to swear allegiance to the would-be God, Satan. For them, it is too late. Their fate is fixed, their doom is certain. Everlasting hell (*gehenna*) awaits the devil and his angels (Matt. 25:41).

SOME FALLEN ANGELS ARE LOOSE

The Bible also seems to indicate that some of the angels who sinned are on the loose. The angels that are not bound in Tartarus are actively engaged in doing the devil's evil work. Paul testified that angels seek to separate believers from God and Jesus Christ (Rom. 8:38). The great apostle also declared that our battle is not against flesh and blood but against the spiritual hosts of wickedness in heavenly places (Eph. 6:12). Angels, under the diabolical direction of Satan, the prince of the power of the air, are at work in the lives of those who, like themselves, are disobedient to God (Eph. 2:2).

Consider all the evil in our world today. If the devil and his angels are not responsible for all the havoc and heartache, then who?

WHY ARE SOME BOUND AND OTHERS FREE?

How do we account for the fact that some of the angels who sinned are bound in Tartarus while others are free to work their evil for Satan? Have some of them been able to break their chains and escape? It is highly doubtful that this could happen. How, then, are we to explain why some are bound and others are free?

Perhaps no Biblical explanation can be given. One speculation is that the angels who assist Satan in his work are angels who chose to leave their estate after the original rebellion. Another speculation is that the angels, along with Satan, have been loosed for "a little season" in accordance with Revelation 20:3. These explanations may not be worth the paper they are written on and if it seems unsatisfactory to the reader, the reader is free to reject them and formulate explanations of his own.

THE CHURCH WILL JUDGE ANGELS

Although we cannot say with any certainty why some evil angels remain unbound, we can know that all angels who have sinned – bound or unbound – will be cast into the lake of fire at the final judgment (Matt. 25:41; Rev. 20:10). The church, so beleaguered by wicked angels, will some day judge them. Paul wrote, "do you not know that the saints will judge the world? . . . Do you not know that we will judge angels?" (1 Cor. 6:2, 3). T. R. Applebury writes,

> . . . The church is God's means of demonstrating to the angels that rebelled against His authority that some men will serve Him out of their love for Him. The church is made up of those who deliberately choose to do God's will and refuse to do the bidding of Satan. If men can do this, angels certainly could have done so. The character and conduct of the saints then becomes a means of judging angels that sinned (*Studies in First and Second Corinthians,* p. 105).

Christians, so long plagued by Satan and his helpers, will take part in his crushing overthrow: "The God of peace will soon crush Satan under your feet" (Rom. 16:20).

11 THE ANGEL OF THE LORD (1)

In the Old Testament there is a very special angel that appears from time to time. He is called "the angel of the Lord" and should be distinguished from any angels simply referred to as "an angel of the Lord." When the Bible refers "to an angel of the Lord," it could be any one of countless thousands that God selected for a certain task or mission. But when we come across the phrase "the angel of the Lord," it appears that reference is being made to a unique messenger.

THE THEOPHANIC ANGEL – WHO IS HE?

From a study of the passages mentioning "the angel of the Lord," it becomes apparent that, at least on several occasions, the angel may be the Lord God Himself, Jehovah. Other references seem to indicate that the special messenger may have been an appearance of the pre-incarnate Christ Himself. In either case, this is what is known as a "theophany," a visible appearance of a divine being in human form. The question then arises, "Who is the theophanic angel?" Is he God Himself appearing, what some have called "a momentary descent of God into visibility"? Is he the pre-incarnate Word, the Lord Jesus Christ? Or is he just a very special angel with special commission from God? Before we attempt to answer these questions, let's look at some actual case histories of people who encountered an appearance of "the angel of the Lord."

HAGAR'S EXPERIENCE

First on our list is Hagar. Twice in her life this woman – so despised by her mistress, Sarah – was favored with a visit from this heavenly personage. In Genesis 16:7 the angel of Lord finds Hagar in the desert. He tells her that He will multiply her seed until they will not be able to be numbered (Gen. 16:10). This is nearly the same language that God Himself used in personally promising a great nation to Abraham (Gen. 12:2; 17:6; 18:18). Hagar, sensing the presence of a Divine Being, called the name of the Lord who spoke to her "You are the God who sees me," adding "I have now seen the One who sees me" (Gen. 16:13). From that day the well where this encounter took place was called "Beer Lahai Roi" which means, "Well of the Living One who sees me."

Later in her troubled life Hagar again is visited by this special angel. Again she has been sent into the desert by her mistress Sarah; again the angel of the Lord ministers to her (Gen. 21:17). Please note that it is "God" who hears the lad Ishmael crying. But it is "the angel of God" who speaks to her from heaven. In verse 19 it is "God" who opens Hagar's eyes so that she can see a well of water, thus preserving both her, the boy, and the nation that will come from her seed.

In both instances, we find an interchange of the words "God" and "the angel of God."

ABRAHAM'S ENCOUNTERS

The next person so favored was Abraham. The Bible says that "the *Lord* appeared to Abraham near the great trees of Mamre" (Gen. 18:1). Abraham looks up and sees three men. Two of these visitors are later identified as angels (cf. Gen. 18:22; 19:1). The third visitor appears to be the Lord Himself. Repeatedly in the account, God speaks to Abraham (see vs. 10, 13, 17).

Like Hagar, Abraham experienced a second visit with the angel of God. On Mount Moriah, about to sacrifice his son of promise, Isaac, Abraham is divinely interrupted. The angel speaks from heaven and arrests the hand of Abraham (Gen. 22:11). The careful reader will note that the angel says, "Now I know that you fear God, because you have not withheld from me your son, your only son" (Gen. 22:12). The angel then assures Abraham of his promise that his descendants will be as numerous as the stars in the sky and the sands on the seashore (v. 17). This of course, was a promise that *God* had made to Abraham earlier in his life (see Gen. 13:16; 15:5).

JACOB'S DREAM AND ORDEAL

The next individual to meet the angel of God was Jacob. He once recounted to his wives, Rachel and Leah, how the angel of God had appeared to him in a dream (Gen. 31:11). The angel, according to Jacob, identified Himself thusly: "I am the God of Bethel, where you anointed a pillar and where you made a vow to me" (Gen. 31:13). The incident of which God is reminding Jacob is when Jacob had another dream – the dream of the ladder between heaven and earth. Angels were ascending and descending the ladder. At the very top of the ladder was the Lord who spoke to Jacob, assuring him, as He had Abraham, that his descendants would be as the dust of the earth in number and that through him all people of the earth will be blessed.

When Jacob is reunited with his estranged brother Esau, he again encounters angels (Gen. 32:1, 2). This time he wrestles all night with an angel/man. The wrestler is called a "man" in verse 24 but an "angel" in Hosea 12:4. In the midst of the all-night wrestling match, the angel changes Jacob's name to Israel because Jacob had actually "struggled with God" (Gen. 32:28). Not to be content with that, Jacob dares to ask the angel to divulge his name. The angel refuses but Jacob names the place where he and the angel wrestled "Peniel" because, according to Jacob, "I saw God face to face, and yet my life was spared" (Gen. 32:30). Peniel means "face of God."

Before he died, Israel (once known as Jacob) praised "the God who has been my Shepherd all my life to this day, the *angel* who has delivered me from all harm . . . " (Gen. 48:15, 16). Again one notes the interchangeable terms of "God" and "angel."

MOSES AND THE BURNING BUSH

Moses becomes the fourth person to be blessed by an appearance from "the angel of the Lord." One day, as Moses was tending his father-in-law's sheep near Mount Horeb, this special angel appeared to him "in flames of fire from within a bush" (Exod. 3:2). Intrigued by this phenomenon – for the bush, amazingly, was not being consumed by the flames – Moses went closer and received the shock of his life! God himself spoke to Moses from the bush! The Almighty instructed Moses to take off his sandals because he was now standing on "holy ground" (Exod. 3:5). God proceeds to identify Himself as "the God of your father, the God of Abraham, the God of Isaac and the God of Jacob." God continued saying He was the great *I AM* (Exod. 3:14). Stephen later verifies this incident in his account of Jewish history (Acts 7:30-35).

It is clear from Exodus 3:2 that "the angel of the Lord" is one and the same as the God who speaks from the burning bush (Exod. 3:4).

THE CHILDREN OF ISRAEL

The promised descendants of Jacob (Israel), led by Moses out of the land of Egypt, were also led by the angel of God. The theophanic angel traveled before them in a pillar of cloud by day and gave them light by night in the form of a pillar of fire. Exodus 14:19 says it was "the angel of God" that performed these wonderful and helpful services for the children of Israel. Yet, Exodus 13:21 says it was "the Lord (who) went ahead of them in a pillar of cloud to guide them on their way and by night in a pillar of fire to give them light, so that they could travel by day or night." Are these contradictory terms? No. They are *complementary* terms: the Lord and the angel of the Lord are synonymous.

The Israelites were also informed by the Lord that He was sending His angel ahead of them to bring them safely into Canaan (Exod. 23:20). They were instructed to pay attention to him and to listen to what he said because "My Name is in him" (Exod. 23:21). If the Israelites would listen carefully to what the *angel* would say, and would do all that *God* told them to do, all would go well with them (Exod. 23:23).

Even after the people sinned at the foot of Mount Sinai, God again promised to provide them with the guidance and protection of His special messenger (Exod. 32:4; 33:2). The prophet Isaiah later records that "the angel of his presence" saved His people in their distress (Isa. 63:9).

The angel of the Lord also rebuked the Israelites at Bokim for their failure to obey God in breaking down pagan altars (Judg. 2:1-5). The angel reminded them, "I brought you out of Egypt and led into the land that I swore to give to your forefathers" (Judg. 2:1). The people wept at the angel's words (Bokim means "weepers") and offered sacrifices to the Lord (Judg. 2:5).

The angel of the Lord also placed a curse on Meroz, a town that failed to come to the aid of Deborah and Barak in their battle against Jabin, king of Canaan. In the song of Deborah we find these words "'Curse Meroz,' said the angel of the Lord. 'Curse its people bitterly, because they did not come to help the Lord, to help the Lord against the mighty'" (Judg. 5:23).

12 THE ANGEL OF THE LORD (2)

BALAAM AND THE BEAST

Sixth, the angel of the Lord, along with a not-so-dumb donkey, stopped the madness of a prophet, Balaam. The latter, a mercenary-minded prophet, was on his way to do business with the Israelites' enemies, the Moabites. He was riding a donkey. Numbers 22:22 says that God was very angry with Balaam, and "the angel of the Lord stood in the road to oppose him." The divine presence was visible to the donkey but not to Balaam. The donkey shied and Balaam proceeded to beat the poor beast. When Balaam finally got the donkey back on the road, the angel again appeared, blocking the way. This forced the donkey against a narrow wall, crushing Balaam's foot. Enraged, the prophet pounded on his donkey. A third time the angel blocked the way. This time the donkey could not turn to the left or right. She proceeded to simply lie down in the road – an act which infuriated Balaam. He whipped out his staff and proceeded to beat the beast unmercifully. Then God did an amazing thing. He opened the donkey's mouth and she began to speak to Balaam! "What have I done to you to make you beat me these three times?" (Num. 22:28). Balaam is so beside himself that he does not know what he is doing – he begins a conversation with his donkey! I wonder what his servants were thinking of this bizarre scene! Finally, God opens Balaam's eyes and he sees what the poor donkey had seen all along – "the angel of the Lord standing in the road with his sword drawn" (Num. 22:31). This frightens the prophet nearly out of his wits. The angel tells Balaam to "speak only what I tell you" (Num. 22:35).

When Balaam finally arrives at his destination he tells the king of Moab, "I must speak only what God puts in my mouth" (Num. 22:38).

JOSHUA AND THE MAN WITH THE DRAWN SWORD

The seventh man to see the angel of God was a man whose name is like unto that of Jesus – Joshua. Both names mean "the Lord is salvation." Just before the fall of Jericho, Joshua was near that fated city when he looked up and saw a man standing before him (Josh. 5:13). Like the figure before Balaam, he has a drawn sword in his hand. Joshua gathers his courage and asks the imposing figure if he is for Israel or Jericho. "Neither," came the strange reply. "But as commander of the army of the Lord I have now come" (Josh. 5:14). Upon hearing this Joshua falls to the ground – and worships! It is highly significant that he is not told to stop worshiping. The awesome figure must have been more than a man, for men are not to be worshiped. The apostle Peter told Cornelius to "stand up" because he (Peter) was also just a man (Acts 10:26). The figure must have been more than an angel as well, because the worship of angels is forbidden in Scripture (Col. 2:18; Rev. 22:8,9). It is not beyond reason to think that the figure was that of God Himself or the pre-incarnate Word, Jesus Christ. In fact, Joshua calls the figure "my Lord" (Josh. 5:14). The response of the commander of the Lord's army is most interesting: "Take off your sandals, for the place where you are standing is holy" (Josh. 5:15). Sound familiar? It should. These are almost the exact words that Moses heard at the burning bush, from God Himself (Exod. 3:5). A coincidence? We think not.

GIDEON'S FIRE-RAISING EXPERIENCE

In the book of Judges, the angel of God appears to Gideon under the oak tree in Ophrah (Judg. 6:11). Gideon has been threshing wheat in a winepress to keep it from the hands of marauding Midianites. The angel tries to assure Gideon that the Lord is with him (Judg. 6:12). Gideon wonders out loud, "If the Lord is with us, why has all this happened to us?" (Judg. 6:13). Note an important change in the text. In verse 14, God Himself speaks to troubled Gideon: "The Lord turned to him and said, 'Go in the strength you have and save Israel out of Midian's hand.'" Gideon calls Him "Lord" in verse 15. He asks Him for a sign that it is really God talking to him. Receiving divine permission, Gideon prepares bread and meat for an offering. Now the angel tells him to put the meat and bread on a rock and to pour out the broth (Judg. 6:20). The angel takes his staff and touches the meat and bread. An incredible thing happens! Fire flares from the rock and consumes the meat and bread. At the same time, the angel disappears. As knowing slowly dawns on Gideon, he exclaims, "Ah, Sovereign Lord! I have seen the angel of the Lord face to face!" (Judg. 6:22). But God has not left Gideon's presence after all, for he hears God speaking, "Peace! Do not be afraid. You are not going to die" (Judg. 6:23). Why would Gideon be assured that he was not going to die if the figure he had encountered was not Deity? Many people had seen angels before and, although thoroughly frightened, were in no danger of dying. The fear of death came because of seeing the Lord (Exod. 19:21). Relieved, Gideon builds an altar unto the Lord and calls it "The Lord is Peace" (Judg. 6:24). He goes on to do great exploits for God.

SAMSON'S PARENTS

The parents of the Bible's strongest man, Samson, were privileged to see the theophanic angel. Samson's mother was the first of the two to be visited by the angel of God. She was barren, unable to have children. One day the angel suddenly appears and tells her that in spite of her barren condition, she is going to conceive and have a son. She is instructed not to drink wine or eat anything unclean because the son is to be a Nazarite. No razor is to touch his head. He will be the deliverer of Israel from the hated Philistines (Judg. 13:2-5).

Samson's mother later describes the angel to her husband, Manoah, a Danite. She said, "A man of God came to me. He looked like an angel of God, very awesome" (Judg. 13:6). Manoah then prays to God and asks if He would send the man back to teach them how to raise the child (Judg. 13:8). God graciously answers Manoah's prayer and the angel reappears to his wife in the field. She runs to get Manoah and he comes and asks for guidance from the angel in how they are to raise the boy. The angel again gives the instructions that he had earlier given Manoah's wife. Afterwards, Manoah invites the angel to stay for supper. The angel consents but says he will not eat the food. He tells them to offer it as a burnt offering to the Lord. At this point in the story we learn that "Manoah did not realize that it was the angel of the Lord" (Judg. 13:16). Perhaps puzzled by the strange request, Manoah (like Jacob) asks the angel his name. The angel replied, "Why do you ask my name? It is beyond understanding" (Judg. 13:18). The King James Version has "secret." The American Standard Version has "wonderful." The Messiah, according to the prophet Isaiah, would be called "Wonderful" (Isa. 9:6).

Manoah takes a young goat and offers it together with a grain offering. As he and his wife watch, the Lord does an amazing thing! Fire blazes up from the altar and the angel of the Lord ascends in a flame! (Judg. 13:19,20). Stunned,

Manoah and his wife fall to the ground, at last realizing it was the angel of the Lord (Judg. 13:21). Manoah bursts forth, "We are doomed to die . . . , We have seen God!" (Judg. 13:22). But his wife reasons that if God had meant to kill them, He would not have accepted their burnt offering (Judg. 13:23). In spite of their having been in the Divine Presence, Manoah and his wife are spared, she has a son, Samson, and he becomes a noteworthy judge in Israel.

DAVID AND THE DESTROYER OF JERUSALEM

The tenth instance of the angel of God appearing to men in the Old Testament is perhaps the most frightening of all. King David, tempted by Satan (himself an angel), numbers the people of Israel (1 Chron. 21:1). The thing displeases the Lord and He punishes Israel. Seventy thousand Israelites fall in a terrible plague (1 Chron. 21:14). The angel of God is then sent to destroy the holy city itself – Jerusalem! (1 Chron. 21:15). In the midst of the process God has pity on Israel and tells the angel to withdraw his hand (1 Chron. 21:15). David, by this time deep in distress, looks up and sees a dreadful sight! The angel of God is standing between heaven and earth. He has a drawn sword in his hand. The sword is extended over Jerusalem! David beseeches God not to let the plague continue on Jerusalem but on himself and his family (1 Chron. 21:17). The angel orders the prophet Gad to tell David to build an altar to the Lord (1 Chron. 21:18). David does so and God answers with fire from heaven. God also speaks to the angel who sheathes his sword and the plague is stayed (1 Chron. 21:27).

ZECHARIAH'S VISION OF THE MAN ON THE RED HORSE

Zechariah, a contemporary prophet with Haggai, received a series of eight visions from the Lord. In the first vision (Zech. 1:7-17), the angel of the Lord appears to

Zechariah in a grove of myrtle trees, astride a red horse. Other riders are with him, mounted on red, brown and white horses. Astounded, Zechariah asks a nearby interpreting angel who these figures are. The rider of the red horse (v. 8) is identified as the angel of the Lord (vs. 12,13). Clarke comments,

> An angel in the form of a man: supposed to have been the LORD JESUS; who seems to have appeared often in this way, as a prelude to his incarnation; see Josh. 5:13; Ezek. 1:26; Dan 7:13; and 10:5. The same, probably that appeared to Joshua with a drawn sword, as the Captain of The Lord's Host. Josh. 5:13-15 (*Clarke's Commentary, Vol. IV*, p, 769).

The riders of the other horses in the myrtle grove are probably angels, who have gone throughout the whole earth (vs. 10,11). Again we cite Clarke:

> Probably pointing out the different orders of angels in the heavenly host, which are employed by Christ in the defense of his Church. The different colours may point out the gradations in power, authority, and excellence, of the angelic natures which are employed between Christ and men (*Ibid.*, p. 769).

The message from the angel of the Lord to Zechariah is this: although God's people have been in Babylonian captivity for 70 long years (1:12), they are going to return to their homeland and, among other things, rebuild the beloved temple (1:16). Indeed, this is the recurring theme in the first half of the book of Zechariah (Chapters 1-8). The last half of the book deals with prophecies concerning the coming of Christ and the glories of His kingdom.

The angel of the Lord and the interpreting angel appear to Zechariah in seven additional visions:

> The four horns and the four smiths (1:18-21), teaching that Israel's enemies are now destroyed and there is no longer any opposition to the building of God's house.
>
> The man with the measuring line (chap. 2), teaching that Jerusalem will expand till it outgrows its walls and God will

be its best defense.

Joshua, the high priest, clad in filthy garments which represent the sins of himself and the people is cleansed and given charge of the temple. He is a type of the Messiah-Branch to come who will take away all iniquity. Chap. 3.

A seven-branched candlestick fed by two olive trees, teaching that the people of God will receive God's grace through their spiritual and temporal leaders, through whose efforts the prosperity of the nation will be accomplished. Chap. 4.

A flying scroll (5:1-4), teaching that the land shall be purified from wickedness when the temple is built and God's law taught.

A woman (typifying the besetting sins of Israel) is carried off in an ephah-measure to the land of Babylon (5:5-11), teaching that God not only forgives the sins of His people, but carries them away from their land (*Zondervan Pictorial Bible Dictionary*, p. 909).

SUMMARY

There are many questions that will have to go unanswered in reading the accounts of "the angel of the Lord." For example, why, if he was "a momentary descent of God into visibility," did not the people die as God had indicated they would (Exod. 19:21)? Is it because they were not seeing God in His pure spirit form? Or could it be because it was not really God at all in these cases we have examined? Was the theophanic angel Jesus in the pre-incarnate state? If the angel with the drawn sword was the pre-incarnate Son of God, how does that coincide with the Christ who said He came to save, not destroy; who, in fact, once told an overzealous follower of His to put up his sword?

And yet we are led to believe that at least in some of the accounts the angel and God are really one and the same. All of this and even more cautions us not to be dogmatic in the matter. The following words of wisdom are in order:

Who is the theophanic angel? To this many answers have been given, of which the following may be mentioned: (1) This angel is simply an angel with a special commission; (2) He may be a momentary descent of God into visibility; (3) He may be the Logos, a kind of temporary pre-incarnation of the second person of the Trinity. Each has its difficulties, but the last is certainly the most tempting to the mind. Yet it must be remembered that at best these are only conjectures that touch on a great mystery. It is certain that from the beginning God used angels in human form, with human voices, in order to communicate with man; and the appearances of the angel of the Lord, with his special redemptive relation to God's people, show the working of that Divine mode of self-revelation which culminated in the coming of the Saviour, and are thus a foreshadowing of, and a preparation for, the full revelation of God in Jesus Christ. Further than this it is not safe to go (John MacArtney Wilson, *The International Standard Bible Encyclopedia*, Vol. 1, p. 134).

To which we say "Amen."

13 THE MINISTRY OF ANGELS (1)

The Bible says that angels are "ministering spirits" (Heb. 1:14). To minister is to serve. The angels of God have special services to do on behalf of man. They do not just roll around heaven all day, reclining on fleecy clouds, "preening their wings" and plucking their harps. The angels have a very real work to do.

THE TWOFOLD MINISTRY OF ANGELS

The ministry of angels can be divided into two simple categories:

(1) They have a *heavenly* ministry to fulfill;
(2) they have *earthly* duties that must be carried out.

This chapter will be devoted to the ministry of angels in heaven.

How do angels spend an average day in heaven? Are they, like God, unhampered by time? Are a thousand years like a day? What do they do?

WORSHIP AND PRAISE

First (and probably foremost), angels worship, adore and praise God the Father and His Son, the Lord Jesus Christ. Jesus taught that the angels of God are in heaven and always see the face of the Father (Luke 18:10). More than just admire God, they worship and adore Him. Revelation

5:11,12 finds the angels singing praise to the Lamb of God who was worthy to be slain.

Beginning in the Old Testament, let's see how the angels in heaven worship the Lord.

At the creation of the world, all the angels "shouted for joy" (Job 38:7). How they must have shouted with delight as the world took shape before their wondering eyes! No wonder they worship and revere the omnipotent Creator.

The Psalmist tells us that the angels are continually praising God. "Praise the Lord, you his angels, you mighty ones who do his bidding, who obey his word. Praise the Lord, all his heavenly hosts, you his servants who do his will" (Psa. 103:20,21).

Isaiah saw a vision of the Lord, seated on a throne, high and exalted. Two six-winged seraphs were crying, "Holy, holy, holy is the Lord Almighty; the whole earth is full of his glory" (Isa. 6:1-3).

An innumerable host of angels encircle the throne of God singing "Worthy is the Lamb, who was slain, to receive power and wealth and wisdom and strength and honor and glory and praise!" (Rev. 5:12). They fall down on their faces before the throne and worship God saying "Amen! Praise and glory and wisdom and thanks and honor and power and strength be to our God for ever and ever. Amen!" (Rev. 7:11,12). How magnificent are the worship scenes around the throne of God and the Lamb!

In the dramatic opening of the seventh seal, seven angels with seven trumpets stand before God. An angel with a golden censer comes and stands at the golden altar before the throne. Incense is given to him to offer, along with the prayers of the saints. Both the incense and the prayers go up before God from the angel's hand (Rev. 8:1-4).

At the sounding of the seventh trumpet by the seventh angel, loud voices are heard in heaven, saying, "The kingdom of the world has become the kingdom of our Lord and of his Christ, and he will reign for ever and ever" (Rev. 11:15).

The picture that is portrayed for us in Scripture of the

angels worshiping God is one of ceaseless praise. From the creation of the world to the ushering in of eternity, the angels worship and praise the Lord and His Christ.

REJOICING IN HEAVEN

Second, the angels in heaven rejoice at the victories of Christians. Angels are extremely interested in redemption, longing to understand the wonderful plan of salvation that God devised for fallen man (1 Pet. 1:12). In spite of the fact that they are unable to experience salvation as man can, they are very happy whenever a sinner repents and turns to God. Angels do not have a jealous or envious heart. They are glad for us.

Jesus taught that there is great joy in heaven among the angels of God over just one sinner that repents (Luke 15:7,10). Just imagine the "tongues of angels" (1 Cor. 13:1) rejoicing over a lowly sinners turning to God! You are important to God – He loves you and sent His only son to die for you. You are important to Jesus – He took your place on the cross, atoning for your sins in His death. You are important to the angels – they rejoiced over your repentance, your turning from sin to God.

Perhaps this is why the Hebrew writer explains, "You have come to Mount Zion, to the heavenly Jerusalem, the city of the living God. You have come to thousands upon thousands of angels in joyful assembly" (Heb. 12:22). If we could only know how much joy we bring to the angels!

Some feel that the "great cloud of witnesses" in Hebrews 12:1 may be referring to the angels in heaven. Although the context (Heb. 11: 4-40) seems to favor the departed heroes of the faith, it certainly is not out of line to say that angels are interested in the activities, struggles and victories of each and every child of God on earth.

ON 24-HOUR CALL TO SERVE MAN

Third, the angels of God stand ready to minister to the saints. Scripture says angels are sent to serve those who will inherit salvation (Heb. 1:14). Numberless hosts of angels are at God's beck and call to speed to earth and do His will. God's will is done in heaven (Matt. 6:10) by the angels who stand ever ready to obey God and aid man.

For example, when Abraham commissioned his faithful servant, Eliezer of Damascus, to go and find a wife for his son Isaac, he encouraged him by saying that God would "send his angel" before him to aid him in the successful selection of a wife (Gen. 24:7, 40). What faith this patriarch had in the ministry of angels! Would God that we could have the same. God's angel helped Eliezer in a marvelous way and a godly wife for Isaac was found, Rebekah.

The ministry of angels is so great that a wicked pagan king, Nebuchadnezzar of Babylon, once praised the true God of the Hebrews because He sent an angel to rescue three of His followers from a furnace of fire. Hear his powerful testimony: "Praise be to the God of Shadrach, Meshach and Abednego, who has sent his angel and rescued his servants" (Dan. 3:28). O, that God's people today could have the same faith that the three Hebrew children did and would have the spiritual awareness of even this pagan king!

Daniel had a wonderful testimony to give to another pagan king, Darius. He declared, "My God sent his angel, and he shut the mouths of the lions" (Dan. 6:22). Surely the angel made haste to help Daniel in his moment of need.

The angel Gabriel told Zacharias that he had been personally sent by God to give him a message. "I am Gabriel. I stand in the presence of God, and I have been sent to speak to you and to tell you this good news" (Luke 1:19). Perhaps no verse more clearly shows us that angels stand in the presence of God to be sent to minister to men's various needs.

A short time later, God sent Gabriel to Nazareth to give

one of the greatest announcements in history: the forthcoming birth of the Son of God. "In the sixth month, God sent the angel Gabriel to Nazareth, a town in Galilee, to a virgin . . . . The angel went to her and said, 'Greetings, you who are highly favored! The Lord is with you . . . . You will be with child and give birth to a son, and you are to give him the name Jesus'" (Luke 1:26-28,31).

The apostle Peter, following a miraculous escape from prison, stated, "Now I know without a doubt that the Lord sent his angel and rescued me from Herod's clutches and from everything the Jewish people were anticipating" (Acts 12:11).

At the end of time God will send his angels to gather the elect and cast the wicked into hell (Matt. 13:41,42; 24:31; Mark 13:27). These are just a few examples of times when angels obeyed the command of God to come to earth and help God's people in different situations. The angels of God stand in His presence, ever ready to be sent to help us.

Reggie Thomas is an evangelist who has traveled more than three million miles visiting 66 countries. He has survived an attempted assassination in Jamaica, a bombing in Hong Kong, the war in Vietnam, a bloody revolution in Chile, a bridge collapse in Guyana, military coups in Nigeria, Ghana, and Haiti. "In all these travels," Reggie testifies, "God has wonderfully delivered me. I cannot account for this in any other way except to say God has delivered me through the ministry of angels."

One story merits telling here. Reggie and his wife were in Ghana, Africa, in 1988, to preach Christ in remote villages. One night, after the service was over, the Thomases and their party had to walk several miles through snake infested jungle to get to their van they had left parked along the road. To complicate things, the battery was dead and the van would only go in high gear. They pushed the van, got it going, and proceeded in high gear.

Soon they came to a steep hill. The van did not have the power to climb the hill in high gear. Soon the engine died. Reggie and his party jumped out of the van and tried to push it uphill. Reggie pushed so hard he broke out into a cold sweat. But the van would not budge. "We realized we were at the end of our human resources," Reggie admitted. "There was nothing else we could do."

"In that moment of absolute hopelessness, our Ghanian evangelist Appiah Danquah, prayed a simple prayer. At the top of his lungs, he cried, 'Jesus! Help us!' Immediately the vehicle started up the hill! And we were not pushing it! Suddenly I realized someone was pushing the van – but it was not any of us. Stunned, we all followed in wonder. No one spoke a word. When we got to the top of the hill we got into the van and these "people," whoever they were continued to push the van in silence until it started again and we drove all the way to Accra, Ghana, a distance of 40 miles, in high gear, without any further difficulty.

"Later, when my wife and I were alone, I said, 'I hesitated to say anything in front of the others because I don't want them to think I'm crazy. But I think God sent angels to help us. Am I crazy?' My wife replied, 'No, you're not crazy. That's exactly what happened.'"

Reggie testifies, "Why should we think this so unusual? Brother Appiah prayed, 'Jesus! Help us!' And Jesus helped us!"

SUMMARY

The ministry of angels in heaven involves three basic things: (1) praising and worshiping the Lord God and His Son, Jesus Christ; (2) rejoicing over the repentance of sinners and the victories of the saints; (3) standing as faithful sentries in the Lord's presence, ready to be sent by God to do His bidding. Praise God for the heavenly ministry of the angels!

14 THE MINISTRY OF ANGELS (2)

We have said that the ministry of angels is twofold: heavenly and earthly. This chapter will begin to examine the ministry of angels on earth. The angels of God have been – and continue to be – very active in the affairs of men on earth. Two phases of their ministry on earth will be considered in the next few pages.

"ANGELGRAMS" AND GABRIEL

One important function of the angels is to carry, announce and even interpret messages. With radar-like accuracy, the angels seek and find the subjects of God's messages. With great clarity of speech they faithfully deliver God's message. Western Union had its messenger boys; the Postal Service has its mailgrams; God uses "angelgrams!"

One angel in particular was used by God to announce vital messages. Gabriel was a special agent who was instrumental in carrying several key communiques. God must have seen in him an extra-special measure of responsibility to entrust to him the important messages that He did. The Hebrew meaning of Gabriel is "man of God." Gabriel was certainly God's "man of the hour" on at least four occasions.

1. Gabriel interpreted Daniel's vision of the two-horned ram and the one-horned goat (Dan. 8:1-27). Daniel could not figure out what the strange vision meant. God sent Gabriel to interpret it for Daniel. Gabriel told him that the two-horned ram represented the kings of Media and Persia while the shaggy one-horned goat symbolized the king of

Greece (Dan. 8:20-21).

2. Later in the book of Daniel, God again uses Gabriel. While Daniel was deep in prayer and confession of sin, Gabriel came to him in "swift flight," about the time of the evening sacrifice (Dan. 9:20,21). His mission this time was to give Daniel "insight and understanding" into Jeremiah's prophecy of the 70 weeks. Thus Gabriel was privileged to announce the coming of the Anointed One, the Messiah, Jesus Christ, who would make atonement for the sins of the people (Dan. 9:20-27).

3. The third time God called on this special messenger was when He sent him to Zacharias to announce the birth of John the Baptist, the forerunner of the Messiah (Luke 1:11-20). Gabriel appears to Zacharias while he is standing by the altar of incense. He assures the old man that he has come from God with this special message. Because Zacharias does not believe the message, Gabriel tells him that he will not be able to speak until the child is born. The angel's word came true (see Luke 1:64).

4. An even greater assignment awaited Gabriel when God selected him to carry the most important news the world would ever hear – that a virgin, Mary would conceive of the Holy Spirit and would bring forth a son, the Son of the Most High, Jesus (Luke 1:26-38). No greater news has ever traveled from heaven to earth! Gabriel assures Mary that he has come from God and that she has found favor with God. She will bear a son, call His name Jesus, and his kingdom will never end. After faithfully delivering the message, Gabriel leaves Mary.

Other angels, besides Gabriel, are used by God to carry messages of significance to men and women. In the Old Testament angels told Hagar to return to Sarah (Gen. 16:7-14; 21:17, 18), informed Abraham and Sarai that they would have a son (Gen. 18:10), warned Lot to flee from Sodom (Gen. 19:12, 13), told Abraham not to slay his son (Gen. 22:11, 12), spoke to Moses from the burning bush (Exod. 3:2-4), gave counsel and warning to the Israelites on their exodus from Egypt (Exod. 23:21), promised Manoah and his wife that they would have a son (Judg. 13:3-20), gave instruction to Elijah before meeting a king (2 Kings 1:3,15), told the prophet Gad to give a message to King David (1 Chron. 21:18), gave numerous messages to the prophet Zechariah (Zech. 1:9-19) et al.

In the New Testament angels continue their work of taking messages to key people. Joseph, husband of Mary, was favored with a number of visits from the angels of God (Matt. 1:19-24; 2:13,19,20). An angelic host announced the birth of Jesus to lowly Judean shepherds (Luke 2:9-15). Angels told the women at the empty tomb that Christ had arisen (Matt. 28:5-7; John 20:12). An angel told Philip to leave his successful work in Samaria and go into the desert (Acts 8:36). Angels instructed Cornelius to send for Peter (Acts 10:3-7), told Peter to get up and leave his prison cell (Acts 12:7,8), and assured Paul that he would not be harmed in a storm at sea (Acts 27:23-25). It was an angel that gave John the revelation of Jesus Christ (Rev. 1:1).

MINISTER TO MAN'S PHYSICAL AND EMOTIONAL NEEDS

Another distinctive feature of the angels' earthly ministry is the aid and assistance they render to men in their weakened physical condition. The Bible relates several instances when God sent angels to minister to the material, physical and practical needs of His people. Truly, they are "angels of mercy."

On two separate occasions Hagar was visited in the desert by an angel of the Lord. The first time the angel gave her "moral support," urging her to return to her mistress, Sarai, and promising her that she would have a child (Gen. 16:7-14). The second time the angel of God ministered to her physical needs as well. Hagar's water supply was gone and she had placed her child, Ishmael, under a shrub because she could not bear to see him die. The angel revealed to her a water source that she had not noticed.

Hagar and Ishmael were spared sure and certain death because of the timely intervention and ministrations of the angel of God (Gen. 21:14-20).

The prophet Elijah was another recipient of a beneficent angel. The prophet was suffering from a severe case of "burn-out." Fresh from a victory over the prophets of Baal at Mount Carmel, Elijah had run into a buzzsaw named Jezebel. "Hell hath no fury like a woman scorned." Elijah was sitting under a juniper tree in the wilderness, asking God to take his life. Wearily he laid down and went to sleep. God took pity on His stressed-out servant and sent an angel who prepared a hot, nourishing meal for Elijah. He awakened the prophet and told him to eat. Elijah ate the welcome food and drank deep draughts of cold water from a jar the angel provided. Then he went back to sleep. A second time the angel repeated the hospitable scene. Refreshed by the sleep and envigorated by the food, Elijah traveled on in his new-found strength and courage for 40 days (2 Kings 19:3-9). Talk about "angel food cake!"

The Psalmist says that the children of Israel partook of "angel's food" in the wilderness (Psa. 78:25). Whether manna was the favored food of angels (angels do eat, see Gen. 18:8; 19:3), or whether this meant that it was actually angels who provided food for the Israelites, is not clear.

An intriguing verse which is not included in some manuscripts is John 5:3,4. The King James Version included the incident and we will discuss it here. Near the Sheep Gate in Jerusalem was a pool surrounded by five covered colonnades. In the Aramaic tongue it was called "Bethesda." Hundreds of physically impaired people – the blind, the lame, the paralyzed – would lie around the edge of the pool, waiting (according to the verses in dispute) for the "moving of the water," What caused this strange turbulence? From time to time, according to the King James Version, an angel would come down and stir the waters. Whoever could then manage to get into the pool first would be healed of whatever ailed him. If the disputed verses are to be considered genuine, this would be another instance of angelic ministry to the physical needs of human beings.

The great apostle Paul was once given some needed "moral support" by an angel of God. On his voyage to Rome – where he was to stand trial before Caesar – a "northeaster" swept down on the sailing vessel upon which he was aboard. The storm raged on for days. The crew was throwing the cargo overboard. Neither the sun by day nor the stars by night could be seen. Soon the men on board gave up all hope. That's when God sent an angel to Paul to tell him that even though the ship itself was going to be lost, not one of them would perish! The angel went on to tell Paul that he would live to stand before Caesar (Acts 27: 13-26).

ANGELS MINISTERED TO JESUS

Of all the times that people were ministered to by angels, most touching are the times when angels ministered to our Lord Jesus Christ. He who was "made a little lower than the angels" was lovingly ministered to by angels on two separate occasions.

The first occasion was just after His baptism in the Jordan River. The account is told in Matthew 4:1-11, Mark 1:12,13 and Luke 4:1-13. Matthew says that Jesus fasted for 40 days in the wilderness and afterwards was hungry. Trying to hit Jesus where He was weakest, Satan slyly suggests that Jesus- – if He really was the Son of God – turn stones into bread. Two other temptations followed. Jesus resisted all of them. When Satan is resisted, he is forced to flee (Jas. 4:7). This the devil did, but only "for a season" (Luke 4:13). Both Matthew and Mark then record that angels came and ministered to Jesus (Matt. 4:11; Mark 1:13).

What all did this angelic attending involve? We cannot say for sure, but it would certainly seem within reason to imagine that the angels provided Jesus with good nourishing food to eat and water to drink as an angel once did with Elijah (1 Kings 19:5-7). Food prepared by angels that could sustain a man for 40 days like it did Elijah could certainly be used to revive a man who had gone without food for 40 days! The human needs of Jesus may have been met by angels in this way.

Perhaps the angels warded off the wild animals that Mark says were present in the wilderness during the temptation (Mark 1:13). God had once before sent an angel to stop the mouths of lions (Dan. 6:22; Heb. 11:33). Surely He could do it again. In His weakened condition, angels may have helped Jesus by keeping the wild animals at bay. Maybe the angels ministered to Jesus in spiritual ways as well, speaking words of encouragement after this titanic struggle with Satan.

During another time of extreme spiritual duress, our Lord was attended to by an angel. On the Mount of Olives, just before His betrayal and arrest, Jesus was agonizing in prayer. Luke, an observing physician, notes that great drops of sweat – like drops of blood – were falling to the ground from the anguished brow of Jesus. It must have broken the Father's heart to hear the cries of His Son. "Yet He, who hath in anguish knelt, is not forsaken by His God!"

God sent an angel in this hour of trial to "strengthen" His Son (Luke 22:43). How did the angel of mercy strengthen the Son of God? We cannot say for sure. Perhaps he bathed His sweating brow – the brow soon to be pierced by cruel thorns – with a cool, wet cloth. Perhaps he gave Him water to drink. Water! O, how He soon would thirst for it on the cross! Perhaps the angel, like Moses and Elijah on the mount of Transfiguration, talked with Him about His departure which He was soon to fulfill in Jerusalem (Luke 9:31). William Bradbury poignantly wrote,

Tis midnight; and from ether-plains
is borne the song that angels know;
unheard by mortals are the strains
that sweetly soothe the Saviour's woe.

Maybe the angel just held Jesus in his arms and rocked Him in the cradle of love like His mother used to do. Whatever the case, our Lord received sufficient strength from the ministering angel that He arose, met His captors and resolutely went to the cross and atoned for our sins. Thank God for that angel who strengthened our Lord that fateful night!

GOD GAVE THE LAW TO MOSES THROUGH ANGELS

The law, which was a schoolmaster to bring people to Christ (Gal. 3:24), was given to Moses through the ministry of angels. Hence, angels have helped all mankind to come to Christ and salvation. Consider the testimony of Scripture:

> 1. You who have received the law that was put into effect through angels but have not obeyed it (Acts 7:53).
> 2. The law was put into effect through angels by a mediator (Gal. 3:19).
> 3. For if the message spoken by angels was binding, and every violation and disobedience received its just punishment, how shall we escape if we ignore such a great salvation? (Heb. 2:2,3).
> 4. And he said, The Lord came from Sinai, and rose up from Seir unto them; he shined forth from mount Paran, and he came with ten thousands of saints: from his right hand went a fiery law for them (Deut. 33:2 KJV).

J.W. McGarvey comments, "These passages show that according to apostolic interpretation, God gave the law to Moses, not by speaking in his own proper person, but by speaking through angels whom he sent to Moses, and who doubtless appeared to him visibly" (*New Commentary on Acts of Apostles*, Vol. 1, p. 131). In his commentary on Galatians he adds, "It was not given directly by divine lips, as was the gospel, but through the intervention of angels (Deut. 33:2; Heb. 2:2); and it was not given personally, but through Moses, a mediator (Deut. 5:5)" (*Commentary on*

Thessalonians, Corinthians, Galatians and Romans, p. 269).

Fred Dickason observes,

> The Law came through angels into the hands of Moses and then to the people (Gal. 3:19). The Jews correctly regarded the Law as ordained by angels, and yet they failed to keep it (Acts 7:38, 52-53). The words of the Law, at least in part if not the whole, are regarded as spoken through angels (Heb. 2:2) . . . . This helps us to understand the Jews' high regard for angels and why the writer of Hebrews takes two chapters to show the superiority of Christ to angels and His replacing of the Mosaic law (Heb. 1,2). (*Angels: Elect and Evil*, p. 96).

If we were to make a simplified "flow chart" to show how the Law came from God to the people it might look something like this:

GOD
▼
ANGELS
▼
MOSES
▼
THE PEOPLE OF ISRAEL

Again, we must point out that since the law was put in charge to lead us to Christ (Gal. 3:24), angels have played a very important role in God's great plan of salvation. The ministry of angels brought God's Law to mankind, the precursor of the saving gospel of Christ.

15 THE MINISTRY OF ANGELS (3)

GUIDING, GUARDING, DELIVERING, DESTROYING

A third work of the earthly ministry of angels is to guide, guard and deliver the saints of God, wherever they may be, whatever their need, and to destroy the enemies of God, whoever they may be. It is not in man to direct his own steps. Men are like sheep – they tend to go astray. Many times the people of God have found themselves in a situation too great for them to understand or with which to cope. Here is where the ministry of angels is not only helpful but necessary. Angels are not jealous. They love God and His people and work diligently on their behalf.

GUIDING ANGELS

When the children of Israel were making their exodus from Egypt, the angel of the Lord led them (Num. 20:15,16). The angel guided them by day in a pillar of a cloud and by night he gave them light in the pillar of fire (Exod. 13:21; 14:19). God instructed the Israelites to pay strict attention to the angel, to listen to whatever he said and not to rebel against him since he represented God Himself (Exod. 23:20-23).

GUARDIAN ANGELS

Angels guard as well as guide. Psalm 34:7 says, "The angel of the Lord encamps around those who fear him, and he delivers them." Those who are wise enough to put their trust in God will be protected from disaster and harm. "For he will command his angels concerning you to guard you in all your ways; they will lift you up in their hands, so that you will not strike your foot against a stone" (Psa. 91:11). In the temptation of Jesus, Satan partially quotes this Scripture in a vain attempt to get Jesus to jump from the pinnacle of the temple. The portion he left out was "to guard you in all your ways" in the first clause. As B.W. Johnson notes, "The promise is limited to those who walk in the way appointed to them" (*The People's New Testament With Notes*, p. 31).

The Israelites were protected by an angel of God in their conquest of Canaan. The angel went before them, driving out their enemies (Exod. 33:2).

Elisha is another case in point. He had proven to be a thorn in the side of the king of Syria. Time and time again Elisha had thwarted his plans by revealing them to the king of Israel. Enraged, the king of Syria sent troops to Dothan to capture the wily prophet. When Elisha's servant arose that morning, he discovered that they were surrounded by the enemy troops. "Not to worry," was Elisha's reply, in effect. He knew that God's secret agents – the angels – were protecting him. He prayed that God would open his servant's eyes and give him supernatural vision. God did, and what the bug-eyed servant saw nearly transfixed him. The hills were alive with horses and chariots of fire! This story is found in 2 Kings 6:8-23. Read it and rejoice! "Those who are with us are more than those who are with them" (2 Kings 6:16). Truly, the angels of God encamp around those who will fear and trust the Lord.

Michael, the mighty archangel of God, is a protector of God's people (Dan. 12:1). In the final days – when there will be distress as never before – Michael will protect and deliver "everyone whose name is found written in the book." How we should thank God for the protection of His angels in times past, the present and in the future!

Perhaps the best-known reference in the Bible to "guardian angels" is Matthew 18:10. In this passage our

Lord said, "See that you do not look down on one of these little ones. For I tell you that their angels in heaven always see the face of my Father in heaven." The care and concern that Jesus had for little children was very real. He loved them, took them up in his arms, told people that if they didn't become like little children they would not enter heaven, and rebuked His own disciples for their attitude toward children. Each child has an angel in heaven who takes a special interest in them – just as our Lord did. They "see the face of the Father" on behalf of the children – many of whom have been totally rejected by their natural fathers and mothers.

Herbert Lockyer asks,

> But what exactly did Jesus mean by his assertion: "In heaven their (the little ones) angels do always behold the face of my Father which is in heaven" (Matt. 18:10)? Do children have angels of their own? When they cease to be children, have they no further need of angelic guardianship? We do not feel that Jesus meant that each child born into the world is given in charge to some individual angel whose responsibility it is to watch over it and, in some way or other, render the child aid in the critical junctures of its life. The language Jesus used suggests that a certain company of angels collectively cared for children in general; the idea is that of collective rather than a personal and particular guardianship. Jesus did not say their several angels, but "their angels," the plural angels favoring corporate rather than individual care. Each among "the little ones" is not to have his own angel, but angels....
>
> Paul, however, reminds us that the care of angels is not confined to children. "Are they not all ministering spirits, sent forth to minister for them who shall be heirs of salvation" (Heb. 1:13,14)? Just how they minister to us, we are not told, but as they ministered to Jesus in the days of his flesh, so they undertake in unseen and unknown ways for the heirs of salvation, the redeemed of the Lord, whether they be young or old (*Everything Jesus Taught*, pp. 448, 449).

Perhaps one of the most difficult questions to answer about angels is the question of a grieving parent, "If there are guardian angels, why did my child die?" Some children, despite the reality of guardian angels, die young, are killed in accidents or are even murdered. What can we say to these parents in pain?

There are instances in the Bible where some children were saved by angelic intervention and others were not. The parents of the Christ Child, for example, were warned by an angel to flee to the safety of Egypt (Matt. 2:13), but many parents in Bethlehem mourned the slaughter of their innocent children, in sad fulfillment of Jeremiah's prophecy (Matt. 2:16-17; Jer. 31:15).

It is most difficult for us to understand why James, the brother of John, was put in prison and then beheaded by Herod (Acts 12:1-2), but in that same prison, just a few days later, Peter was wonderfully released, escaping execution, at the intervention of an angel (Acts 12:3-19). Why did God allow Peter's angel (Acts 12:15) to rescue him, but did not allow James' angel to do the same? What would you say to the grieving families of James, Stephen, and Antipas – and a veritable host of other "faithful martyrs" (Rev. 2:13) who were not spared death by the heavenly host?

We do not wish to question the wisdom of an all-wise God. "It is not mine to question the judgments of my Lord. It is but mine to follow the leadings of His Word" (C. Austin Miles). We can learn something from the ancient sufferer Job. This good man lost all his children – seven sons and three daughters – in one day's time. But his response to this tragedy was magnificent. "The Lord gave, and the Lord has taken away; blessed be the name of the Lord" (Job 1:21). In all this tragedy, the record says, "Job did not sin nor charge God with wrong." In fact, Job's faith was such that he could later truthfully affirm, "Though He slay me, yet will I trust in Him" (Job 13:15).

"RESCUE SQUADS"

Many times God has sent angelic rescue squads to deliver His people. Angels reached out and jerked Lot back into his own house, rescuing him from a mob of homosexuals (Gen. 19:10). The next day they evacuated Lot and those of his family who would listen from the coming holocaust (Gen. 19:15,16).

Young Isaac, who was born according to the promise of God, was divinely spared from being sacrificed on the altar when an angel of the Lord stayed the upraised hand of Abraham (Gen. 22:10-12). Talk about deliverance at the last minute!

When Jacob was dying, he blessed the Lord for His angel who had delivered him from harm all the days of his life (Gen. 48:16). Perhaps he was referring to the time just before he met his wronged and estranged brother Esau. On that occasion, the angels of God met Jacob (Gen. 32:1). In any event, you and I should be as observant and thankful for the ministry of angelic deliverance as Jacob was on his deathbed.

God sent a rescue team of one to deliver the three Hebrew children from death in the furnace (Dan. 3:28). The Hebrew writer may have had this in mind when he spoke of those who "quenched the fury of the flames" (Heb. 11:34).

An angel spared Daniel from a violent death when he muzzled the hungry beasts (who later devoured Daniel's enemies before they hit the ground). Again, the Hebrew writer refers to those who "shut the mouths of lions" (Heb. 11:33).

The apostles of Christ were put on display, "like men condemned to the arena." Paul said, "We have been made a spectacle to the whole universe, to angels as well as men" (1 Cor. 4:9). Angels did more than just observe the apostles' trials in sympathetic silence. They delivered the apostles from prison (Acts 5:19). Peter was broken out of jail by an angel on his execution eve (Acts 12:6-11). In his last inspired document Paul writes that he was "delivered from the lion's mouth" (2 Tim. 4:17). While some see the lion as the devil (the devil is likened to a lion in I Peter 5:8), it may be a reference to an actual deliverance from a wild beast, perhaps in an arena where many Christians were cast to lions. In 1 Corinthians 15:32 Paul wrote, "If I fought wild beasts in Ephesus for merely human reasons, what have I gained?" Again, some see the reference to wild beasts as human beings, but it is not unreasonable to think that Paul may indeed have been delivered from wild animals. If so, it would not surprise us to find angels as his source of deliverance.

THE DEATH ANGEL

Not only do angels guide, guard and deliver the saints of God from trouble, they turn around and trouble the enemies of God – even to the point of death! I would not want to be the enemy of God! The angel of the Lord, according to Psalms 35:5,6, pursues those who fight against God and His people. "May they be like chaff before the wind, with the angel of the Lord driving them away; may their path be dark and slippery, with the angel of the Lord pursuing them."

For example, angels smote the men of Sodom with blindness (Gen. 19:11). The same thing happened to an entire Syrian army (2 Kings 6:18). Psalms 78:49 informs us that it was a "band of destroying angels" that unleashed the 10 plagues that thundered across ancient Egypt.

On one fateful night, the angel of the Lord smote 185,000 Syrian soldiers causing Sennacherib, king of Assyria, to lift his siege against Jerusalem (2 Kings 19:35). When David sinned by numbering the people, an angel destroyed 70,000 Israelites and was about to destroy all Jerusalem when God stayed his hand (2 Sam. 24:15-17). David saw the awesome angel standing between heaven and earth, a drawn sword in his hand stretched out over the holy city (1 Chron. 21:15). The destroying angel "killed many Israelites who murmured" (1 Cor. 10:10).

An angel of the Lord immediately smote King Herod because he did not give God the glory for his oratorical ability. He was greatly afflicted with worms and he died a horrible death (Acts 12:21-23).

In the book of Revelation, the seven angels with the seven last plagues wreak absolute havoc on the enemies of God. "Men gnawed their tongues in agony and cursed the God of heaven because of their pains and sores, but they refused to repent of what they had done" (Rev. 16:10.11). Wave after wave of awful punishment is inflicted on stubborn and unrepentant mankind by the angels of God.

SUMMARY

What have we learned? That angels are sent from God to guide His people, to guard them from danger and harm, to deliver them from evil. By the same token, angels are used by God to afflict, punish and even execute His enemies. Let us strive to live like godly Abraham who was called "the friend of God." Let us be careful that we do not become friendly with the ways of the wicked world for "Anyone who chooses to be a friend of the world becomes an enemy of God" (Jas. 4:4).

16 THE MINISTRY OF ANGELS (4)

Angels are sometimes called "watchers" in the Bible (Dan. 4:13,17, 23 KJV). This title indicates their interest in and guardianship of believers. Angels have always watched over God's people. The church is no exception to this rule. Angels watch over God's new society, the church.

ANGELS WATCH THE CHURCH

In the context of the church at worship, Paul states that angels observe us (1 Cor. 11:10). The church (*ekklesia*) is God's called-out people. He has called them out of a world of sin and into a glorious fellowship made possible through the shed blood of His Son, Jesus Christ. God purchased the church with His own blood (Acts 20:28). Christ loved the church and gave Himself for her (Eph. 5:25). Angels – even though they have not experienced redemption through the blood – love the church too. They are very interested in it – i.e., you and me.

The angels in heaven rejoice when a sinner on earth repents of sin and turns to God (Luke 15:10). Think for a moment how the angels must have celebrated on the day of Pentecost when about 3,000 souls repented and were baptized in the name of Jesus Christ for the forgiveness of sins (Acts 2:38). That account goes on to say that those who gladly received the Word were baptized, the Lord added them to the church, and they continued in the Christian life with gladness (Acts 2:41,47). If there was joy in Jerusalem, there must have been hilarity in heaven!

ANGELS INTERESTED IN OUR PRAYERS

One spiritual exercise in which the early Christians continued steadfastly was prayer (Acts 2:42). Prayer was a very important part of their Christian life, both publicly and privately. They prayed to God through His Son, Jesus Christ. Prayer, to be effective, must be offered to God in Jesus' name (John 14:6, 13,14). But in Revelation 8:3,4, we discover an added dimension – an angel stands before God and is given the prayers of the saints. He, in turn, offers them up to God. "Another angel, who had a golden censer, came and stood at the altar. He was given much incense to offer, with the prayers of all the saints, on the golden altar before the throne. The smoke of the incense, together with the prayers of the saints, went up before God from the angel's hand."

This does not mean that we are to pray to angels. Such is forbidden in Scripture. We are not to worship angels (Col. 2:18; Rev. 22:8,9). Nor are we to offer incense to the Lord. But we are to be aware that the ministry of angels and the prayers of the saints are intertwined. Angels are interested in the prayers of the church.

ANGELS OBSERVE THE CHURCH AT WORSHIP

Angels are also interested in the worship of the church. Perhaps this is why Paul cautioned the women worshippers in the church at Corinth about praying to God with their heads uncovered – "because of the angels" (1 Cor. 11:10). It is evident (although the meaning of this passage is not generally agreed upon) that angels are heavenly observers of the worship assemblies of the church. What do they see when they "visit" each Sunday? Worshippers or whisperers? Singers or sleepers? Participants or pew-sitters?

Paul also saw fit to caution a young minister, Timothy, about showing favoritism in the selection and appointment of church leaders. "I charge you, in the sight of God and

Christ Jesus and the elect angels, to keep these instructions without partiality, and to do nothing out of favoritism. Do not be hasty in the laying on of hands, and do not share in the sins of others" (1 Tim. 5:21, 22). The presence of angels should serve as an incentive as to how we, too, ought to conduct ourselves in the house of God, which is the church (1 Tim. 3:15). Realizing that angels are present and watching should add some much-needed decorum and dignity to our worship assemblies.

ANGELS INTERESTED IN THE MESSAGE OF REDEMPTION

Although the angels of God have not experienced redemption through the blood of Jesus, they have a strong desire to know more about this wonderful theme. The apostle Peter writes that angels, like the prophets of old, seek to know more about salvation.

> Concerning this salvation, the prophets, who spoke of the grace that was to come to you, searched intently and with the greatest care, trying to find out the time and circumstances to which the Spirit of Christ in them was pointing when he predicted the sufferings of Christ and the glories that would follow. It was revealed to them that they were not serving themselves but you, when they spoke of the things that have now been told you by the Holy Spirit sent from heaven. Even angels long to look into these things (1 Pet. 1:10-12).

The prophets, who share this intense desire with angels, were informed that the reason they could not understand their own Spirit-inspired prophecies regarding the Redeemer was because they were not serving themselves. They were serving us! What "privileged characters" we are! The angels, who also long to understand the wonderful plan of salvation, are not allowed to fully fathom the mysteries of the gospel because they, too, were sent to serve those who would inherit salvation (Heb. 1:14) – you and me!

Does this deter the holy angels from trying to learn more? No. And there is nothing wrong with this either. God did not rebuke the prophets or the angels for trying to gain a greater understanding of spiritual things. In fact, from Ephesians 3:10, it appears that God even wants the angels to know about the gospel. In that passage, Paul testifies that God gave him grace to preach to the Gentiles the unsearchable riches of Christ and to make plain to everyone the mystery, which, for ages past was kept hidden in God. But then notice what he adds. "His intent was that now, through the church, the manifold wisdom of God should be made known to the rulers and authorities in the heavenly realms." Who are these rulers and authorities in the heavenly realms? None other than angels (see also Eph. 1:21; Col. 1:16; 2:10). B.W. Johnson points out that the manifold wisdom of God was to be made known by preaching of the gospel to three groups; (1) to the Jew, (2) to the Gentile, (3) to the angels.

How enlightened are the holy angels by the teaching and preaching in our churches? How much do they learn about the gospel by listening to the lessons taught in our Bible classes? What are they discovering about the greatest story ever told in the sermons our preachers are preaching? Or is it the greatest story never told? Paul professed to know nothing but "Jesus Christ, and him crucified" (1 Cor. 2:2). Angels must have learned much by "eavesdropping" on his teaching and preaching. What are they learning from the teaching and preaching in your congregation?

THE ANGELIC THEATER

The angels in heaven are also very interested in our day-to-day struggles. Paul wrote, "For it seems to me that God has put us apostles on display at the end of the procession, like men condemned to die in the arena. We have been made a spectacle to the whole universe, to angels as well as to men" (1 Cor. 4:9).

A.S. Joppie comments,

> The word spectacle (Gr. *theatron*) refers to the old Roman theater or Colosseum which seated 80,000 people. In this great theater the so-called gladiators fought to entertain the emperor and pleasure-loving Romans. The wicked hearts of the Romans became so depraved that men fought savage beasts of all kinds, wild bulls, half-starved lions and the like. Rome reached the depth of her depravity when human beings – the Christians – were brought in and subjected to all kinds of torture for entertainment. St. Paul says this world is like a great theater and that the angels are looking down and watching. Angels are watching every day how you stand up for Jesus Christ. They observe how you fight for truth and right (*The Ministry of Angels*, p. 72).

Paul himself testified, "I fought wild beasts in Ephesus" (1 Cor. 15:32). Were these "wild beasts" merely men with beast-like behavior or were they actually wild animals to whom Paul was thrown? He would not be the first godly person to be thrown to wild beasts and delivered by angels (Dan. 6:22). And did not the great apostle also testify, "And I was delivered from the lion's mouth" (2 Tim. 4:17)? This could be a reference to Satan, the "roaring lion" (1 Pet. 5:8). or to actual wild beasts. When Jesus was tempted in the wilderness, wild beasts were present but angels may have protected Him in His weakened physical state (Mark 1:13).

Angels witness the spiritual struggles of God's saints on earth. Perhaps they saw Stephen's face, for the Bible says that during his ordeal before the Sanhedrin, his face was "like the face of an angel" (Acts 6:15). Some feel that Hebrews 12:1, the "great cloud of witnesses," is a reference to angels watching us. If so, all around us angels are watching, hoping, straining with us in the spiritual fight.

"This world is a great theater! Angels are beholding us! What a solemn warning to every one of us! How carefully we should walk! How carefully we should talk! For the angels are near!" (*The Ministry of Angels*, p.73).

17 THE MINISTRY OF ANGELS (5)

ANGELS ARE PRESENT AT DEATH

One of the most fascinating and comforting aspects of the angels' service on behalf of the saints is the fact that they minister to us, even in death. The service that they render on our behalf does not end at death but continues until we are "safe in the arms of Jesus." We depend upon the angels of God more than we will ever know.

WHAT HAPPENS AT DEATH?

What happens when a person dies? Where does his spirit go? How does it get there? Is there any difficulty in it getting from Point A to Point B? Are there any forces that would seek to prevent its safe arrival?

These are not trivial questions. They are extremely important and deserve straight-forward, Biblical answers. Interestingly, angels play an important part in these answers.

The Bible says, "Blessed are the dead who die in the Lord" (Rev. 14:13). Death, for the believer, is a blessed or happy event. What wonderful assurance it gives us to know that our sins are forgiven and that we have a home awaiting us in heaven (1 John 5:13).

The apostle Paul testified that to be "absent from the body" was to be "present with the Lord (2 Cor. 5:8). When a Christian dies, his spirit departs to be "with the Lord" (Phil 1:23). Where is the Lord? He is in heaven, seated at the right hand of God (Mark 16:19; Heb. 1:3; Acts 2:33 et al.). Where does the spirit of a believer go at death? To be "with the Lord" – in heaven!

THE PARADE FROM PARADISE

Before Christ arose from the grave and ascended into heaven, "leading captivity captive" (Eph. 4:8 KJV), the spirits of just men went to Paradise.

THE INTERMEDIATE STATES OF THE DEAD

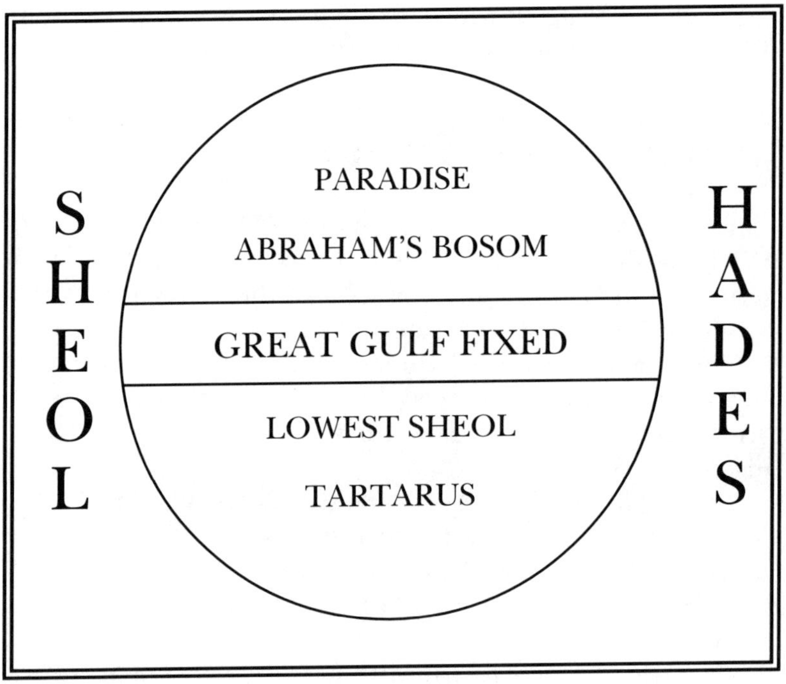

Jesus Himself told the repentant thief that he would be with Him in Paradise (Luke 23:43). At death their spirits went to that place. Paradise was a place much like heaven.

It was a place of rest and comfort (Luke 16:25). It was one of two compartments in Hades, the unseen abode of the dead. It was separated from Tartarus, a horrible place of suffering, by a great gulf (Luke 16:26).

Now that Jesus has ascended to His home on high (taking with Him the "spirits of just men made perfect"), those who die in the Lord go directly to be with the Lord in heaven. What comfort and blessing this gives us who have loved ones "die in the Lord."

HOW DOES THE SPIRIT GET FROM HERE TO THERE?

How does the spirit of a believer in Christ get from earth to glory? By the continuing ministry of the angels of God! Jesus declared that when the beggar Lazarus died, he was "carried by the angels into Abraham's bosom" (Luke 16:22). The angels are our source of transport to heaven when we die.

Death is the separation of the spirit from the body. James wrote, "The body without the spirit is dead" (Jas. 2:26). When a person dies, his body is consigned to the earth where it returns to its original element, dust. But the spirit – "the real you" – goes back to the Creator who gave it life.

Wise Solomon spoke of the death experience and declared with the wisdom God gave him that when a man goes to his "eternal home" the dust (body) returns to the earth from whence it came, but the spirit returns to the God who gave it (Eccl. 12:5,7). We know how the body returns to dust. We lovingly consign the bodies of our loved ones to the bosom of Mother Earth. But how does the spirit return to God? It is completely out of our hands. But the spirits of our departed are in good hands! The spirit of a believer is lovingly transported to the bosom of Abraham, or God, by the angels (Luke 16:22). Thank God for the caring, constant and continuing ministry of angels!

The apostle Paul described death as "the last enemy" (1 Cor. 15:26). But even in death the believer is triumphant. The body, consigned to earth, shall eventually be resurrected when Jesus returns. Hence, the grave has no victory (1 Cor. 15:55). The spirit has already winged its way home to God so there is no "sting" in death.

'TWIXT HEAVEN AND EARTH

Between heaven and earth is a vast expanse of seemingly endless space. If the spirit is to "return to God," it must pass through this incredible stretch of atmosphere. And Scripture warns that Satan, the enemy of the soul, is the "prince of the power of the air" (Eph. 2:2). The devil and his evil angels rule this air space. Paul also adds that our battle is not against flesh and blood but against the evil spirit world – against rulers, against the authorities, against the powers of this dark world and against the spiritual forces of evil in the heavenly realms (Eph. 6:12).

In life, evil angels seek to separate believers from God and Christ (Rom. 8:38). There is no reason to think that they suddenly give up their Satanic efforts when a believer dies. If Satan desired the body of Moses (Jude 9), how much more would he be interested in wresting the spirits of believers from God? So God sends his angels to transport the spirits of His children safely home. Note that it is more than just an angelic escort; the angels carried Lazarus to his eternal home.

If only our eyes could somehow be opened like Elisha's servant, we would see the eternal conflict that is taking place every moment in the heavens above! It is all for our sake, for our good. What a battle must be raging in the unseen heavenly realms for the souls of men – both in life and in death. Think how bravely and faithfully the angels of God protect the spirits of the departed who have boarded "Flight Final" to the New Jerusalem! Think of how daring and devilish must be the efforts of the angels of Satan who would abort this mission if they could. But they cannot. Peter writes that our eternal home is guarded by the power of God (1 Pet. 1:5). The Greek language indicates a "garrison of protectors." God placed Cherubim and a flaming sword in Eden to guard the tree of life from those who would seek entry into the garden (Gen. 3:24). He has placed faithful sentinels in heaven to guard our mansions. No evil forces can strip the angels of their priceless cargo.

HOW FAR TO HEAVEN?

How far is this final flight to heaven? How long does the flight take? Anybody who has ever traveled with small children knows how important questions like these are. "How far is it? Are we almost there? How many more miles? How many more minutes?" God wants His children to know about this journey.

According to Paul, it sounds like a matter of only seconds – "absent from the body, present with the Lord" (2 Cor. 5:8). Charles Spurgeon said, "Just one sigh and we are there."

Consider how far it is to heaven. Modern astronomers tell us it is at least 10 billion light-years to the edge of our universe. A light-year is calculated as the distance light can travel in one year, moving at the speed of 186,282 miles per second. This means it would take 10 billion years, traveling at the speed of light, just to reach the edge of our universe! And beyond that is heaven!

Not to worry. We have already learned that one astounding characteristic of the angels is their incredible swiftness with which they can move from one point to another. When God dispatches His angels, they travel faster than the speed of light. This defies the laws of nature, but angels are above the laws of nature. They are *supernatural* beings who can do supernatural things because they are endowed with supernatural power from a supernatural source – Almighty God. Angels come and go in "swift flight" (Dan. 9:21). Talk about a "space shuttle!"

WE ARE NEVER ALONE

The Christian does not have to cross "chilly Jordan" alone. We are not alone when we walk through the valley of the shadow of death (Psa. 23:4). The Lord has promised that He will never leave us nor forsake us (Heb. 13:5). Jesus promised His disciples that He would not leave them without comfort. He sent them the Comforter, the Holy Spirit (John 14:16, 26). Nor has He left us to fend for ourselves. We have the indwelling presence of the Holy Spirit to comfort, convict and counsel. And we have the everabiding presence and watchcare of the angels of God. The presence of angels in our lives – particularly at the moment of death – verifies the Biblical fact that we are never alone. Jefferson Hascall caught a picture of the angels' ministry in death when he wrote the hymn, "O Come, Angel Band." He writes of his impending death ("My latest sun is sinking fast"). He senses eternal gain ("I know I'm nearing holy ranks"). He also senses the approach of angels ("I've almost gained my heavenly home, My spirit loudly sings; The holy ones, behold they come, I hear the noise of wings"). The chorus contains his dying cry:

> *O come, angel band;*
> *come and around me stand,*
> *O bear me away on your snowy wings,*
> *to my eternal home!*

Can we say, with Jefferson Hascall, "Even so, come ye bands of angels!"?

18 ANGELS AND THE SECOND COMING OF CHRIST

More than 300 times the writers of the Bible declare that Jesus Christ is coming again. Every writer in the New Testament heralds the second advent of our Lord (Matt. 24:31; Mark 8:38; Luke 21:27; John 14:3; 1 Thess. 4:16; Jas. 5:8; 1 Pet. 5:4; Jude 14,15 et al). The doctrine of Christ's second coming is firmly set in Scripture. What is also clearly seen is the important role the angels of God will play in that long-awaited event.

ANGELS WILL PERSONALLY ACCOMPANY CHRIST

Jesus is coming again but He is not coming alone. He will be accompanied by the angels of heaven in His grand return. Angels announced the birth of Christ, ministered to Him after the temptation and before the betrayal and arrest, stood ready to help Him at the cross and will return in triumph with Him in the second advent.

We have Jesus' own word on this: "For the Son of Man is going to come in his Father's glory with His angels, and then he will reward each person according to what he has done" (Matt. 16:27). The angels, the lifelong companions of Jesus before His birth and first coming to earth, will be with Him when He returns a second time. What a glorious sight that will be to see Jesus descending with hundreds of thousands of angelic beings!

The accompanying angels are described as being "holy" and "mighty." They are called "holy" in Matthew 25:31, Mark 8:38 and Luke 9:26. "Holy" implies that they are spiritual and pure in nature. They are angels of righteousness. They are also called "mighty" in 2 Thessalonians 1:7 and Jude 14. "Mighty" suggests their awesome physical strength. The angels who come with Christ will be both spiritually and physically equal to their tasks.

THE SOUND OF THE TRUMPET

When the angels descend with Christ at the end of time, they will do so at the sound of a trumpet. "And he will send his angels with a loud trumpet call . . ." (Matt. 24:31). Paul also mentions the sounding of the trumpet in 1 Corinthians 15:52. The blast from the trumpet will be the signal for the angels in heaven to begin their descent with Christ to earth. Do you suppose they ask each other, "Do you think this will be the day?" We know from Scripture that they do not know the day nor the hour when Jesus will return (Matt. 24:36).

ANGELS WILL GATHER THE ELECT

Why are the angels coming? Why does God send them with Jesus? The Bible says it is because they are to gather the saved from the four corners of the earth. The angels know where they are. They have been observing them and protecting them for many years. Jesus said, "And he will send his angels and gather his elect from the four winds, from the ends of the earth to the ends of the heavens" (Mark 13:27).

Paul wrote, "Then the end will come, when he hands over the kingdom to God the Father after he has destroyed all dominion, authority and power" (1 Cor. 15:24). The return of Christ will spell doom for the evil angels. At the same time, the holy angels will be used to gather the elect to be delivered to the Father.

HEAVENLY HARVESTERS

The angels who come with Jesus will sever the wicked from among the just. Listen to our Lord: "This is how it will be at the end of the age. The angels will come and separate the wicked from the righteous . . ." (Matt. 13:49). The angels will know who is a child of God and who is a child of the devil. They will make no mistakes. In the parable of the tares (weeds) that were sown among the wheat (Matt. 13:24-30, 36-39), Jesus identified the subjects as follows:

The sower	Jesus, the Son of Man
The field	The world
The good seed	The sons of the kingdom
The tares (weeds)	The sons of the evil one (Satan)
The enemy that sowed them	The devil
The harvest	The end of the world (age)
The harvesters	The angels

It will be the solemn duty of these "heavenly harvesters" to weed out of Christ's kingdom all those who do evil and cause others to sin (Matt. 13:41). The insincere will be weeded out by the angels – there will be no more hypocrites in the church! The angels will know who is sincere and who is insincere, who are righteous and who are self-righteous, who are sinners and who are saints. The angels will collect the tares (the sons of the devil) and will bind them to await sentence (Matt. 13:30).

ANGELS WILL HEAR CHRIST CONFESS OR DENY MEN

The angels who will work with Christ on that fateful day will hear Him either confess or deny men. This must be one of the most chilling and yet thrilling aspects of their work.

Jesus said that whoever had confessed Him before men when they were on earth, "him shall the Son of Man also confess before the angels of God" (Luke 12:9 KJV).

We can almost imagine His words. "Yes, Father, this is one who was not ashamed to confess Me before his friends, his family, his fellow workers. He is worthy to enter heaven." How the angels will rejoice! But can you imagine the looks of sorrow and shame that will come over their faces when the Son of God denies and disowns men? The Bible says that Christ will deny, or disown men who have denied Him "before the angels of God" (Luke 12:9). If Peter wept bitterly when he denied Christ, think how awful the weeping will be when Christ denies men. We find these words of doom in Matthew 7:23, "Then I will tell them plainly, 'I never knew you. Away from me, you evildoers!'"

It will be a thrilling experience for the angels to hear Christ confess men before them. It will be a chilling experience for them to hear Christ say, "Depart! I never knew you!" What a bittersweet day that will be for the angels.

EXECUTORS OF ETERNAL JUDGMENT

The Bible says that the angels of God will be the final executors of judgment. Jude, the brother of our Lord, cites Enoch, the seventh from Adam, saying, "See, the Lord is coming with thousands upon thousands of his holy ones to judge everyone, and to convict all the ungodly of all the ungodly acts they have done in the ungodly way, and of all the harsh words ungodly sinners have spoken against him" (Jude 14,15).

Those whom the angels have gathered and bound will be punished with everlasting destruction, shut out forever from the presence of the Lord (2 Thess. 1:8,9). It will be the sad duty of the angels to "throw them into the furnace of fire" where there shall be "wailing and gnashing of teeth" (Matt. 13:41,42,49,50).

It will not be just the sinners and pretending believers who will be thrown into the lake of fire. The devil himself and all his evil angels will be cast into hell. Hell, in fact, was "prepared for the devil and his angels" (Matt. 25:41). In Revelation 20, John sees an angel coming down out of heaven who seizes Satan, binds him and locks him in the Abyss for a thousand years (Rev. 20:1-3). Later, the devil is thrown into the lake of fire where he is tormented day and night for ever and ever (Rev. 20:10). Who throws him in? We would not be surprised at all if it were the same angel, for that is the duty of angels.

SUMMARY

With the casting of Satan and his angels into hell, the grim work of the angels of God will be finished. Never again will they have to battle the forces of evil. No more will they have to leave the beauty of heaven to speed to the earth of wickedness and woe. Together with the saved of all ages they will enjoy a life of peace and praise in heaven.

19 ANGELS IN THE BOOK OF REVELATION

Of special interest to many are the angels mentioned in the book of Revelation. There are about 30 special angels that appear in the pages of this unique book. Of course, there are "myriads" of angels that worship and serve God.

Since much of Revelation is written in highly figurative or symbolic language, we will not concern ourselves by giving our interpretation of each angel and his work. The reader may do so, if he is so inclined. This chapter will simply summarize the ministry of angels in the book of Revelation by categorizing what the Bible says they said, did or looked like.

REVELATION GIVEN BY AN ANGEL

To begin with, Revelation 1:1 says that God made the revelation of Jesus Christ known to John by sending an angel to the Patmos-bound disciple. An angel is a messenger. The message of Revelation was given to John by an angel from heaven. How God must have trusted this angel! How privileged was this angel – to serve as a "middleman" for this great book.

THE SEVEN EVANGELISTS

The seven stars of Revelation 1:16 are identified by Jesus to be the seven angels, or messengers, of the seven churches (Rev. 1:20). The basic meaning of *angelos* is "messenger." A messenger can be human or divine. In this case we believe that the angels were human messengers, or evangelists. Look at the word "ev*angel*ist." What root word do you see? Angel.

Each of the seven churches of Asia had an angel, or human messenger, evangelist. The angel of each church is mentioned (Ephesus, Rev. 2:1; Smyrna, Rev. 2:8; Pergamum, Rev. 2:12; Thyatira, Rev. 2:18; Sardis, Rev. 3:1; Philadelphia, Rev. 3:7; Laodicea, Rev. 3:14). Some believe that these angels were actually divine beings that watched over each church. That may be. One thing for sure, from chapter three on the angels certainly appear to be divine in nature.

THE MIGHTY ANGEL AND THE SCROLL

In Revelation 5:2 a "mighty" angel is mentioned. He proclaims with a loud voice, "Who is worthy to break the seals and open the scroll?" When no one in heaven or earth is found to open the scroll, great weeping occurs. When the Lamb of God is finally found to open the scroll, there is great rejoicing. "Many angels, numbering thousands upon thousands, and ten thousand times ten thousand" encircle the throne and with a loud voice sing, "Worthy is the Lamb, who was slain, to receive power and wealth and wisdom and strength and honor and glory and praise!" (Rev. 5:11, 12).

FOUR ANGELS AT THE CORNERS OF THE EARTH; THE ANGEL WITH THE SEAL

In the seventh chapter, John sees four angels standing at the four corners of the earth (Rev. 7:1). They are holding back the four winds of the earth. Then John sees another angel coming from the east (Rev. 7:2). This angel has the seal of the living God in his hands. The angel cries out in a loud voice to the four angels who are holding back the four winds, "Do not harm the land or the sea or the trees until we put a seal on the foreheads of the servants of our God" (Rev. 7:3). The 144,000 are then sealed and all the angels who are standing around the throne fall down and worship God (Rev. 7:4, 11).

SEVEN ANGELS WITH SEVEN TRUMPETS; THE ANGEL WITH THE GOLDEN CENSER

Seven angels stand before God in Revelation 8:2. Each of them receives a trumpet. Another angel, carrying a golden censer, approaches the altar. He is given incense to offer, along with the prayers of the saints (Rev. 8:3). Both ascend up to God from the angel's hand. Then the angel does a strange thing. He fills the censer with fire from the altar and hurls it to the earth! Great peals of thunder roll, lightning flashes and a rumbling earthquake takes place (Rev. 8:4).

In chapters eight and nine, the first six angels sound their trumpets. The following occurs when each trumpet is sounded:

1. The first angel (Rev. 8:7). Hail, fire and blood fall upon the earth. One third of the trees, grass and earth are burned up.
2. The second angel (Rev. 8:8,9). A burning, mountain-like object is thrown into the sea. A third of the sea turns to blood, a third of the sea creatures die, a third of the ships are destroyed.
3. The third angel (Rev. 8:10,11). A great, blazing star named "Wormwood" streaks from the sky and contaminates one third of the earth's water. Many people die from the bitter water.
4. The fourth angel (Rev. 8:12,13). A third of the sun, moon and stars are stricken so that they turn dark. As John watches, an eagle in midair cries, "Woe! Woe! Woe to the inhabitants of the earth, because of the trumpet blasts about to be sounded by the other three angels!"
5. The fifth angel (Rev. 9:1-12). A star falls from the sky

to the earth. He is given a key to the Abyss. He opens the Abyss and amidst great plumes of smoke, locusts emerge. The locusts are given power to torment, but not to kill, those who do not have the seal of God on their foreheads. The locusts do so for five months. Their king is the angel of the Abyss. In Hebrew his name is "Abaddon." In Greek, "Apollyon." Both names mean "destroyer." This locust-king is Satan.

6. The sixth angel (Rev. 9:13-21). A voice is heard coming from the golden altar before God. It tells the sixth angel to "Release the four angels who are bound at the great river Euphrates" (Rev. 9:14). The four angels are released and one third of mankind is killed. Those who are not killed continue in their unrepentant state, worshiping demons, idols, committing murder, practicing the magic arts, sexual immorality and theft.

THE RAINBOW ANGEL

Another mighty angel appears in chapter 10. He comes down from heaven robed in a cloud, with a rainbow above his head; his face is like the sun and his legs are pillars of fire (Rev. 10:1). He holds a little book in his hand and straddles the land and sea. When he gives a lion-like shout, the voices of seven thunders are heard. John is about to write down what they said but is forbidden to do so. The angel lifts his right hand to heaven and declares that when the seventh angel sounds his trumpet, the mystery of God will be accomplished. John is told to take the little scroll from the angel and eat it. The angel tells him to do so but warns him that though it will taste sweet in his mouth, it will turn sour in his stomach. He tells John to continue his prophecy about peoples, nations, languages and kings.

THE DREADED SEVENTH ANGEL

The much feared seventh angel finally sounds his trumpet in chapter 11. God's temple in heaven is opened! Lightning flashes, thunder rolls, the earth quakes and a great hailstorm ensues. Inside the temple, the ark of God's covenant can be seen!

ANGELIC WAR IN HEAVEN

A titanic struggle ensues between Michael and his angels and the devil and his angels in Revelation 12:7-9. Some see this as describing a pre-Eden event and others see it as happening during the "end times." In any event, Satan and his angels are not strong enough to prevail. They lose their place in heaven. They are cast down in defeat to the earth.

A TRIO OF FLYING ANGELS

The 14th chapter of Revelation opens with the first of three angels flying through the air. The angel has the everlasting gospel that is to be proclaimed to "every nation, tribe, language and people" (Rev. 14:7).

The second flying angel follows and cries, "Fallen! Fallen is Babylon the Great . . ." (Rev. 14:8).

The third flying angel cries in a loud voice that if anyone worships the beast or his image and receives his mark that he will drink of God's fury. He adds that they will be tormented "in the presence of the holy angels and the Lamb" (Rev. 14:10). He urges the saints of God to continue patient endurance in obeying God's commandments and faithfulness to Jesus (Rev. 14:12).

SEVEN ANGELS WITH THE SEVEN LAST PLAGUES

Chapter 15 begins with a great and marvelous sign in heaven: the seven angels with the seven last plagues – "last, because with them God's wrath is completed" (Rev. 15:1). The angels emerge from the temple, dressed in shining linen with golden sashes. Each one is given a golden bowl, filled with deadly contents – the wrath of God (Rev. 15:7). In chapter 16 they are instructed to pour out the contents of their bowls upon the earth (Rev. 16:1). They proceed to do so as follows:

1. The first angel (Rev. 16:2). His bowl is poured out on the land. Ugly, painful sores break out on those who have the mark of the beast and who worship his image.

2. The second angel (Rev. 16:3). He pours out his bowl on the sea. It turns to blood. Every living thing in the sea dies.

3. The third angel (Rev. 16:4-7). This angel pours out his bowl on the rivers and springs of water. They too, turn into blood. The angel in charge of water declares that this judgment is just because the enemies of God have shed the blood of God's saints and prophets (Rev. 16:5,6). Poetic justice, as it were.

4. The fourth angel (Rev. 16:8,9). The sun is the target of the fourth plague. The sun intensifies its heat and the enemies of God are seared and scorched with intense heat. Do they repent? No. They curse the God who is causing these plagues and continue in their rebellion and sin.

5. The fifth angel (Rev. 16:10,11). His bowl is poured out on the throne of the beast. A direct hit! The beast's kingdom is plunged into darkness. An awful scene ensues. Men gnaw their tongues in agony. They hurl curses at God because of their pain. "But they refused to repent of what they had done" (Rev. 16:11).

6. The sixth angel (Rev. 16:12-16). The Euphrates river is the target of the sixth angel's bowl. The water is dried up to allow three frog-like evil spirits to emerge from the

mouths of the dragon, beast and false prophet. These are actually demon-spirits who go out to gather the kings of the earth for a great battle, Armageddon.

7. The seventh angel (Rev. 16:17-21). The last plague, like the 10th and final plague in ancient Egypt (Exod. 12:29), was the worst. The seventh angel pours out his bowl into the air. A great cry emanates from the temple, from the throne, saying, "It is done!" (Rev. 16:17). Again the thunder rolls, lightning flashes and this time an earthquake unparalleled in history occurs. The great city of Babylon is split into three parts. Cities of the nations suffer total collapse. God, remembering the sins of Babylon the Great, gives her a cup "filled with the wine of the fury of his wrath" (Rev. 16:19). One-hundred-pound hailstones fall from the sky upon men. They scream and curse God because the plague is so terrible.

THE INTERPRETIVE ANGEL

Sensing John's bewilderment, one of the seven angels who poured out one of the bowls invites John on a journey to understand what has happened (Rev. 17:1). The angel carries John "away in the Spirit into a desert" (Rev. 17:3). John sees a woman sitting on a seven-headed, ten-horned scarlet beast. She holds a golden cup, filled with filth. Written on her forehead is this title:

MYSTERY
BABYLON THE GREAT
THE MOTHER OF PROSTITUTES
AND OF THE ABOMINATIONS OF THE EARTH

The woman is drunk with the blood of saints. John's astonishment increases. The angel offers to explain the mystery of the woman and the beast she rides (Rev. 17:7). The angel's interpretation is found in the balance of the chapter (Rev. 17:8-18). He cautions that it "calls for a mind with wisdom" to understand it (Rev. 17:9).

THE ILLUMINATING ANGEL

After receiving the interpretation from the angel, John sees another angel coming down from heaven. This one has great authority and "the earth was illuminated by his splendor" (Rev. 18:1). With a mighty voice he shouts, "Fallen! Fallen is Babylon the Great!" There follows a long list of her sins (Rev. 18:2-20).

THE ROCK-THROWING ANGEL

Following the lengthy denunciation of Babylon by the illuminating angel, another angel, mighty in strength, picks up a boulder "the size of a large millstone" and casts it into the sea (Rev.18:21). He then explains that this is to symbolize the violent downfall of Babylon (Rev. 18:21-24).

THE ANGEL WHOM JOHN ATTEMPTED TO WORSHIP

A strange thing happens, or almost happens, in chapter 19. The angel who has been telling John to write all these things down becomes the would-be object of John's worship! The angel had been dictating to John, "Write: 'Blessed are those who are invited to the wedding supper of the Lamb.'" He also added, "These are the true words of God" (Rev. 19:9). Upon hearing these twin statements, John falls at the angel's feet to worship him. Why? Perhaps these words were so indicative of the Lord that John thought that's who was addressing him. But the angel rebukes him, saying, "Do not do it! I am a fellow servant with you and with your brothers who hold to the testimony of Jesus. Worship God! For the testimony of Jesus is the spirit of prophecy" (Rev. 19:10).

Does poor John learn the lesson? No. Later, in Revelation 22, the same thing happens. John again falls down before the revealing angel and attempts to worship him. The angel gives the same rebuke (Rev. 22:8,9).

THE ANGEL WHO STOOD IN THE SUN

After receiving a magnificent vision of the Rider on the White Horse (Rev. 19:11-16), John sees an angel "standing in the sun" (Rev. 19:17). This angel has a strange announcement to make. He invites the birds of the air to a great feast – rotting flesh of kings, generals, soldiers, horses, freemen, slaves, small and great (Rev. 19:17,18). These are the victims of the great battle, Armageddon, which is described in verses 19 and 20. The birds gorge themselves on the mountains of flesh.

THE ANGEL WITH THE KEY TO THE ABYSS

John sees what must have been a welcome sight in Revelation 20:1. An angel comes down from heaven with a key to the Abyss (bottomless pit, KJV). The Abyss is the abode of unclean spirits (demons) and fallen angels. It is mentioned seven times in Revelation (9:1,2,11; 11:7; 17:8; 20:1,3). The welcome angel also has a chain in his hand. He seizes Satan! What a cheer must have gone up from the watching angels! He binds him for "a thousand years" and throws him into the Abyss, locking it with the key (Rev. 20:2,3). Later, the devil will be loosed and will enjoy a brief time of deceiving the nations (Rev. 20:7,8). He causes them to surround the people of God but at the last minute, fire falls from heaven, destroying the enemies (Rev. 20:9). Satan is then thrown into the lake of fire where he is tormented for eternity (Rev. 20:10).

THE ANGEL WHO SHOWED JOHN THE HOLY CITY

John now is privileged to view the Holy City, the New Jerusalem (Rev. 21:1, 2). After all the wonderful but terrible things John had seen in his visions, this must have been a sight for sore eyes! One of the seven angels involved in the seven last plagues comes to John and offers to give him an aerial view of the Holy City (Rev. 21:9). John is carried away in the Spirit to a high mountain and shown "the Holy City, Jerusalem, coming down out of heaven from God" (Rev. 21:10). The angel had with him a golden measuring rod with which he measured the city. John recorded the measurements and other fascinating details (Rev. 21:15-27).

The last chapter of Revelation (indeed, of the entire Bible) opens with this angel showing John another magnificent sight – the river of life, "clear as crystal," flowing from the throne of God (Rev. 22:1). The angel tells John that his words are trustworthy and true and that God has sent him to show His servants the things that must soon take place (Rev. 22:6). John then hears the voice of Jesus Himself, saying, "Behold, I am coming soon! Blessed is he who keeps the words of the prophecy in this book" (Rev. 22:7). Perhaps mistaking the angel for Jesus, John again fell down to worship him but was forbidden (Rev. 22:8-9).

THE LAST MESSAGE FROM AN ANGEL

The angel then tells John not to seal up the prophetic book yet, "because the time is near" (Rev. 22:10). He then gives the last message we find by an angel in the Bible: "Let him who does wrong continue to do wrong; let him who is vile continue to be vile; let him who does right continue to do right; and let him who is holy continue to be holy" (Rev. 22:11). Solemn words, those. And how appropriate that the last word spoken by a holy messenger sent from a holy God was "holy."

THE LAST MENTION OF AN ANGEL IN THE BIBLE

The Lord Jesus Christ Himself testifies in Revelation 22:16 that it is He who sent this angel to John to record the message for the churches. "I, Jesus, have sent my angel to give you this testimony for the churches. I am the Root and the Offspring of David and the bright Morning Star." This is the last reference to angels in Scripture.

20 DO ANGELS EXIST TODAY?

Do angels still exist? Are they present with us today? Do they still intervene in the affairs of men? Questions like these may have been running through your mind throughout this study of what the Bible says about angels.

These are perfectly legitimate questions to ask. They deserve honest, Biblically-based answers. It is all well and good to read the exciting accounts of angels in the Bible. Who has not thrilled to the story of Daniel's deliverance from the lion's den? "My God hath sent his angel!" exulted Daniel (Dan. 6:22). Great! Wonderful! Tremendous! But what of us mortals today? Does God still have His angels? Does He still send them to help us? Do they still intervene on our behalf? If so, why don't we sense their presence more than we do? Why don't we see them like Abraham, Jacob, Gideon and many others did?

THE ANSWER IS YES

Angels are still with us. There is not a shred of Biblical evidence that points to their sudden withdrawal from human affairs. God has not "recalled" the angels. Since they do not die (Luke 20:36), we know they are not dead. Neither are they dormant. The Bible still says that angels are sent to be ministering spirits to those who will inherit salvation (Heb. 1:14). If that isn't you and me, then who is it? All those who have been saved by the power of God are ministered to by the angels of God.

ANGELS: A NEW TESTAMENT DOCTRINE

The writers of the New Testament constantly wrote of the presence and ministry of angels in their day. Some may foolishly object to New Testament angelology, claiming, "Angels did exist – in the Old Testament." But that is pure nonsense. Time and time again the presence and ministry of angels is mentioned in the New Testament.

Paul even tells us that our present-day battle is not against flesh and blood. That's what some like to narrow it down to – the seen. Today it isn't sophisticated or rational to believe in angels or demons. But Paul says our battle is "against rulers, against the authorities, against the powers of this dark world and against the spiritual forces of evil in the heavenly realms" (Eph. 6:12). Was Paul just seeing things? Was he hallucinating when he wrote that? We think not. Our battle is still the same; our source of help unchanging – the angels of God.

ENTERTAINING ANGELS UNAWARE

A third argument to substantiate the continuing ministry of angels is Hebrews 13:2. The Hebrew writer indicates that some of God's people have entertained an angel of God without knowing it. How do you know that you have not entertained an angel unknowingly? The possibility always exists. As long as there are angels, there will be opportunities for hospitality (lit., "love of strangers").

Some may wonder (and rightfully so), "How do I know that stranger at my door is not an angel?" Or a hitchhiker along the road, for that matter. We do not know. Perhaps that is why the Bible encourages us to do good to all men, especially those of the household of faith (Gal. 6:10). But back to the beggar or bum at the door. If an angel did appear to you, his actions and behavior would always be consistent with Biblical virtues (i.e., truth, honesty, virtue, diligence, etc.).

EXPLAINING DELIVERANCE AND PROTECTION

Fourth, if angels do not exist anymore or intervene in the affairs of men, how do we account for the many experiences that believers have had in being providentially protected from injury or even divinely delivered from death? Does not the Bible say that the angel of the Lord encamps around those who fear God and delivers them (Psa. 34:7)? Those who put their trust in God and make Him their habitation are promised angelic protection. God's angels will guard us in all our ways (Psa. 91:9-11). Even the devil knows that verse and once quoted it to Jesus in a vain attempt to get Him to abuse His powers (Matt. 4:6). Why should the devil have all the good verses? Why don't the people of God – for whom the verses were written claim them, believe them, live by them?

> The great majority of Christians can recall some incident in which their lives, in times of critical danger, have been miraculously preserved – an almost-plane crash, a near-car wreck, a fierce temptation. Though they may have seen no angels, their presence could explain why tragedy was averted. We should always be grateful for the goodness of God, who uses these wonderful friends called angels to protect us. Evidence from Scripture as well as personal experience confirms to us that individual guardian, guiding angels attend at least some of our ways and hover protectively over our lives (*Angels: God's Secret Agents*, pp. 106,107).

Several years ago I was visiting in the home of a former college classmate in Sacramento, California. We were sitting at breakfast when my host, Henry Smith, told me this amazing story. As best as I can recall, here is his story.

"I was driving from Iowa to California during the Christmas vacation," said Henry (one of the most rational and level-headed people I know.) "Somewhere in the middle of Nebraska I drove into a raging blizzard. It was terrible. You could hardly see in front of you. My car slid off the road and became stuck in the snow. I did everything I could to get the car back on the road, but to no avail. It was getting dark and temperature was falling.

"Suddenly I saw the headlights of a car approaching me from the rear. The car stopped and the driver got out. Together we managed to get my car back on the road. I thanked him profusely, for he may have saved my life. As I got back into my car, the stranger pulled around me and drove down the road, ahead of me. I saw his taillights disappear into the swirling snow and gathering gloom.

"I started my car and drove on into the teeth of the storm. And would you believe that later that night my car slid off the road again! I was stuck. There was virtually no traffic on the road. This time I really thought I would freeze to death.

"Now, what I am about to tell you may be hard to believe, but once again, when I had nearly given up all hope, I saw in my rearview mirror, approaching headlights. A car pulled up behind me, stopped, and a figure emerged. It was the same car – the same stranger – who had helped me earlier in the night! Once more he helped me get my car out of the drift and onto the road, and once more I thanked him fervently. Again he drove around me and into the storm. I never saw him again."

When Henry told me this story, I said, "Henry, do you think that stranger might have been an angel?" Henry looked at me, mouth open, his coffee cup suspended in midair. "I never thought of that!"

Here is another true story, as told by my father, who possesses as rational, logical and analytical mind as anyone. But what happened to him one day on a busy Los Angeles freeway was neither rational or natural. Let my dad, Dale V. Knowles, tell you the story.

"I felt hands upon my own as I gripped the steering wheel of my car when another vehicle merged into my lane of traffic, causing me to swerve onto the shoulder of the road, with a huge concrete bridge abutment straight ahead.

"I still marvel how my car barely missed the bridge while scraping the fender of another car.

"What were those hands upon my own?

"My unwavering thought has been that they were the hands of an angel.

"Be that so, then 'over on the other side of this life' I want so much to see that angel with fervent thankfulness to him for his ministry to me."

Our family has a dear friend, Jan Clifton. Before he died, Jan experienced something very unusual. My dad tells the story.

"Jan Clifton was one of many who was baptized into Christ in my ministry at Hamburg, Iowa in the early 1950's.

"Jan served as a preacher and an elder in years following.

"In 1988 cancer rapidly ravaged his body.

"In my last visit with him only a few days before his death he asked me if I believed in angels and their ministry 'for them who should be heirs of salvation.' (Hebrews 1:14)

"My reply was in the affirmative, of course, telling him of my personal experience related above.

"He told me that in the deep hours of one night previously he was in fervent prayer for forgiveness of all sins and for assurance of God's acceptance of his soul in eternity when he felt "someone" sit on the side of his bed and felt a hand laid on his own.

"No one was seen or heard, but a sweet gentle peace swept over him, after which the weight of 'someone' sitting on the edge of his bed was lifted.

'Was that an angel being an answer of comfort and assurance to me in answer to my prayer?' he asked.

"Could I deny it?"

No Christian knows how often and in how many ways angels have ministered unto them.

All Christians should want to include the desire to personally thank the angels in eternity for their ministries to them on earth, as well as thanks to God the Father, the Lord Jesus Christ and the Holy Spirit for their salvation from sin and welcome into the heaven of everlasting joy.

ANGELS CONTINUE TO WATCH THE CHURCH

If the church is still at worship, then the angels are still in business. As long as the church exists on earth, so will the angels. Why? Because one of the duties of the angels is to watch the church. They watch it (us) for a variety of reasons: to rejoice over repentance (Luke 15:7); to hear the prayers of the saints (1 Cor. 11:10); to learn more about the wonderful story of redemption (Eph. 3:10).

Jesus promised that the gates of Hades (death) would never prevail against His church (Matt. 16:18). They have not. The church still exists. As long as there is a church on earth, there will be angels to observe and watch.

FROM HERE TO ETERNITY

Finally, for our very soul's sake, angels had better still exist because they are our ticket to eternity. Jesus said that when a person dies, his spirit is "carried by the angels" into the presence of God (Luke 16:22). We had better hope the angels are still around when it comes time to die. But that is not the best time. The best time is now! If we believe it at death, we should believe it in life. A faith no good to live by is certainly not a faith to die by.

WHY DON'T WE VISIBLY SEE THEM?

If all this is true, why don't we actually see angels today? People in the Bible did, often recognizing them as messengers from heaven, falling down on their faces, even attempting to worship them. Perhaps the reason angels are no longer visible to Christians as such and no longer reveal themselves to believers as such is because we are living in the age of the Spirit. We are to live in the Spirit and to walk in the Spirit (Gal. 5:25). The angel started Philip on his mission but the Holy Spirit took over and guided Philip the rest of the way (Acts 8:26, 29, 39). God wants us to walk by faith, not sight (2 Cor. 5:7). Does this mean we do not believe in the reality of things we cannot see? Of course not. That is the very meaning of faith. Faith is "being certain of what we do not see" (Heb. 11:1). I cannot see God but I believe with all my heart that He exists, cares and helps me in my daily life. I believe in angels for the very same reasons.

WHY DON'T WE SENSE THEIR PRESENCE MORE?

A good question. Brace yourself for the answer. Without meaning to sound harsh, let us consider that it is not the angels' fault. It is not God's fault, either. Nor is it the Bible's fault. "We have met the enemy and they is us." Terrible grammar but excellent logic. The fault lies with us.

We don't sense the presence of angels enough because, for the most part, God's people have lived in total ignorance of the angels. Most Christians have never even thought about angels, except at Christmastime. Most ministers have never preached a sermon or taught a class on the angels. Like people, like priest. God declared, "My people are destroyed from lack of knowledge" (Hosea 4:6). Ignorance is not bliss. It can be fatal.

The angels will become more real to us when we start thinking more about them. Paul told the Athenians that God "is not far from everyone of us" (Acts 17:27). The same is true of the angels. They are not far from us either. The more we come to understand about the nature and mission of angels, the more we will appreciate them and the work they do on our behalf. Angels will become more real to us when a study of what the Bible says about angels becomes real to us!

21 ATTITUDES TOWARD ANGELS

After studying angels, what should our attitude be toward these messengers of God? Our understanding of what the Scriptures say about angels will help us to develop and maintain the correct attitude toward angels and their work. Faulty theology will lead to wrong attitudes and actions. If our theology is wrong, even concerning angels, our whole life will be off-base.

There are two major attitudes toward angels that are demonstrated in the religious world. Both are extremes and both are to be avoided. One attitude is somewhat seen in Catholicism; the other in mainline Protestantism. What are these contrasting attitudes toward angels that you and I should avoid at all costs?

ADORING ANGELS

Since the angels are spiritual and holy in nature, since they dwell in the presence of God and Jesus Christ, some people have made the mistake of worshiping the angels. But the adoration, veneration and worship of angels is forbidden in Scripture.

Paul warns of such in his letter to the Colossians. "Do not let anyone who delights in false humility and the worship of angels disqualify you for the prize. Such a person goes into great detail about what he has seen, and his unspiritual mind puffs him up with idle notions" (Col. 2:18). William Barclay notes that the Jews had a highly-developed doctrine of angels and the Gnostics believed in all kinds of intermediaries. When they spoke of the worship of angels, both groups would justify the practice by saying that God is so high and holy that we can never have direct access to Him. Hence, we must be content to pray to the angels. (*The Daily Study Bible Series, The Letter to the Colossians*, p. 146).

John the Revelator, himself an apostle of Christ, twice nearly made this mistake. When he heard the revealing angel say to him, "Blessed are those who are invited to the wedding supper of the Lamb!" and "These are the true words of God" (Rev. 19:9), John fell at the angel's feet to worship him. But the angel said to John, "Do not do it! I am a fellow servant with you and with your brothers who hold to the testimony of Jesus. Worship God! For the testimony of Jesus is the spirit of prophecy" (Rev. 19:10). Later, John hears the voice of Christ saying, "Behold, I am coming soon! Blessed is he who keeps the words of the prophecy of this book" (Rev. 22:7). Again he falls to worship at the feet of the angel who had been giving him the revelation and again he is rebuked: "Do not do it! I am a fellow servant with you and with your brothers the prophets and of all who keep the words of this book. Worship God!" (Rev. 22:9).

Angels and men – no matter how holy they may be or appear to be – are never to be worshiped. When the apostle Peter entered the house of Cornelius, the latter fell at Peter's feet to worship him. But Peter said, "Stand up, I am only a man myself" (Acts 10:26). Once Paul and Barnabas were mistaken for the gods Zeus and Hermes. Even the priest of Zeus wanted to offer a sacrifice to them. But Paul argued, "Men, why are you doing this? We too are only men, human like you. We are bringing you good news, telling you to turn from these worthless things to the living God, who made heaven and earth and sea and everything in them" (Acts 14:15).

Satan himself is an angel who had the audacity to try and get Jesus to worship him (Matt. 4:9). The answer that Jesus gave him is still the answer for all who would worship any other than God: "Worship the Lord your God, and serve him only!" (Matt. 4:10). Incredibly, there are men and women today who opt for the worship of this fallen angel, Satan. Satanism, though not a major world religion, has enough adherents to make one uneasy.

Even demons (as we will see in Part II of this book) are worshiped by men. Such unbelievable and abominable practices have been the practice of men for centuries, continuing even today (see Lev. 17:7; Deut. 32:17; Psa. 106:37; 1 Cor. 10:20; Rev. 9:20; 13:4)

Catholicism, with its "invocation of the saints," images and relics, is in violation of the clear teaching of Scripture in this matter. God alone is to be worshiped. Not Satan, not men, not apostles, not saints, not Mary, not angels, not demons. Worship God!

IGNORING ANGELS

The second major error religious men make concerning the angels is to ignore them. To ignore the angels is as bad as to adore them. It is going from one extreme to the other. Modern Protestantism largely ignores angelology. This failure to recognize the existence, purpose and work of angels is inexcusable. Angelology is a Biblical topic, as nearly 300 references in Scripture attest. Yet the average churchman knows precious little about these precious beings.

Paul did not want the Thessalonians to be "ignorant" about the second coming and so he wrote two letters to them on the subject. God does not want us to be ignorant about His holy angels. He has inspired the writers of the Bible to mention them time and time again. Why has the church viewed them with stone blindness? Is it because Satan, the fallen angel, has somehow blinded our eyes to the reality of the true angels of God? He would like nothing better. Both angels and demons seek to separate believers from the love of God that is in Christ Jesus our Lord (Rom. 8:38,39). They must be succeeding in their efforts when there is such woeful ignorance about the holy angels.

Why is the church so ignorant of angels? We have suggested one reason already; Satan and the demons. Another reason is ministers of the gospel who fail to study the Word. If the preachers are ignorant of the angels, how can the people to whom they preach be informed? Hosea says both will be destroyed for their lack of knowledge (Hos. 4:6). A third reason is because the people themselves are failing to read the Bible for themselves. God's Word is chock-full of references to angels. The church needs to take up God's Word and read. Read for your life!

PROPER ATTITUDES TOWARD ANGELS

What should our attitude be toward the messengers of God? We should have the following feelings toward them.

1. *Have faith in their existence, presence and ministry.* Without faith it is impossible to please God (Heb. 11:6). God has sent them to minister to our needs (Heb. 1:14). The Bible says that angels are for real. Read the Bible. Believe the Bible. "Faith comes from hearing the message, and the message is heard through the word of Christ" (Rom. 10:17). What did Jesus say about the angels? Study the Bible. Your faith in angels will grow and you will receive a greater blessing from their ministry as you see what the Bible says about angels.

2. *Be thankful for their presence and work in your life.* Were it not for the untiring and ceaseless labors of the angels, we might be injured or even dead. How we need to thank God for His angels who guide, guard, defend and deliver. Even a pagan king, Nebuchadnezzar, did this (Dan. 3:28). Are we less thankful than he? The more thankful we are to God for the ministry of angels the more God will bless us with their presence; the more ungrateful we are, the less we will experience the work of angels in our lives. Have you thanked God for your angel today?

3. *Be constantly aware of the angels of God.* Realize that we are not alone – that we do not have to fight the battle by ourselves. Abraham had the faith that angels go on before us to prepare the way (Gen. 24:7, 40). May we have that same calm and comforting assurance. Why not trust God to send His angels before you? You can depend on the angels. They will never let you down. Having a constant awareness of the angels will bring a calming assurance into our lives that will relieve us of needless fears and hours of lonclincss.

4. *Cooperate with the angels.* If God wants us to so live as to make it easy on those earthly leaders who watch for our souls (Heb. 13:17), how much more should we live so as to make our heavenly watchers' task a joy and not a grief? Why live in willful sin and put the angels in a position where they must rescue you from injury or death? If angels rejoice over our repentance, what must they do when we backslide? Do they weep? Why cause a holy angel to cry? So live as to bring them constant joy. How often do they hear you pray? See you in church? Hear you sing?

SELECTED MEMORY VERSES ON ANGELS

In order to increase your awareness of angels and enhance your appreciation for their ministry in your life, the following verses have been selected to memorize. When we build God's truth into our lives, including the truth of God's Word on angels, we will be a stronger, more spiritual people. Memorize and internalize one verse a month and by the end of the year angels will be more real to you. Write each verse on 3x5 index card and read it aloud each morning when you get up and each night before you go to bed. By the end of the month, God's truth on angels will be built into your life.

Here are Scripture selections for twelve months:

1."The Lord, before whom I walk, will send his angel with thee, and prosper thy way." (Genesis 24:40 KJV).

2. "The angel of the Lord encamps around those who fear him, and he delivers them." (Psalm 34:7).

3. "For he will command his angels concerning you to guard you in all your ways." (Psalm 91:11).

4. "See to it that you do not look down on one of these little ones. For I tell you that their angels in heaven always see the face of my Father in heaven." (Matthew 18:10).

5. "I tell you, whoever acknowledges me before men, the Son of Man will also acknowledge him before the angels of God. But he who disowns me before men will be disowned before the angels of God." (Luke 12:8-9).

6. "Likewise, I say unto you, there is joy in the presence of the angels of God over one sinner that repenteth." (Luke 15:10 KJV).

7. "And it came to pass, that the beggar died, and was carried by the angels into Abraham's bosom; the rich man also died and was buried." (Luke 16:22 KJV).

8. "For I am convinced that neither death nor life, neither angels nor demons, neither the present nor the future, nor anything else in all creation, will be able to separate us from the love of God that is in Christ Jesus our Lord." (Romans 8:38, 39).

9. "For it seems to me that God has put us apostles on display at the end of the procession, like men condemned to die in the arena. We have been made a spectacle to the whole universe, to angels as well as to men." (1 Corinthians 4:9).

10. "Are not all angels ministering spirits sent to serve those who will inherit salvation?" (Hebrews 1:14).

11. "But you have come to Mount Zion, to the heavenly Jerusalem, the city of the living God. You have come to thousands upon thousands of angels in joyful assembly, to the church of the firstborn, whose names are written in heaven." (Hebrews 12:22,23).

12. "Do not forget to entertain strangers, for by so doing some people have entertained angels without knowing it." (Hebrews 13:2).

22 ANGELS IN HYMNOLOGY

The influence that the subject of angels has had on the great hymn writers of the church is significant. This special study does not pretend to be all inclusive or exhaustive. Only three church hymnals were consulted. Yet, about 100 hymns were found to contain references to the angels of God. Many more songs and hymns that mention angels could be found by searching other hymnals. These will suffice for this brief study. The hymn writers, generally speaking, stayed within Scriptural bounds in describing in poetic fashion the person and work of angels. A few are questionable, some fanciful, others unscriptural (without Biblical foundation). Upon examination of nearly 100 hymns, it seemed helpful to categorize in chronological order the ministry of angels as seen by the hymnists. This outline will be followed:

I. Angels in the Life of Jesus Christ
  A. At the Incarnation
  B. At the Agony in the Garden
  C. In the Atonement
  D. In the Death, Burial and Resurrection
  E. In the Ascension and Coronation
  F. In the Second Coming

II. Angels' Ministry to Believers
  A. In Life
  B. In Death
  C. In Meeting the Foe

III. Angelic Activity in Heaven
  A. Angels Singing, Singing, Singing
  B. Waiting for Saints to Enter Heaven
  C. Interest in the Gospel

ANGELS IN THE LIFE OF JESUS

At the Incarnation

The best-known hymns that mention angels would of course be the beloved Christmas songs. In *While Shepherds Watched Their Flocks* (Nahum Tate), "The angels of the Lord came down, and glory shone around." The remaining four verses recount the angel's message of Christ's birth in poetic fashion.

The traditional *The First Noel* has the angel speaking to "certain poor shepherds in fields as they lay." The message is "Noel, Noel, born is the King of Israel."

Frederick Oakley's *O Come All Ye Faithful* urges all to come to Bethlehem and behold Him who is "born the King of angels." The second stanza admonishes "choirs of angels" to "sing in exultation, O sing, all ye bright hosts of heav'n above."

The beautiful song *O Little Town of Bethlehem* (Phillips Brooks) describes the angels "gathered all above, while mortals sleep, the angels keep their watch of wondering love." Then, the "morning stars together proclaim the holy birth; and praises sing to God the King, and peace to men on earth." The fourth stanza says, "We hear the Christmas angels the great glad tidings tell: O come to us, abide with us, Our Lord Emmanuel!"

We cannot overlook Charles Wesley's famous *Hark! The Herald Angels Sing* where the angels sing "Glory to the newborn King." Nor would we forget the peaceful *Silent Night* by Joseph Mohr where "glories stream from heaven afar" and "Heavenly hosts sing Alleluia."

In *It Came Upon a Midnight Clear* (Edmund H. Sears) all four vèrses end with the angels singing. The first verse describes the angels "bending near the earth, to touch their harps of gold." "Peace on the earth, good will to men" is their message. The second stanza reads, "Still thro' the cloven skies they come, with peaceful wings unfurled, and still their Heavenly music floats, o'er all the weary world:

Above its sad and lowly plains they bend on hovering wing; and ever o'er its Babel sounds the blessed angels sing."

In addition to the well-known Christmas songs, there are other good hymns that describe the angels and the birth of Christ. For example, in Fanny Crosby's *Tell Me the Story of Jesus* we find this: "Tell how the angels, in chorus, sang as they welcomed His birth, 'Glory to God in the highest! Peace and good tidings to earth.'" In *Wonderful Story of Love* (J. M. Driver), "angels with rapture announce it, shepherds with wonder receive it."

At the Agony in the Garden

Several hymn writers captured the moment of angels ministering to Jesus as He agonized in prayer in the Garden of Gethsemane. Among the best-known is the haunting, *'Tis Midnight; And On Olive's Brow* by William B. Tappan. The suffering Savior, who "weeps in blood," is not forsaken by His God for "from ether-plains is borne the song that angels know; unheard by mortals are the strains that sweetly soothe the Savior's woe."

Charles H. Gabriel (appropriately named) describes the garden scene as well in his song, *My Savior's Love*. However, both Gabriel and Tappan have angels (plural) attending Christ while Luke says only one came (Luke 22:43). Gabriel writes, "In pity angels beheld Him, and came from the world of light to comfort Him in the sorrows He bore for my soul that night."

In W. B. Waldrop's *Gethsemane*, Christ, "soul-wounded and weary" goes to Gethsemane to pray. As shadows creep and dark skies weep "the angels bear witness to Jesus divine." But later, when Christ is crowned King, the angels "exclaim" and chime "sweet music" because a "golden day" has broken in old Gethsemane and now we all, "with a halo," travel the pathway to God.

The song *I Love Him Because He First Loved Me* (Frank E. Rousch) says, "Angels from blessed realms of light gave strength to His aching heart that night." Dr. J. Wilbur Chapman's beloved *One Day* has Jesus, alone in the garden. But then "angels came down then to keep sacred vigil, weighted with sin, my Redeemer is He." Some hymnals have altered this to "angels came down o'er His tomb to keep vigil."

In the Atonement

In *He Could Have Called Ten Thousand Angels*, the chorus, based on Christ's statement to Peter at His arrest in the garden, repeatedly reminds us that Jesus could have called ten thousand angels "to destroy the world, and set Him free." But "He died alone, for you and me."

Dr. J. M. Gray reminds us that "No angel could His place have taken" in his hymn *What Did He Do*. Only Christ could atone for man's sin.

When Christ shed His blood on the cross, S. J. Henderson sees "the angels rejoicing because it is done" in the hymn *Saved By the Blood*.

In the Death, Burial, and Resurrection

The "heart of the gospel" – the death, burial and resurrection of Christ (1 Cor. 15:1-4) – is wonderfully portrayed in several hymns. *Lead Me to Calvary* (Jennie Evelyn Hussey) has angels keeping vigil over the tomb: "Show me the tomb where Thou wast laid, tenderly mourned and wept; Angels in robes of light arrayed guarded Thee whilst Thou slept."

Dr. Chapman's *One Day* has the stone "rolled away from the door." Though angels are not specifically mentioned in this instance, we know that an angel rolled away the stone in the Biblical account (Matt. 28:2).

The resurrected Christ is praised by both men and angels in Charles Wesley's stirring *Christ, the Lord is Risen Today*.

"Sons of men and angels say: Alleluia!"

Thomas Kelly, in *The Lord Is Risen Indeed*, describes "attending angels, hear! Up to the courts of heav'n with speed, the joyful tidings bear." The fourth stanza says, "Then wake your golden lyres, and strike each cheerful chord; Join, all ye bright celestial choirs, To sing our risen Lord."

In the Ascension and Coronation

The glories of our Lord's ascension and coronation in heaven are grandly described by the hymnists. Anne Richter, in *We Saw Thee Not*, writes, "But we believe that angels said, 'Why seek the living with the dead?'"

The coronation of Christ is given great treatment by John Bakewell in *Hail, Thou Once Despised Jesus!* "Jesus, hail! enthroned in glory, There forever to abide; all the heavenly hosts adore Thee; Seated at Thy Father's side." In the fourth stanza he implores the angels to, "Help, ye bright angelic spirits; Bring your sweetest, noblest lays; Help to sing our Saviour's merits: Help to chant Immanuel's praise!"

Thomas Kelley's *Look, Ye Saints, The Sight Is Glorious* has Christ "from the fight returned victorious." In verse two: "Crown the Savior, angels, crown him; Rich the trophies Jesus brings." In the third stanza: "Saints and angels, crowd around Him, Own His title, praise His name."

The angels are also mentioned in *Crown Him With Many Crowns* (Matthew Bridges). "The Heavenly anthem drowns all music but its own." When the Lord of love reveals His hands and side, "no angel in the sky can fully bear that sight, But down-ward bends his wondering eye At mysteries so bright."

Edward Perronet's majestic *All Hail the Power of Jesus' Name* sees "angels prostrate fall." They "bring forth the royal diadem, and crown Him Lord of all."

Holy, Holy, Holy (Reginald Heber) has the saints "casting down their golden crowns around the glassy sea."

"Cherubim and Seraphim" fall down before God. In the old Crusader Hymn, *Fairest Lord Jesus*, the Lord is described as shining brighter and purer "Than all the angels heav'n can boast."

In the Second Coming

When the Roll is Called Up Yonder (James M. Black) begins with "When the trumpet of the Lord shall sound." Angels will come at the sound of the trumpet (Matt. 24:31; 1 Thess. 4:16).

In *What a Gathering That Will Be* J. H. Kurzenknabe writes, "When the angel of the Lord proclaims earth-time shall be no more." Later in the hymn we find these words: "the golden harps are sounding, and the angels bands proclaim."

In *Christ Returneth* (H. L. Turner), the "hosts cry Hosanna, from heaven descending, With glorified saints and the angels attending."

ANGELS' MINISTRY TO BELIEVERS

In Life

The Bible says that angels are ministering spirits sent to serve those who will inherit salvation (Heb. 1:14). The hymnwriters of the church have captured this concept of angelic ministry in a number of songs.

Precious Memories has "unseen angels" being sent "from somewhere to my soul." In *Count Your Blessings*, Johnson Oatman Jr. urges us not to be discouraged with life because "angels will attend, help and comfort give you to your journey's end."

Like the angel that went before the Israelites in a cloud by day and a pillar of fire by night, Thomas Hasting's *Guide Me, O Thou Great Jehovah* has similar encouragement: "Let the fiery, cloudy pillar, Lead me all my journey thro'."

The English melody *The Lily of the Valley* mentions "a wall of fire about me, I've nothing now to fear, with His manna He my hungry soul shall fill." Angels fed the Israelites with manna in the wilderness (Psa. 78:25).

John Newton's *Glorious Things of Thee Are Spoken* has "round each habitation hovering, See the cloud and fire appear for a glory and a cov'ring, showing that the Lord is near! He who gives us daily manna, He who listens to our cry, to Him raise the glad hosanna, rising to His throne on high."

In *Now the Day Is Over*, Sabine Baring-Gould refers to our guardian angels watching over us as we sleep at night: "Thru the long nightwatches, May Thine angels spread their white wings above me, Watching 'round my bed."

James Edmeston (*Savior, Breathe An Evening Blessing*) writes of the protection of angels. "Tho' destruction walk around us, Tho' the arrows past us fly. Angel guards from Thee surround us; We are safe if Thou art nigh."

In Death

Never are the hymnists more given to detail than in their descriptions of the angels' ministry to believers at the hour of death. The Bible teaches that angels carry the spirits of those who die in the Lord to heaven (Luke 16:22). This special ministry is seen in the following hymns.

J. S. Torbett's *Will the Angels Come For Me?* asks, "Will they bear me on their pinions o'er the dark and stormy sea?" and "Will the angels bear me upward to that home so bright and fair?" The chorus assures us that, indeed, the angels "will take us home to God."

In *O Come, Angel Band*, Jefferson Hascall describes dying and the approach of the angels: "I've almost gained my Heavenly home, My spirit loudly sings; The holy ones, behold they come! I hear the noise of wings." The refrain goes, "O come, angel band, come and around me stand, O bear me away on your snowy wings, To my immortal home."

J. W. Welsh (*The Sinless Summerland*) longs for the band of angels to come. "I am longing for the coming of the snow-white angel band, That shall bear my weary spirit To the sinless summerland."

In Shepherd's *Must Jesus Bear the Cross Alone?*, angels "from the stars come down and bear my soul away." *Beyond the Sunset*, says a hand will guide me "To God, the Father, whom I adore." The hand may be that of an angel because angels have charge of the dead.

In *Lord, Dismiss Us With Thy Blessing* (John Fawcett), we are borne from earth to heaven by the angels. "So, when e'er the signal's given Us from earth to call away, Borne on angel's wings to heaven, Glad the summons to obey."

Elizabeth Prentiss, in her song *More Love to Thee* writes, "Let sorrow do its work, Send grief and pain; Sweet are Thy messengers, Sweet their refrain, When they can sing with me, More love, O Christ, to Thee."

Austin Taylor, in *Home On the Banks of the River*, said, "Soon the angels will come and carry me over, To that beautiful home of God." The chorus goes, "Home on the bank of the river . . . Home with the angels forever."

The blind poetess Fanny Crosby wrote the comforting hymn, *Safe in the Arms of Jesus*. In it she hints that the angels are the ones who bear us to the arms of Jesus: "Hark! 'tis the voice of angels, Borne in a song to me, Over the fields of glory, Over the jasper sea."

In Mary Lathbury's *Day Is Dying in the West*, the Lord of life gathers those who seek His face when "the deepening shadows fall." How? By means of the angels. The fourth stanza says, "When forever from our sight Pass the stars, the day, the night, Lord of angels on our eyes Let eternal morning rise, And shadows end." The chorus is angelic in nature as well: "Holy, Holy, Holy, Lord God of Hosts! Heav'n and earth are full of Thee! Heav'n and earth are praising Thee, O Lord Most High!"

In Meeting the Foe

The angel hosts are sometimes portrayed in battle scenes, fighting for the Lord, for His people, for truth and right. Sir Robert Grant writes with bold pen, "His chariots of wrath the deep thunderclouds form, And dark is His path on the wings of the storm" in his song *O Worship the King*. Angels are sometimes referred to in Scripture as the chariots of God (see Psa. 68:17).

A rousing hymn by Mrs. Ch. H. Morris, *The Fight Is On* says, "The Lord of hosts is marching on to victory, The triumph of the right will soon appear." "Hosts" is a term describing the vast number of the angels.

Before the angel hosts, all enemies flee. Sabine Baring-Gould, author of the militant *Onward Christian Soldiers*, has Satan's host on the run, thoroughly routed by the more powerful forces of God. "At the shout of triumph Satan's host doth flee." Baring-Gould waxes eloquent with the very foundations of hell "quivering" at the shout of praise; with brothers lifting their voices in the triumph song that "men and angels sing."

Another famous hymn that refers to the devil and his angels is Martin Luther's *A Mighty Fortress Is Our God*. Luther wrote, "For still our ancient foe Doth seek to work us woe." He adds, "this world with devils filled" (referring to either fallen angels or demons). He also writes that "The Prince of Darkness grim" (Satan) is doomed.

ANGELIC ACTIVITY IN HEAVEN

Angels Singing, Singing, Singing

By far and away, the favorite feature of angels as seen by hymnwriters is the singing that angels have done, are doing, and will continue to do throughout eternity. "I shall see the King, where the angels sing" wrote W. C. Poole in his song *I Shall See the King*.

This emphasis is not undue because the Bible repeatedly mentions the fact that angels sing praises to God and Jesus Christ. They could no more stop singing than the sun could stop shining. Praising God is as natural to them as breathing is to us.

Perhaps the best known hymn in this category is the good old *Doxology* or *Old Hundreth* by Thomas Ken. "Praise Him above, ye Heavenly host; Praise Father, Son, and Holy Ghost."

Fanny Crosby's stirring *Praise Him! Praise Him!* has "highest archangels in glory" giving "strength and honor" unto "His holy name!"

A song based on Psalm 148, *Hallelujah, Praise Jehovah!*, says "All His angels praise proclaim, All His hosts together praise Him."

L. H. Jameson's stately *There Is a Habitation* has "Within its pearly portals, Angelic armies sing, With glorified immortals, The praises of its King." Jameson was a member of the Christian Church.

In *Our King Immanuel* (James Rowe), "Celestial praises swell; Where cherubim and seraphim Now join us when we cry: All hail, Our King Immanuel!"

Christopher Wordsworth's *O Day of Rest and Gladness* reads "On Thee, the high and lowly, Thro' ages joined in tune, Sing 'Holy, holy, holy,' To the great God Triune."

Kempthorne's *Praise The Lord* has "Praise Him, angels in the height . . . Praise Him, all ye stars of light."

Samuel Medley's wishful *O Could I Speak* we find these words, "O could I sound the glories forth Which in my Saviour shine, I'd soar, and touch the Heavenly strings, And vie with Gabriel while he sings in notes almost divine."

In addition to Gabriel, Michael the archangel is implied in Mrs. J. B. Karnes's *An Empty Mansion*. "I'll exchange this old home for a mansion up there And invite the archangel as guest."

The harps of angels are mentioned in several hymns. Harps are mentioned several times in the Bible, especially in Revelation (Rev. 5:8; 14:2; 15:2; 18:22). H. E. Blair (*Meet*

Me There) writes, "Where the harps of angels ring, and the blest forever sing."

Choirs of angels are also described in the hymns of the church. In the song by E. M. Bartlett, *Just a Little While*, we find these words: "Then we'll hear a choir of angels, Singing out the victory song."

The *clothing* of angel choirs is given some attention as well. H. R. Palmer, in *There Is a Home Eternal*, describes "White-robed angels" singing "around the bright throne." In *A New Name in Glory*, C. Austin Miles refers to "the white-robed angels" who "sing the story, 'A sinner has come home'." Robert Lowry sees "bright angel's feet" that have trod at the beautiful river that "flows by the throne of God" in his song, *Shall We Gather at the River?*

The *voices* of angels are seen in contrasts by the hymnists. Sometimes they are loud, in jubilant shouts of triumph or praise. At other times, the voices of angels are pictured as soft and sweet. "Soft as the voice of an angel" wrote Alice Hawthorne in *Whispering Hope*.

"Sweetest note in seraph song" was William Hunter's description in *The Great Physician*. Even though she was blind, Fanny Crosby still visualized "Angels descending, bring from above, Echoes of mercy, whispers of love" in her beloved *Blessed Assurance*.

A. S. Bridgewater sensed the sweet sounds of angel voices: "the angels so sweetly are singing" (*How Beautiful Heaven Must Be*).

Some of the hymnists see both angels and saints singing together the praises of God. T. N. Pannell in *I'll Be Satisfied* wrote, "When I meet the ransomed over on the golden shore . . . There I'll join the angels singing praises evermore." E. P. Stifles describes "Angels with the white robed throng" joining in "the sweet redemption song" in his hymn *Beulah Land*.

"We'll sing and shout with angels around the throne" says Morgan Williams in *It Won't Be Very Long*. Ada Powell speaks wistfully of departed saints in *Sing To Me of Heaven*. The second stanza states, "Sing to me of heaven, as I walk along, Dreaming of the comrades that so long have gone; in a fairer region, 'mong the angel throng, They are happy as they sing that old, sweet song."

James W. Gaines wrote, "With the angels we'll extol, Christ who is our Lord and King" in his hymn *In That Home of the Soul*. F. M. Lehmen's moving hymn *The Love of God* had "the saints' and angels' song." What is their song? "Redeeming grace to Adam's race."

Waiting For Saints To Enter Heaven

Several hymns indicate the angels are waiting for us in heaven, lingering, even beckoning to us to come. Although this thought may be only somewhat implied in Scripture, the hymnists nonetheless elaborate the point. For example, in the haunting invitation hymn *Almost Persuaded* (P. P. Bliss), we note that "Angels are lingering near" as "prayers rise from hearts so dear."

Nearer, My God, To Thee (reported to have been sung by the ill-fated passengers and crew of the *Titanic* as she sank beneath the frigid waters of the North Atlantic) has "Angels to beckon me, nearer, my God to Thee."

D. W. C. Huntington's *O Think of the Home Over There* says, "all the saints and the angels up there Are watching and waiting for me.

The rollicking *This World Is Not My Home* (Albert C. Brumley) tells us that "the angels beckon me from heaven's open door."

John Newman (*Lead, Kindly Light*) has smiles on the faces of the waiting angels: "And with the morn those angel faces smile."

In *Is My Name Written There?*, Mary Kidder writes, "Where the angels are watching." J. W. Vaughan has "Angels and loved ones are looking this way, Hoping to greet us some wonderful day" in his song, *Inside the Gate*.

Interest in the Gospel

Angels were denied the ministry of reconciliation. That ministry was left to man (2 Cor. 5:19). This thought is the theme of Dr. E. T. Cassel's hymn *The King's Business*. He writes of the message "angels fain would sing." But in heaven, the angels will be able to sing along with us about this great message. In Elton Roth's *In My Heart There Rings a Melody* we find these words: "Twill be my endless theme in glory, With the angels I will sing."

E. M. Bartlett (*Victory in Jesus*) tells "about the angels singing, and the old redemption story." Tillit S. Teddlie, a member of the Church of Christ, wrote *Singing Redemption's Song*. In it he states, "Angels are singing redemption's sweet song, Wonderful theme, Glorious theme!"

Perhaps the greatest hymnwriter of all was Charles Wesley. The son of a poor preacher in the Church of England, Wesley composed an average of three hymns a week for 57 years. Of his 8,989 religious poems, 6,500 are considered hymns. In one of them, *And Can It Be That I Should Gain?*, Wesley intimates that the angels, so long deprived of understanding God's wonderful plan of redemption, will at last fully fathom it and will rejoice with the saved:

Tis mercy all! Let earth adore:
Let angel minds inquire no more.

Part Two:

DEMONS

23 WHY STUDY DEMONS?

Why would a Christian want to study about demons? A Christian is to have his mind fixed on things above (Col. 3:2). A Christian is to think about things that are pure, lovely and of good report (Phil. 4:8). Why should believers clutter up their minds with things that are impure, unlovely and of an evil report?

The subjects of this study are so repugnant and repulsive to the spiritual mind that perhaps we would be better off if we left it alone. But leaving it alone will not make it go away. Demons, whether we like it or not, are in the Bible. Worse yet, they are in the world. Our world. We must face the subject because the subject faces us.

Learning about angels is one thing; the demons are quite another. Demonology is not a topic that naturally draws to it those who are trying to have the mind of Christ. Why study, then, about demons? For at least five good reasons we should consider these evil beings known as "demons."

A BIBLICAL TOPIC

The concerned child of God should study demons because they are a Scriptural subject. What does the Bible say about demons? Much. By learning what God has to say about these creatures we can be better prepared to withstand their evil efforts. "All Scripture is God-breathed and is useful for teaching, rebuking, correcting and training in righteousness, so that the man of God may be thoroughly equipped for every good work" (2 Tim. 3:16,17). Knowing what the Bible says about demons can be very useful and helpful for those whose battle is not against flesh and blood (Eph. 6:12).

To be forewarned is to be forearmed. If we fail to equip ourselves for the battle we are in, we may fall prey to the "doctrines of demons" (1 Tim. 4:1). They certainly have their teachings, or doctrine. We had better know God's doctrine, or teaching, about demons. Demons are not inspired of God but the inspired Word of God clearly describes their evil presence, power and performance. That is reason enough to learn about demons.

MENTIONED MANY TIMES

An intense study of demons should be undertaken because of the sheer number of times they are mentioned in Scripture. There are at least 80 references to demons in the Bible. We will consider each of them as we progress in this study. God has much to say about the demons and how believers in Jesus can be thoroughly equipped to withstand them.

Have you ever considered that the Lord's Supper is not mentioned very many times in the Bible? Yet we give much attention to it – and rightly so. It is a joy to gather around the table of the Lord each Sunday and partake of the bread and the cup. This Jesus has asked us to do, "in remembrance" of Him (1 Cor. 11:25). Demons are mentioned many more times in Scripture (not that they are spiritual). Shouldn't we also learn what the "table of demons" and the "cup of demons" means? Both are mentioned in 1 Corinthians 10:20, 21. We certainly don't want to be "partakers with demons."

JESUS TOOK DEMONS SERIOUSLY

A third reason why demonology should be studied is because our Lord took their existence very seriously.

Demons are mentioned in connection with Jesus more than anywhere in Scripture. Demons were no figment of the imagination to Jesus. He recognized their evil presence and power in the lives of people in His day and cast them out by the Spirit of God. If Jesus Christ took demons seriously, what of you and me?

THE DEVIL'S DEVICES

Another valid reason to learn about demons is to increase our awareness of Satan's devices. Demons are subject to Satan and do his evil will. Like their malevolent master, they seek to devour us (1 Pet. 5:8). God does not want this to happen. He warns us in His Word that we are not to be ignorant of the devil's devices (2 Cor. 2:11).

Since the beginning of sin, the demons have been an effective device of Satan. How they have hounded and hassled the children of God! To be unaware of their existence and evil work – whether because of ignorance, indolence or unbelief – can be fatal. Maybe we need a big warning label affixed to our Bibles: "Warning! Ignorance of demons can be hazardous to your spiritual health!" We are in an all-out, no-holds barred struggle for spiritual survival. The more we know about our enemy the better equipped we will be to meet our "ancient foe."

TO HELP OTHERS

Fifth, we should want to learn about demons and how they operate so that we can be ready to help others understand what they need to know about these evil agents of Satan. There are many people who need to know what the Bible says about demons. They have been troubled, needlessly so, by the inordinate attention demons have received in movies, music, literature and even "harmless" table games. Their view of demons is wildly distorted. This does not mean that demons are not real. They are. But the Biblical picture of demons is a far cry from the picture the demon "obsessed" portray.

The devout Christian should always be ready to help others with whatever need they have: physical or spiritual. Many troubled and enquiring souls have questions about Satan and the occult. Some may even feel that they are "possessed" by a demon. How are we to respond to these people? With answers from the Word of God! Christians are to be clad in the "full armor of God so that you can take your stand against the devil's schemes" (Eph. 6:10). We are to take "the sword of the Spirit, which is the word of God" (Eph. 6:17). God's Word will equip us against the spirit world. It will help others defend themselves against the demons of Satan as well. Their only hope is found in the Bible.

Demonology is not a pleasant topic. But it is a Biblical one. The spiritual person will take whatever time is necessary to learn more about Satan and his demons. Our very spiritual lives depend upon what we know about them and how to defeat them. So do the lives of our family and friends. God's Word contains the answers. Let's dig in and find them.

24 ARE DEMONS FOR REAL?

Yes, Virginia. There really are demons.

To affirm belief in the existence of demons goes against the grain in this "age of enlightenment." How can a "rational" individual believe that such beings ever existed, let alone believe they exist today? The "enlightened" person would say that he has progressed way beyond such superstition and nonsense. And yet millions of dollars are being made by opportunists who sell their fanciful and frightening concepts of demons to the general public by means of demented movies, demonic music and distorted novels. Such irony! On one hand the world denies the Biblical concept of demons, calling such ideas "irrational" and/or "outdated." Yet at the same time they shell out big money to buy (literally) the off-beat and twisted picture of demons.

Putting both ancient superstition and modern skepticism aside, there is good reason to believe in the reality of demons. Why? For at least three intelligent reasons.

THE AUTHORITY OF GOD'S WORD

Why believe in the reality of demons? Because the only truly inspired document in all literature says demons exist. The Bible is the God-breathed Word of God (2 Tim. 3:16, 17). God's Word is truth (John 17:17). It is impossible for God to lie (Titus 1:2). If the Bible says there are demons then there must be demons. And the Bible does, dozens and dozens of times. The Scripture cannot be broken (John 10:35).

When the Bible speaks on demons, it is speaking truth. There is no error in the Word of God. Alexander Campbell declared, "There is nothing so certain, so durable, so unchangeable as the word of the Lord. There is no error in it. There can be no error in the most strict and exact conformity to it: for it shall stand forever. Truth, like its author, is eternal and unchangeable" (*The Millennial Harbinger*, Vol. 3, Mar. 1832, p. 99). Any subject the Bible addresses, from Angels to Zion, is truth from beginning to end. The Bible says it, we believe it, that settles it.

THE TESTIMONY OF JESUS CHRIST

Second, we believe in the reality of the demon world because Jesus addressed the subject as something real. If we cannot trust Jesus then whom can we trust? Jesus was a man who went around doing good. What He did was good. What He taught was good (i.e., truth). Good men tell the truth. Jesus said that demons exist. Whose word shall we believe? The Son of God or the modern skeptic?

Jesus was more than a good man – He was the God-man. He was Immanuel, "God with us." He was God manifested in the flesh (1 Tim. 3:16). Jesus was with God in the beginning, was God, and was made flesh, dwelling among men as a man, displaying the glory of the Father (John 1:1,14). Note the testimony of the apostle Peter: "God anointed Jesus of Nazareth with the Holy Spirit and power, and how he went around doing good and healing all who were under the power of the devil, because God was with him" (Acts 10:38). Part of the good that Jesus did was to rid men of the demon powers that possessed them.

Jesus was without sin (Heb. 4:15; 2 Cor. 5:21; 1 John 3:5). That means He never told a lie, never deceived anyone. The Bible says, "He committed no sin, and no deceit was found in his mouth" (Isa. 53:9; 1 Pet. 2:22). Jesus spoke of the demons as a reality in His day. He addressed them as real and powerful forces. If we cannot believe Jesus on the reality of demons, we cannot take His word on the existence of the king of demons, Satan. Following this pattern, we should soon be stripped of all our beliefs on anything that Jesus ever taught. Jesus was a teacher "sent from God" (John 3:2). He taught with the authority of God. If His teachings are not true, neither is His source. We can chuck it all out the window and "do our own thing." Nothing would please the devil and his demons more!

What Jesus said about demons is true. If He was "off" on that subject then on what subject can we trust Him? Sin? Atonement? Redemption? Grace? The Second Coming? Judgment? Heaven? Hell? Where do you draw the line? You don't. The line has already been drawn – Christ has spoken. We dare not cross over that line!

Commenting on the credible testimony of Jesus and the Scriptures, Merrill F. Unger observes,

> . . . there is not a hint that Jesus or any of the New Testament writers had the slightest doubt as to the real existence of either Satan or demons. They believed in their reality quite as much as in the existence of God, or of the good angels. Only slight investigation is necessary to expose the extreme crudity, destructiveness, and the untenability of the rationalistic and mythical view of Satan and demons. It not only jeopardizes the character and truthfulness of the Son of God himself, but challenges the authenticity and reliability of the whole Bible. For if the teachings of Scripture on the subject of Satan and demons are judged mythical, any other doctrine of Holy Writ may likewise be declared mythical at the caprice of the critic, who is disposed to offset his opinions against those of the prophets, apostles, and the Lord himself (*Biblical Demonology*, pp. 36, 37).

PROOF FROM PHYSICAL AND HUMAN NATURE

In his classic work, *Biblical Demonology*, Merrill F. Unger notes that the existence of demons can be proved from both physical and human nature as well as Scriptural testimony.

1. Proof from physical nature:

> To any reverent student, the witness of the Scripture to the existence of demons is amply sufficient, and further proof is unnecessary. But for those who are not disposed to accept the testimony of the Bible, other evidence, both scientific and philosophical, is not lacking. Nature, which has often been called God's "oldest Testament," lifts eloquent voice, as is frequently the case, in authentication and illustration of Scriptural truth. Everywhere in the natural world there are illustrations that suggest such beings as Satan and demons in the spiritual world. In the plant kingdom there are pests, insects, and blight that continually harass the farmer. In the animal kingdom there is not a creature that does not have its deadly enemy, killing and feeding upon it. Even the human family is perpetually besieged by a vast multitude of hostile germs awaiting their chance to storm the citadel of the human body and cause disease and death. However, this is not at all to suggest a causal connection between pests, parasites and disease germs of the natural realm and demons of the spiritual realm . . . It seems obviously deducible from the facts at hand that the tormenters and troublers that afflict every sphere of the natural realm are meant to be illustrations of the host of evil, malignant, invisible agencies that exist in the spiritual realm. The witness of nature is such as forever to disencumber the doctrine of demons from the common objections urged against it, that it is neither scientific nor philosophic. It is both (*Biblical Demonology*, p. 37).

2. Proof from human nature. T. Witton Davies, author of *Magic, Divination, and Demonology Among the Hebrews and Their Neighbors* declares, "The belief in evil spirits is universal." Unger then observes,

> How is the practical universality of such a conviction to be accounted for? That the belief has ofttimes been vitiated by extravagant superstitions, though perhaps no more than beliefs in God, or Satan, is beside the question. The problem of a widely prevailing predisposition and of an inveterate tendency on the part of the human race remains a subject for scientific inquiry. What vital truth has not suffered

> distortion and violence at the hands of fallen mankind? For sensible people to discard the doctrine of Satan and demons, because it has been abused, is folly. Following a similar irrational procedure would result in repudiating every vital doctrine of the Word of God, for every aspect of revelation has suffered endless distortion and misrepresentation.
>
> But how is the preponderance of human belief in demons, from the most ancient times to the present day, to be explained? Is it a mere chance occurrence, a kind of colossal accident? Or is demonism only an invention perpetuated by superstition? Or is it a phenomenon built upon the facts of an original revelation of truth, preserved by human instinct, and nurtured by the facts of experience and observation? . . . The only valid conclusion . . . is that belief in Satan and demons, like other religious convictions which have expressed themselves in multifarious ways in different ages, is not an invention at all, nor the fancy of insane men, but it can be traced to its ultimate source in a primitive divine revelation. The basic facts of this revelation have been perpetuated by a God-implanted and ineradicable human instinct and are supported by experience and observation (*Ibid.*, pp. 38,39).

Some may reject this point as being subjective in nature. But it is subjective experience that is grounded in objective truth – the Word of God. The Bible clearly teaches that demons – unclean spirits – took possession of men, body and soul (mind). Demon possession did not end at the Cross. Time and time again we read accounts of demonic activity in the book of Acts, the epistles, and the book of Revelation. There are people today who were once involved with demonic activity that have been delivered and saved by the power of Jesus Christ. Their testimony is not to be disregarded or denied.

One such man is Ben Alexander, a personal friend of mine. Ben was a spiritualist medium for many years in England. He came to America to found a spiritualist society. Instead he found Christ. The power of the Holy Spirit of God came into his life, expelling the unholy spirit of the "god of this world" – Satan. Ben's story can be read in the exciting book *Out From Darkness: The True Story of a*

Medium Who Escaped the Occult (Miranda Press, 1993).

Many godly missionaries have recounted incidents that can only be attributed to demonic powers. Merrill F. Unger writes,

> It is, moreover, a hasty conclusion to infer that there are no cases of demon possession now. The testimony of missionaries to heathen lands is unequivocally to the contrary. Phenomena similar to those described in the Gospels are still met, not only in rude and savage districts, but also in countries of ancient pagan civilization, such as India and China. There the gospel coming to a head-on collision with entrenched Satanic opposition and the pagan darkness of centuries, brings the operation and power of evil supernaturalism into sharper focus, and reveals demonic activity amazingly similar to that which occurred in the days of our Lord's earthly ministry (*Biblical Demonology*, pp. 82, 86).

These three reasons lead us to believe in the reality of demons. They are mentioned as a matter of fact in Holy Scripture. Our Lord had many encounters with demons and addressed them as real beings. Some people living today have had personal encounters with the spirit world.

We repeat: Yes, Virginia. There really are demons. Demons are for real!

25 WHAT IS A DEMON?

What in the world – or above or beneath the world – is a demon? This will not be an easy question to answer. The subject of demonology is both evil to behold and elusive to grasp.

There are two basic views or beliefs concerning demons. One view is that demons are fallen angels. Despite the lack of hard evidence in Scripture, many scholars hold this view. For this view, see Jack Cottrell, *What the Bible Says About God the Creator*, pp. 133, 265, 289. Also see John Walvoord, commentary on *The Revelation of Jesus Christ.* A list of sources for further reading can be found in Terry Miethe, *A Compact Dictionary of Doctrinal Words,* p. 71. The other point of view is that demons are the spirits of the wicked dead. That is the viewpoint that will be presented in the following pages.

Perhaps one of the most intelligible writings on this subject was done by the noted 19th Century Restoration Movement scholar Alexander Campbell in an "Address on Demonology," delivered before the Lecture Club in Nashville, Tennessee, March 10, 1841.

CAMPBELL'S SEVEN REASONS WHY DEMONS ARE DEPARTED SPIRITS OF MEN

Campbell's proposition was this: "We have, from a careful survey of the history of the term demon, concluded that the demons of Paganism, Judaism and Christianity were the ghosts of dead men." He then proceeded to present seven "pillars" or points to prove his proposition. They are as follows:

1. All pagan authors of note, whose works have survived the wreck of ages, affirm the opinion that demons were the spirits or ghosts of dead men. From Hesiod down to the more polished Celsus, historians, poets and philosophers occasionally express this opinion.

2. The Jewish historians, Josephus and Philo, also avow this conviction. Josephus says, "Demons are the spirits of wicked men, who enter into living men and destroy them, unless they are so happy as to meet with speedy relief." Philo says, "The souls of dead men are called demons."

3. The Christian fathers, Justin Martyr, Irenaeus, Origen, depose to the same effect. Justin, when arguing for a future state, says, "Those who are seized and tormented by the souls of the dead, whom all call demons and madmen." Lardner, after examining with the utmost care the works of these and all the other fathers of the first two centuries, says, "The notion of demons, or the souls of dead men, having power over living men, was universally prevalent among the heathen of these times, and believed by many Christians."

4. The evangelists and apostles of Jesus Christ so understood the matter. As this is a very important, and, of itself, a sufficient, pillar on which to rest our edifice, we shall be at more pains to illustrate and enforce it. We shall first state the philological law or canon of criticism, on the generality and truth of which all our dictionaries, grammars and translations are formed. Every word not specially explained or defined in a particular sense, by any standard writer of any particular age and country, is to be taken and applied in the current or commonly received signification of that country and age in which the writer lived and wrote. If this canon of translation and of criticism be denied; then we affirm there is no value in dictionaries, nor in the acquisition of ancient languages in which any book may be written, nor is there any confidence to be placed in any translation of any ancient work, sacred or profane; for they are all made upon the assumption of the truth of this law.

We have, then, only to ask, first, for the current signification of this term *demon* in Judea at the Christian era; and, in the second place, Did the inspired writers ever give any special definition of it? We have already found an answer to the first in the Greeks and Jews of the apostolic age, and of the preceding and subsequent ages. We have heard Josephus, Philo, Lucian, Justin and Lardner, from whose writings and affirmations we are expressly told what the universal acceptation of the term was in Judea and in those times. In the second place, the apostles and our Lord, as already said, use this word in various forms seventy-five times, and on no occasion give any hint of a special, private or peculiar interpretation of it; which was not their method when they used a term either not generally understood, or understood in a special sense. Does any one ask the meaning of the words Messiah, prophet, priest, elder, deacon, presbytery, altar, sacrifice, sabbath, circumcision? We refer him to the current signification of these words among the Jews and Greeks of that age. Why, then, should any one except the term *demon* from the universal law? Are we not, therefore, sustained by the highest and most authoritative decision of that literary tribunal by whose rules and decrees all works sacred and profane are translated from a dead to a living tongue? We are, then, fully authorized to say that the demons of the New Testament were the spirits of dead men.

5. But as a distinct historic evidence, and as confirmatory rather of our views than of the authority of the inspired authors, I adduce a very explicit and decisive passage from the epistle to the Smyrneans, written by the celebrated Ignatius, the disciple of the apostle John. He quotes the words of the Lord to Peter when Peter supposed he saw a spirit or a ghost. But he quotes him thus: Handle me and see, for I am not – *daimon asomaton* – a disembodied demon – a spirit without a body. This places the matter above all doubt that with those of that day demon and ghost were equivalent terms.

6. But we also deduce an argument from the word *angel*. This word is of Bible origin, and confined to those countries in which that volume is found. It is not found in any of the Greek poets, orators or historians, so far as known to me. Of that rank of beings to whom Jews and Christians have applied this official title, the Pagan nations seem never to have had the first conception. It is therefore certain that they could not use the term *demon* interchangeably with the word *angel*, as indicative of an order of intelligent beings above men and intermediate between them and the Divinity. They had neither the name nor the idea of an angel in their mythology. Philo the Jew has, indeed, said that amongst the Jews the word *demon* and the word *angel* were sometimes used interchangeably; and some have

thence inferred that lapsed angels were called demons. But this is not logical inference; for the Jews called the winds, the pestilence, the lightnings of heaven, angels, as indicative of their agency in accomplishing the will of God. In this sense, indeed, a demon might be officially called an angel. But in this sense demon is to angel as the species to the genus: we call a demon an angel but we cannot call an angel a demon – just as we can call every man an animal, but we cannot call every animal a man.

Others, indeed, have imagined that the old giants and heroes, said to have been the fruit of the intermarriage of the sons of God with the daughters of men before the flood, were the demons of all the world Pagan, Jews and Christians. Their most plausible argument is, that the word hero and the word love are identical; and the loves of the angels for the daughters of men was the reason that their gigantic offspring were called heroes; whence the term was afterwards appropriated to persons of great courage as well as of great stature. This is simply ridiculous.

But to refer to the word *angel*. It is a Bible term, and not being found in all classic, in all mythologic, antiquity, could not have entered into the Pagan ideas of a demon. Now, that it is not so used in the Christian Scriptures is evident from the following reasons:

1st. Angels were never said to enter into any one.

2nd. Angels have no affection for bodies of any sort, either as habitations or vehicles of action.

3rd. Angels have no predilection for tombs and monuments of the dead.

In these three particulars angels and demons stand in full contrast and are contradistinguished by essentially different characteristics: for –

1st. Demons have entered into human bodies and into the bodies of inferior creatures.

2nd. Demons evince a peculiar affection for human bodies, and seem to desire them both as vehicles of action and as places of habitation.

3rd. Demons also evince a peculiar fondness for their former mortal tenements; hence we so often read of their carrying the possessed into the graveyards, the tombs and sepulchres, where, perchance, their old mortalities lay in ruins.

From which we argue, as well as from the fact that the Pagans knew nothing of a devil, nor an angel, nor Satan, before the Christian era, that when they, or the Christians or

Jews, spoke of demons, they could not mean any intermediate rank of spirits apart from the spirits of dead men. Hence in no instance in Holy Writ do we find *demon* and *angel* used as convertible terms. Is it not certain, then, that they are the ghosts of dead men? But here remains yet another pillar.

7. Among the evidences of the Papal defection intimated by Paul, he associates the doctrine concerning demons with celibacy and abstinence from certain meats, as chief among the signs of that fearful apostasy. He warrants the conclusion that the purgatorial prisons for ghosts and the ghostly mediators of departed saints, which, equally with the command to abstain from lawful meats and the prohibition of marriage to the clergy, characterize the times of which he spoke, are attributes of the same system, and indicative of the fact that *demons* and *ghosts* are two names for the same things. To this we add the testimony of James, who says the demons believe and tremble for their doom. Now, all the eminent critics concur that the spirits of wicked men are here intended; and need I add that oft-repeated affirmation of the demoniacs? – We know thee, Jesus of Nazareth: art thou come to torment us before the time?" Thus, all the scriptural allusions to this subject authorize the conclusion that demons are wicked and unclean spirits of dead men. A single saying in the Apocalypse makes this most obvious. When Babylon is razed to its foundation, it is said to be made the habitation of demons – of the ghosts of its sepulchred inhabitants.

From these seven sources of evidence – viz. the Pagan authors, the Jewish historians, the Christian fathers, the four Evangelists, the epistle of Ignatius, the acceptation of the term *angel* in its contrast with *demon*, and the whole of the New Testament – we conclude that the demons of the New Testament were the ghosts of wicked men.

McGARVEY: DEMONS ARE SPIRITS OF THE WICKED DEAD

To Alexander Campbell's sagacious and lengthy reasoning, we would add these brief comments of the wonderful Bible expositor J. W. McGarvey, the man whom *The London Times* described at his death in 1911 as being the greatest Bible scholar on earth.

> Matthew, Luke and Mark all concur in pronouncing demons unclean; that is, wicked. They thus corrected the prevailing Greek notion that some of the demons were good. The word "demon," as used in our Saviour's time by both Jews and Greeks, meant the spirits of the departed or the ghosts of dead men, and the teaching of that and prior ages was that such spirits often took possession of the living men and controlled them (*The Fourfold Gospel*, p. 167).

VICTOR HOVEN ON DEMONS

Victor E. Hoven, former professor at Northwest Christian College, Eugene, Oregon, is another respected man of learning of more recent years. In his popular *Outlines of Biblical Doctrine* he has this to say about demons:

> In the Authorized Version of the New Testament the word for demons is incorrectly rendered "devils"; there is but one devil. "Demons" and "unclean spirits" are used interchangeably (Mk. 3:14,15; Matt. 10:1), but never with reference to fallen angels, for they are not said to enter into anybody; only demons do that.

Hoven then examines the meaning of the word "demon."

> The rule for ascertaining the meaning of a word is, "That meaning given it by those to whom it is addressed." What, then, was the meaning of the term demons in the time of Jesus and His apostles?
>
> The Jewish belief is given by Josephus who speaks of 'demons, which are no other than the spirits of the wicked (dead), that enter into men that are alive." Philo said, "The souls of dead men are called demons."
>
> The Greeks believed that demons were the spirits of dead men deified, hence when Paul preached to the

Athenian philosophers Jesus and the resurrection they said, "He seemeth to be a setter forth of strange gods" (marg.."foreign demons," Acts 17:18). Hesiod, as quoted by Plutarch, says: "The spirits of mortals become demons when separated from their earthly bodies."

Jesus used the term demons without definition or explanation differing from the popular meaning current in His day. It is not thinkable that He was deceived, or intended to deceive, in this matter. This popular conception is confirmed by Paul in his treatment of the "spirit of divination" in a maid at Philippi (Acts 16:16-18). And he wrote to the Corinthians that the Gentiles "sacrifice to demons," the spirits of dead heroes (1 Cor. 10:20). (*Outlines of Biblical Doctrine*, pp. 40,41).

MEANING OF "DEMON"

What, then, is a demon? We will have a better understanding when we look at the meaning of the word. The Greek noun for demon (*daimon*) at first signified, among Pagan Greeks, an inferior deity, whether good or bad. We have already seen that the New Testament corrects that notion. W. E. Vine says, "in the N. T. it denotes an evil spirit" (*Vine's Expository Dictionary of Old and New Testament Words*, Vol. 1, p. 291). Seth Wilson, long-time Academic Dean of Ozark Christian College, offers these thoughts on the meaning of "demons:"

1. Not the same as the Greek word for "devil." There is only one devil but many demons.

2. Oldest meaning: divine power, deity. Homer (c. 850 B. C.) used it interchangeably with the word God.

3. A being between man and God. Plato attempted to fix this definition. He used it in both a good and bad sense. Plato held that they included departed spirits of good men. Socrates spoke constantly of his "demon." Ignatius says that Jesus told His disciples after the resurrection, "I am not a disembodied demon." This shows his way of expressing what Luke 24:37-39 says. See also Luke 4:33, "spirit of an unclean demon."

4. Elsewhere in the New Testament demons are always

evil spirits, messengers and ministers of Satan.

a. Heathen deities (Acts 17:18; 1 Cor. 10:20; Rev. 9:20).

b. Ones who believe and tremble (or bristle) but are lost (James 2:19).

c. They recognize Jesus as the Son of God (Matt. 8:29; Mark 1:23,34; 3:11; Luke 4:41).

d. Agents of Satan (Matt. 12:24-26; Luke 10:17, 18; 11:15-22). (*Learning From Jesus*, pp. 302, 303).

Plato, in Symposium, derived "demon" from *daemon*, "knowing" or "intelligent." Campbell traced *daiman* to an ancient verb which meant "to discriminate, to know." As we will see, demons have vast knowledge. They are the "knowing ones."

ARE DEMONS ACTUALLY DISEASES?

Those who would try to explain away the reality of demons, even in Biblical times, suggest that demons were actually diseases. Consider McGarvey's insightful response:

> But whatever these demons were, the Scripture, both by its treatment of them and its words concerning them, clearly indicates that they were immaterial, intelligent beings, which are neither to be confused with maladies and diseases of the body, nor with tropes, metaphors, or other figures of speech. In proof of this we adduce the following Scriptural facts:
>
> 1. The legislation of the Old Testament proceeded upon the assumption that there was such a thing as a "familiar spirit" (Lev. 19:31).
>
> 2. In the New Testament they are spoken of as personalities (Jas. 2:19; Rev. 16:14). Jesus even founded a parable upon their habits (Luke 11: 24-26).
>
> 3. Jesus distinguished between them and diseases, and so did His disciples (Matt. 10:8; Luke 10:17-20).
>
> 4. Jesus addressed them as persons, and they answered as such (Mark 5:8; 9:25).
>
> 5. They manifested desires and passions (Mark 5: 12,13).
>
> 6. They showed a superhuman knowledge of Jesus (Matt. 8:29).

"It would be impossible to regard demon possession as a mere disease without doing violence to the language used in every instance of the expulsion of a demon" (*The Fourfold Gospel*, p. 167). To this fine testimony we could add that of Albert Barnes, renowned Bible commentator.

> It has been maintained by many, that the sacred writers meant only by this expression to denote those who were melancholy or epileptic, or afflicted with some other grievous disease. This opinion has been supported by arguments too long to be repeated here. On the other hand, it has been supposed that the persons so described were under the influence of evil spirits, who had complete possession of the faculties, and who produced many symptoms of disease not unlike melancholy, and madness, and epilepsy. That such was the fact, will appear from the following considerations:
>
> 1st. That Christ and the apostles spoke to them, and of them as such: that they addressed them, and managed them, precisely as if they were so possessed, leaving their hearers to infer beyond a doubt that such was their real opinion.
>
> 2nd. They spake, conversed, asked questions, gave answers, and expressed their knowledge of Christ, and their fear of him –things that certainly could not be said of diseases, Matt. 8:28.
>
> 3rd. They are represented as going out of the persons possessed, and entering the bodies of others, Matt. 8:32.
>
> 4th. Jesus spoke to them, and asked their name, and they answered him. He threatened them, commanded them to be silent, to depart, and not to return, Mark 1:25; 5:8; 9:25.
>
> 5th. Those possessed are said to know Christ; to be acquainted with the Son of God, Luke 4:34; Mark 1:24. This could not be said of diseases.
>
> 6th. The early fathers of the church interpreted these passages in the same way. They derived their opinions probably from the apostles' sentiments.
>
> 7th. If it may be denied that Christ believed in such possessions, it does not appear why any other clear sentiment of his may not in the same way be disputed. There is, perhaps, no subject on which he expressed himself more clearly, or acted more uniformly, or which he left more clearly impressed on the minds of his disciples (*Barnes' Notes on the New Testament*, p. 18).

ARE DEMONS "EASTERN METAPHORS?"

A companion argument to the one that suggests that demons were actually diseases is that demons were only "Eastern metaphors." This argument, if indeed it can be called that, drew the wrath of Alexander Campbell, a master of sarcasm. How the men of the Nashville Lecture Club must have pounded the tables and "rolled in the aisles" when the sapient Campbell took this argument apart!

> It ought, however, to be candidly stated that there have been in later times a few intellectual dyspeptics, on whose nervous system the idea of being really possessed by an evil spirit produces a frenzied excitement. Terrified at the thought of an incarnate demon, they have resolutely undertaken to prove that every demon named in Holy Writ is but a bold Eastern metaphor, placing in high relief dumbness, deafness, madness, palsy, epilepsy, &c.; and hence that demoniacs then and now were and are a class of unfortunates laboring under certain physical maladies called unclean spirits. *Credat Judoeus Apella, Non Ego*.
>
> On the principle that every demon is an Eastern metaphor, how incomparably more eloquent than Demosthenes or Cicero, was he that had at one time within him a legion of Eastern metaphors struggling for utterance! No wonder, then, that the swineherds of Gadara were overwhelmed by the moving eloquence of their herds as they rushed with such pathos into the deep waters of the dark Galilee! (*Popular Lectures and Addresses*, p. 389).

We cannot conclude this chapter without first allowing Campbell a final burst of trenchant wit. He is commenting on the man who was repossessed by seven demons more wicked than the first (Matt. 12: 43-45).

> The first state of the Jews compared to a metaphor! – compared to a nonentity – compared to a fiction! This is even worse than representing a trope coming out of a man's mouth, "crying with a loud voice," "wandering through dry places" – unfigurative language, I presume – seeking a period, and finding a comma – and at length, tired and

> fatigued, returning with seven fiercer metaphors more wickedly eloquent than himself, repossessing the orator, and making him more eloquent than before. It will not help the matter to say that when a disease leaves a man it wanders through dry or wet places, through marshes and fens, through deserts and prairies, and, finding no rest for its foot, takes with it seven other more violent diseases, seeks for the unfortunate man from whom the doctors expelled it, and, reentering his improved condition, makes that its eternal abode (*Ibid.*, p. 391).

What are demons? Demons are unclean spirits, the spirits of the wicked dead.

26 THE ORIGIN OF DEMONS

Where did demons come from? How did they originate? Have they always existed? Are they created beings? How can we account for the existence of these evil beings?

Keep in mind that we are attempting to discover what the Bible says about demons. We are not at all concerned with the fanciful, foolish or frightening ideas that men have had about demons, both past and present. Again we quote from Campbell's "Address on Demonology":

> Think not, however, that I intend to visit the fairy realms and enchanting scenes of wild romance, or that I wish to indulge in the fascinating fiction of poets, ancient or modern; think not that I am about to ascend with old Hesiod into his curious theogony of gods and demigods, or to descend with the late Sir Walter Scott to the phantasmatic realms of Celtic and Scottish ghosts and demons. I aim at more substantial entertainment, at more sober and grave realities, than the splendid fancies of those gifted and fortunate votaries of popular applause.

Our aim should be to discover what God in His Word has said about demons, nothing less, nothing more. The best answer to these questions, really, the only answer, is "What does the Bible say?" "Let God be true, and every man a liar" (Rom. 3:4).

Demonology, like angelology or any other Biblical topic, should be treated intra-Biblically (what God has revealed in His Word) rather than extra-Biblically (what men have said about demons). Superstition, folklore, fables, myths, etc., must yield to the Word of God.

DEMONS, UNLIKE ANGELS, NOT CREATED

The origin of demons is difficult to determine. The angels were created at the command of God (see Neh. 9:6; Psa. 148:2, 5; Col. 1:17). They rejoiced at the creation of the world. Some, however, "did not keep their positions of authority" (Jude 6) but joined the Satanic rebellion and lost their place in heaven (2 Pet. 2:4; Rev. 12:8). But it does not appear that the fallen angels became demons. There is no clear support in Scripture for this assertion. The word for angels (*angelos*) has no connection with demons (*daimon*). Angel means "messenger" while demon means "knowing one." Both are spirit beings but that is where the similarity ends. Angels could assume a human body when appearing to men. Demons actually took over, or possessed, the bodies of existing people. Angels appeared to men as men to minister to them. Demons invaded the bodies of men, women and children to mistreat them. Though both fallen angels and demons are under the control of Satan, they are not one and the same.

THEORIES OF DEMONIC ORIGIN EXAMINED

Wayne Jackson had this to say about the origin of demons in *Christian Courier* (Vol. 20, No. 2, June, 1984):

> What is the truth concerning this matter? What were the demons of biblical fame? Where did they come from? What powers did they possess? Why did they enter certain persons and not others? Do they still possess people today? These questions engage the attention of thinking people.
>
> The answers to the foregoing queries will not be found in the cheap books and shoddy movies of this perverse society. Rather, any information with which the human race has been indulged will be in the inspired Scriptures. The truth of the matter is, the Bible does not give a systematic treatment of demons. When one has examined every biblical reference to the subject, there are still many unanswered questions. The subject of demons is only introduced in the

New Testament as the topic relates to other matters of importance; it is therefore incidental and so we are merely given sufficient minimal information – information necessary for the establishment of more important truths. The subject of demonology was thus obviously not an end within itself in New Testament doctrine.

Demon possession was a historical reality of first century society and no one, who respects the accuracy of the New Testament record, will deny this. Spiritual entities, known as demons, did inhibit and afflict human bodies during that age.

The question of demon origin is not spelled out in the Scriptures. Several theories have been advanced by respectable Bible students, some of which, incidentally, may be dismissed immediately. Some, for instance, have suggested that demons were disembodied spirits of a strange pre-Adam race of men that once lived upon the earth in an alleged "gap period" that is supposed to fall between Genesis 1:1 and 1:2. The problem with that theory is this: there is not a shred of Biblical evidence that any such gap period ever existed! That idea was born in the feverish minds of those who were panicked by the assertions of the evolutionists, and who thus sought to force the Bible into harmony with evolutionary chronology. How could there have been a pre-Adam race often if Adam was the first man (1 Cor. 15:45)?

Others have contended that demons resulted from the cohabitation of angels with some of those ancient women who lived before the Flood. This theory is based upon a misunderstanding of Genesis 6:1-4, "the sons of God came in unto the daughters of men, and they bore children unto them." But this cannot be correct since Christ clearly taught that angels are sexless beings, incapable of such union (cf. Matt. 22:30). In that Genesis context the "sons of God" were the righteous lineage of Seth, while the "daughters of men" represented the wicked descendants of Cain.

The two more plausible views of the identity of demons are as follows. First, demons may have been the spirits of wicked dead men whom God, in harmony with his divine purposes, permitted to leave the Hadean realm to indwell some people. Alexander Campbell argued this position in his lecture entitled "Demonology," which is found in his volume, "Popular Lectures and Addresses." Second, others have contended that demons were fallen angels who were allowed to escape their confinement to similarly accomplish some component in the divine plan (cf. Jude 6). Charles Hodge, in his "Systematic Theology," contends for this viewpoint.

Regardless of the problem of origin, the New Testament clearly recognizes the fact of first century demoniacs.

GENESIS: THE BOOK OF BEGINNINGS

It is the viewpoint of this author that demons are the spirits of the wicked dead. But as far as the origin of demons is concerned, we simply do not know. We would assume that since demons are the unclean spirits of the wicked dead, they have existed since the beginning of man.

The Book of Genesis is the "book of beginnings." In the very first verse we learn of the beginning of the five "Manifestations of the Unknowable" – time, force, energy, space and matter. The balance of the chapter lets us know about the beginning of the three kingdoms; mineral, vegetable and animal. Genesis teaches us about the first man, the first woman, the first marriage, the first family, the first sin, the first murder, the first city, the first nation, etc. Indeed, it is the book of beginnings.

It would be fairly safe to assume, therefore, that the beginning of demons is hinted at in Genesis. Demons are inseparably connected with idolatry (see Deut. 32:17; Isa. 13:21; 34:14; 65:3,11; 1 Cor. 10:20,21; Rev. 9:20). The worship of idols appears early on in Genesis. Terah, the father of Abraham, worshiped idols (cf. Gen. 11:31; Josh. 24:2). Rachel, Jacob's second wife, stole her father's images (Gen. 31:19). Jacob found it necessary to tell his family to get rid of such abominable things (Gen. 35:2). W. E. Vine says, "Demons are the spiritual agents acting in all idolatry. The idol itself is nothing, but every idol has a demon associated with it who induces idolatry, with its worship and sacrifices" (*Expository Dictionary of Old and New Testament Words*, Vol. 1, p. 291).

Merrill F. Unger adds this concluding thought:

Biblical demonology, then, as it exists in its elemental though essential form in the earlier chapters of Genesis, is the ultimate source and basis of all demonology – ethnic, later Biblical, Jewish, and Christian. Genesis as the book of beginnings catalogues the beginning of the earth and the human race, the beginning of human sin and death and the beginning of human government and language. It also suggests the origin of demons . . . . In the Book of Genesis the author assumes the existence of demons just as plainly as he assumes the existence of God or the fall of Satan and his angels (*Biblical Demonology*, pp. 19,20).

27 THE NATURE OF DEMONS

What is the basic nature of demons? Are some good and some bad? Or are they always evil? Are they spiritual or earthly in nature? Do they assume bodily form, like the angels? Or do they merely possess, for a time, other people's bodies?

The basic nature of demons, according to the Bible, is twofold: (1) as to their actual state of being they are spirit; (2) as to their moral character they are unclean. Demons are unclean spirits.

SPIRIT BEINGS

Angels, of course, are spirit beings as well. "Are not all angels ministering spirits..." (Heb. 1:14). But they are sent by God to serve the saints. This could hardly be said of demons. They are emissaries of Satan who seek to afflict saint and sinner alike. Demons are spirit beings all right, but there is nothing spiritual about them or their work.

How do we know that demons are spirit beings? Do you remember when Jesus appeared to His disciples after His resurrection? At first they were frightened. Why? Because they thought they had seen a spirit! "They were startled and frightened, thinking they saw a ghost" (Luke 24:37). Jesus calmed their fears by showing them His hands and feet, saying, "Look at my hands and my feet. It is I myself! Touch me and see; a ghost does not have flesh and bones, as you see I have" (Luke 24:39). Spirit beings – whether good (like angels) or evil (like demons) – are just that; spirit in nature. The angels of God, though spirit in nature, could take on bodily form. They did not have human bodies as such. Nor did they possess the bodies of men like demons. As messengers from God, they appeared in human form to human beings. Demons would enter the bodies of men and women, either by invitation (like the mediums who contacted the spirits of dead men) or by force, (possession).

The gospel writers knew that demons were spirit beings in nature. Matthew, for instance, records that at Capernaum many "demon possessed" were brought to Jesus (Matt. 8:16). Then he says that Christ "drove out the spirits with a word." The two terms, demons and spirits, were synonymous with him. In Mark's account of the Gadarene demoniac, the words "demons" and "evil spirits" are likewise used interchangeably. A man with an "evil spirit" comes to Jesus (Mark 5:2). The "demons" later beg Jesus to send them into a herd of swine (Mark 5:12). Jesus gave them permission and the "evil spirits" came out of Legion and entered the pigs (Mark 5:13).

From these Scriptures and others like them, it is clear that demons are spirit beings. But they differ from angelic beings and human beings. The "spirits of righteous men made perfect" are with God in heaven (Heb. 12:23). The spirits of unjust men who have died are suffering in Tartarus (Luke 16:23) or are roaming the earth in search of rest (i.e., human embodiment).

UNCLEAN ENTITIES

The Bible also makes it plain that demons are unclean spirits. In the Old Testament they are usually referred to as "familiar" spirits (Lev. 19:31; Deut. 18:11; 1 Sam. 28:3; 2 Chron. 33:6; Isa. 8:19 et al). A rare exception is Zechariah 13:2 where they are called "unclean" or "impure." Throughout the New Testament, demons are called "unclean."

For example, in Matthew 12:43 Jesus said, "When the evil spirit comes out of a man it goes through arid places seeking rest and does not find it." The New International Version footnote has "unclean." Later in the text Jesus indicated that the spirit "goes and takes with it seven other spirits more wicked than itself, and they go in and live there" (Matt. 12:45). Demons are called "foul spirits" in Revelation 18:2 (KJV). Evil. Wicked. Unclean. Foul. These are terms the Bible uses to describe demons.

All of this is to say that Scripture knows nothing of "good" demons. Again and again the Bible calls demons "unclean" or "evil." Man has suggested that some demons were actually good and benevolent beings.

It does appear, however, that there are degrees of wickedness among the demons. While none are good, some are less wicked than others. Satan, obviously, is the worst, being called the "prince of demons" (Matt. 12:24). Jesus taught that some demons were more wicked than others. Referring to a vanquished evil spirit, Jesus said, "it goes and takes seven other spirits more wicked than itself, and they go in and live there" (Luke 11:26).

The teaching of our Lord is clear: demons are unclean spirit beings.

28 CHARACTERISTICS OF DEMONS

When we speak of the nature of something, we are talking about the inherent character or basic constitution of a person or thing. The essence of Biblical demons, as we have already seen, is that of an unclean spirit. When we mention the *characteristics* of demons, we mean the distinctive marks or *peculiarities* of these vile beings. Demons are clearly marked by their unusual, unearthly, ungodly action and behavior.

INSATIABLE DESIRE TO INHABIT LIVING BODIES

One characteristic of demons is their intense craving to invade and inhabit a living body. When a person – good or bad, saved or unsaved – dies, his spirit departs from his body (Jas. 2:26). The dead body eventually returns to dust (Gen. 3:19). But the spirit of the deceased returns to the God who gave it life (Eccl. 12:7). God does one of two things with that spirit. He either accepts it into His presence or He sends it from His presence.

When Lazarus died, he was "carried by the angels" into Abraham's bosom (Luke 16:22). But when the rich man died, he was "tormented" in Hades, the unseen abode of the unrighteous dead (Luke 16:23). The spirits of the wicked dead are consigned to the compartment of suffering in Hades, Tartarus.

The apostle Peter mentions both "the spirits in prison" (1 Pet. 3:19) and the "angels that sinned" (2 Pet. 2:4) as being in a place of darkness and suffering, awaiting judgment. Yet, we know that some evil angels and unclean spirits were loose in the days of Jesus, the apostles and the early church. Today, too, for that matter. As to why some angels and demons are confined and others are free to do their evil work is a mystery. The Bible yields no clear clue and we must be content to let the secret things belong to the Lord (Deut. 29:29).

One thing is clear, however. Demons have a burning desire to occupy living bodies. Jesus once spoke of a demon who had been cast out of a man (Matt. 12:43-45; Luke 11:24-26). He said that the excommunicated spirit walked through "dry places," seeking rest but finding none. What does this mean? We know that Satan himself constantly goes "roaming through the earth and going back and forth in it" (Job 1:7). Peter warned, "Your enemy the devil prowls around like a roaring lion looking for someone to devour" (1 Pet. 5:8). Should we be surprised that his vile helpers walk about too?

What are these "dry places?" Could it be desert areas? Christ was tempted by the devil in such a place (Matt. 4:1). A dry and arid place is a place without water. The spirits of the wicked dead know what a terrible thing thirst can be (Luke 16:24). Are they reminded of this horrible place when they walk through "dry places," wherever they may be? Hell is also a place where there is no rest, day or night (Rev. 14:11). The Bible says demons "seek rest" but don't find it. Do these desolate places where demons roam remind them of their torment to come? Is that why they seek rest in human embodiment? And what kind of "rest" do they experience, once ensconced in their new "house?"

The desire for inhabiting a living body is so great among disembodied spirits that they would even prefer animal embodiment to no embodiment at all! When the demons who possessed the man who called himself "Legion" encountered Jesus, they asked His permission to enter a herd of about 2,000 pigs (Matt. 8:31; Mark 5:12; Luke 8:32). They preferred dwelling in the body of a pig to those dreadful days of roaming dry places. Jesus granted their strange request and the demons invaded the herd of swine.

The reaction of the pigs was both startling and immediate. They stampeded "violently" down a steep slope and drowned in the foaming sea. How strange! The demons preferred to live in a pig rather than walk in dry places; the pigs chose to drown in the water rather than be possessed by these strange beings.

The teaching of Jesus on this characteristic of demons is clear. "When an evil spirit comes out of a man, it goes through arid places seeking rest and does not find it. Then it says, 'I will return to the house I left.'" (Matt. 12:43). Evil spirits desire to indwell living beings.

INJURIOUS AND MURDEROUS INTENT

A second characteristic of Biblical demons is that they seek to injure and even destroy – those whom they possess. This seems self-defeating, even sheer madness, but no one has ever said the demons always act in a rational manner. Indeed, their behavior can only be called irrational at times. It is not enough that they seek to invade people – they want to injure them as well.

This strange behavior is seen in several accounts of demon possessed people in Jesus' day. A man who was possessed by a demon in Capernaum was "torn" or "shaken violently" by the vile spirit before he came out at Christ's command (Mark 1:26). It was as though the demon wanted to get in one last act of violence.

The Gadarene demoniac is another case in point. Night and day this poor fellow would scream and cut himself with stones (Mark 5:6). Many times the demon who lived in him had caused the man to break his bonds and run into the desert (Luke 8:29). We can only imagine what the demon tried to do to this unfortunate creature during those wild runs. How his poor body must have been covered with scars and sores from the demon-inspired attacks on his body! This is to say nothing of the games the demons played with the poor man's mind.

Even children were not immune from the foul work of evil spirits. A young lad had been possessed by a demon from childhood (Mark 9:21). The demon, according to the testimony of the lad's father, would often throw the boy into a convulsion. He would gnash his teeth and foam at the mouth (Mark 9:18). After Jesus rebuked the demon, the unclean spirit came out of the boy but not before convulsing him once more. So violent was this final convulsion that onlookers thought the boy was dead (Mark 9:26).

In Ephesus a demon-possessed man caused bodily harm to others (Acts 19:16). He leaped on the seven sons of Sceva and beat them so severely that the brothers fled "naked and bleeding."

The demons seem to take an unholy delight in causing bodily harm, pain and suffering. It leads us to wonder if some of the terrible things that people do today – even to members of their own family – are not demon-inspired. How else can we explain some of the inhuman things that happen? Especially parents who perform such atrocities on their children. And sometimes vice versa.

Not only do demons seek to violently injure those whom they inhabit, they actually desire to kill them! This, as we have said, would seem to be self-defeating for at death they would be forced to roam the feared and dreaded arid places once more. Be that as it may, it must be remembered that demons are under the dark control of their evil master Beelzebub, the prince of demons (Luke 11:15). And what is Satan's desire? To devour believers (1 Pet. 5:8). The devil, according to Jesus, is a "murderer from the beginning" (John 8:44). It was Satan who caused Cain to rise up and murder his own brother in cold blood (Gen. 4:7,8). Is it any wonder that he seeks to assassinate as well as afflict? Murder is the ultimate mission of the demons. To injure is not enough. Only death satisfies the demons.

This is seen in several places in Scripture. One of the most terrible incidents of attempted murder was the demon who possessed the boy of Mark 9. Not content to batter and bruise the boy, the demon would often attempt to drown him by throwing him in the water. He would also throw him into a fire in a wicked effort to burn the boy to death (Mark 9:22). Again we are led to wonder how many people today who suffer from suicidal mania are being afflicted by Satanic spirits. Surely no persons in their right mind would throw themselves into water or fire. Is it possible that King Saul committed suicide at the urging of the spirits that had plagued him for so long? Was the demonized Legion trying to kill himself when he cut himself with sharp stones (Mark 5:5)? How cruel and heartless are the demons of hell!

29 ORGANIZATION AMONG DEMONS

The Scriptures indicate that the demons operate under a highly organized system of authority, even though that system is totally corrupt and wicked. Demons do not "do their own thing." They do not act on their own. They are a part of a diabolical, highly efficient, well-oiled machine. This organization exists to harass, interrupt and even stop the work of God.

SATAN, THE KING OF DEMONS

Jesus Christ is the head of His kingdom, the church (Eph. 1:20-23). Satan is at the helm of his evil empire. The unclean spirits are subject to him. Jesus taught this truth when He recognized that a woman who had a "spirit of infirmity" had, indeed, been bound by Satan for a long time. "And, behold, there was a woman which had a spirit of infirmity eighteen years, and was bowed together, and could in no wise lift herself up" (Luke 13:11 KJV). The Lord had compassion on her and set her free from this spirit-induced infirmity. Then he told the onlookers, "Should not this woman, a daughter of Abraham, whom Satan has kept bound for eighteen long years, be set free on the Sabbath day from what bound her?" (Luke 13:18). Satan uses his demons to bodily afflict people. The spirit that crippled this woman was an agent of the devil acting in accordance with his dark master. However – as is the case in every account in the gospels – the spirits must submit to the still greater authority of Jesus.

On at least two occasions Jesus was accused of casting out demons by Beelzebub, the prince of demons. The Jewish thought of Jesus' day was that Beelzebub, or Satan, was the ruler of demons. "But when the Pharisees heard this, they said, 'It is only by Beelzebub, the prince of demons, that this fellow drives out demons'" (Matt. 12:24). Our Lord then proceeded to show his critics how ludicrous and self-defeating it would be for Him to cast out demons by Satan: "If Satan drives out Satan, he is divided against himself. How then can his kingdom stand?" Would Satan be so stupid as to divide his kingdom? Demons are the willing servants of the devil.

The devil is "the ruler of the kingdom of the air, the spirit who is now at work among those who are disobedient" (Eph. 2:2). Weymouth's translation says, "the prince of the powers of the air, the spirits that are now at work in the hearts of the sons of disobedience." In other words, the demons are actually at work today in the lives of disobedient people. They are under Satan's rule and they rule the lives of sinners.

We know that our battle against Satan is not against flesh and blood. Paul writes that it is against rulers, authorities, the powers of this dark world, the spiritual forces of evil in the heavenly realms (Eph. 6:12). Satan is the acknowledged leader of both fallen angels and unclean spirits. They both do his bidding. They both battle against the forces of righteousness.

IMPRISONED SPIRITS UNDER SATAN'S RULE

Not only are the angels and demons that are "loosed" under Satan's domination, even the spirits which remain in prison in the Hadean realm are subject to the devil. The Abyss, "the abode of demons, out of which they can be let loose" (W. E. Vine), is mentioned a number of times in Revelation (Rev. 9:1, 2, 11; 11:7; 17:8; 20:1,3). Those confined in the Abyss have a king over them, "the angel of the Abyss" (Rev. 9:11). In Hebrew his name is "Abaddon" and in Greek, "Apollyon." Both names mean "Destroyer." Burton W. Barber comments:

> Satan is the personification of destruction. He never builds, never lifts, but tears down and destroys. He destroys men's faith in God and love for Him. He destroys character, homes and nations. He desires no good to come to God or men and only tolerates it long enough to perfect and execute a plan that will destroy everything that God and men build if he possibly can (*The Ruin and Redemption of Man*, p. 33).

Satan himself is bound, cast and sealed in the Abyss for a thousand years (Rev. 20:1-3). Satan is king of his kingdom but not of Christ's!

DEGREES OF DEMONIC STRENGTH AND EVIL

The holy angels of God, though ultimately subject to God and Christ, are also under the authority of an archangel, Michael by name (Jude 9). The prefix, "arche," means "prince." Michael is the prince of the holy angels. "Arche" is found in "principalities" (Rom. 8:38; Eph. 1:21; Col. 1:16). There are good princes and evil princes. Satan is the "prince of the power of the air" (Eph. 2:2). There does not seem to be any "archdemon" in Scripture other than Satan.

However, Jesus taught that there are degrees of wickedness among the demons. All are unclean, wicked, evil and foul. There are no good demons, contrary to popular Greek thought. But some are more wicked than others. Hear Jesus on the matter: "When an evil spirit comes out of a man, it goes through arid places seeking rest and does not find it. Then it says, 'I will return to the house I left.' When it arrives, it finds the house swept and clean and put in order. Then it goes and takes seven other spirits more wicked than itself, and they go in and live there. And the final condition of that man is worse than the first" (Luke 11:24-26). All demons are evil but some are more evil than others.

Degrees of demonic wickedness can be seen in those demons who violently attacked the people whom they possessed. Especially it is seen in the demons who sought to kill those whom they inhabited. Some spirits were content to "merely" afflict people with blindness (Matt. 12:22), deafness (Mark 9:25), muteness (Matt. 9:32; Luke 11:14) or curvature of the spine (Luke 13:11). But other demons, more wicked, would go beyond impairment of speech, sight and hearing. Consider the following:

"The evil spirit shook the man violently . . ." (Mark 1:23). Violence is an earmark of demonism.

"A spirit seizes him and he suddenly screams; it throws him into convulsions so that he foams at the mouth. It scarcely ever leaves him and is destroying him...the demon threw him to the ground in a convulsion" (Luke 9:39-42). What makes this all the worse is the victim was a young boy. Demons have no mercy. Mark adds that the demon would often throw the poor lad into the water to drown him or the fire to burn him to death (Mark 9:22).

"Night and day among the tombs and in the hills he would cry out and cut himself with stones" (Mark 5:5). Demons seek the death of people, even by their own hand.

In addition to teaching that there are degrees of wickedness among demons, our Lord also indicated that certain types of demons required more effort for them to be expelled from their victims. In the case of the epileptic boy, the disciples of Jesus had failed in their effort to help the lad. After Jesus rebuked the demon and cast him out, the disciples asked Jesus why they had not been able to do so. His reply: "This kind does not go out except by prayer and fasting" (Matt. 17:21). Some demons were so wicked that it took more spiritual effort to overcome them. The fact that Jesus was a man of prayer and fasting accounts for His success where the disciples had failed.

In the demon kingdom there are spirits who are more vile and wicked, more injurious and violent, more successful in resisting the efforts of men who have not given themselves to prayer and fasting. Though they have no "archdemon" (such as Michael with the angels), they are subject to Satan, king of the Abyss. He is their acknowledged ruler and reigns supreme in his evil kingdom.

ULTIMATELY UNDER CHRIST

Even so, the demons are subject to the greater power and authority of the Lord Jesus Christ! There has never been a demon who was able, or is able, to successfully withstand Christ's ringing order to come out of the unfortunate people whom they possessed. They would emit terrible shrieks, convulse their victims violently, leaving them as though dead – but ultimately yielded to the greater authority of Christ (Mark 9:26). How they must have hated to do so! How Satan must have gnashed his teeth in frustration, hatred and rage! His own minions of malice, surrendering in defeat to his archenemy, Jesus Christ!

The entire kingdom of demons will someday bow before Jesus and confess that He is Lord. At the name of Jesus every knee will bow, of things in heaven (angelic beings), and things in earth (human beings), and things under the earth (demonic beings). Every tongue – including the tongues of angels and demons – will confess that Jesus Christ is Lord, to the glory of God the Father (Phil. 2:10,11).

Yes, demons are under the domination of their sworn leader, Satan. But whether they like it or not – both in Jesus' day, today and at the Judgment – the demons are subject to the power and authority of the Son of God.

30 THE FAITH OF DEMONS

Amazing as it may sound, demons are believers. James, the brother of our Lord, made this Holy Spirit-inspired assertion. "You believe that there is one God. Good! Even the demons believe that – and shudder" (Jas. 2:19).

TWO KINDS OF FAITH

However, the Bible teaches that there are two kinds of faith. The first kind of faith is a faith which works by love. "For in Jesus Christ neither circumcision availeth any thing, nor uncircumcision; but faith which worketh by love" (Gal. 5:6 KJV). Genuine Biblical faith will work and that work will be motivated by love for God and man. Of this kind of faith the demons know nothing. Their belief in God is from the head, not the heart. They do not love God, let alone man. They seek to discredit God and destroy man.

The other kind of faith the Bible describes is "faith without works" (Jas. 2:26). Demons, although mentally assenting to the existence of God, have no good works to accompany or complement their faith. All their works are evil. Their lack of good deeds and abundance of evil works completely nullifies their "faith."

Consider three things about the demons' faith:

DEMONS ARE MONOTHEISTIC

The Bible says that demons believe in the existence of one God – Jehovah. Listen to James: "You believe that there is one God. Good! Even the demons believe that – and shudder" (Jas. 2:19). James is writing to Jews who prided themselves in the fact that they believed in God. So what? Most Americans, according to the religious polls, believe in God. But our country is waxing worse and worse. Sin is growing by leaps and bounds. What good is religious faith if good moral character does not accompany it? That is James' message to Christian Jews. You believe in God? Good. Great. Then live like it! Don't be like the demons who acknowledge the existence of God but live (literally) for the devil.

In one sense, however, demons are wiser than some men. Remember, one derivation of "demon" is "wise or knowing ones." At least demons believe in the existence of God. In other words, they are not atheists! There are no atheists in hell. Or Tartarus. Or the Abyss. Demons know there is a God. By personal experience.

Nor are demons fools. "The fool says in his heart, 'There is no God'" (Psa. 14:1; 53:1). In this sense, demons are wiser than many men. They are not so foolish as to deny the reality of God's existence. Will this faith save them? No. Their faith comes from the head, not the heart. Their works of evil abrogate their belief in God. Beside this, they are lost – doomed. They had their chance.

Demons are not polytheists either. James says they believe that there is *one* God. This is the repeated testimony in Scripture. "Hear, O Israel: The Lord our God, the Lord is one" (Deut. 6:4). Jesus quoted this Scripture in His remarks to an inquiring lawyer (Mark 12:29). The apostle Paul writes, "There is . . . one God and Father of all" (Eph. 4:4,6). Demons are not dummies. They have not fallen for polytheism, a belief in many gods. They are wiser than the ancient Greeks and modern man. They believe in the oneness of God. This fact causes them to tremble and shudder. The Greek word for "shudder" (*phrisso*) means to be rough, to bristle. When demons hear of God, it causes the hair to stand up! This reminds us of Eliphaz, one of Job's friends. In describing a dream he had, he recounts a "hair-raising" experience. "Amid disquieting dreams, in the night, when deep sleep falls on men, fear and trembling seized me and made all my bones shake. A spirit glided past my face, and the hair on my body stood on end" (Job 4:13-15). The thought of one God, before whom the demons will stand one day, gives them goosebumps!

But doesn't the Bible say that without faith it is impossible to please God? Yes (Heb. 11:6). Demons believe in God. Why, then, won't they be saved? Because the Bible also calls for a life of good works, as well as faith. The demons are like many ungodly men; "They claim to know God, but by their actions they deny him. They are detestable, disobedient and unfit for doing anything good" (Titus 1:16). They were wicked before the grave. They are wicked after the grave.

DEMONS BELIEVE IN THE DEITY OF CHRIST

The Bible also indicates that demons believe that Jesus Christ was more than a man. They believe Him to be the very Son of God, the Holy One of God. Again, demons are more astute than many men who claim to be "wise" but foolishly reject the claims to Christ's deity. Paul says, "Where is the wise man? Where is the scholar? Where is the philosopher of this age? Has not God made foolish the wisdom of the world? For since in the wisdom of God the world through its wisdom did not know him, God was pleased through the foolishness of what was preached to save those who believe" (1 Cor. 1:20, 21).

Demons are not as foolish as men. They believe in the existence of God and in the deity of Jesus Christ. Untold millions today believe in God but not in Jesus Christ. Consider Judaism. Consider Islam. Adherents to both faiths recognize God. Jews call Him "Yahweh" and Muslims call Him "Allah," but neither recognizes Jesus Christ to be the Son of God. Neither can come into the presence of God because Jesus said, "I am the way and the truth and the life.

No one comes to the Father except through me" (John 14:6).

Demons are not modernistic or liberal in their theology. They never slurringly addressed Jesus as the son of Joseph, "the carpenter's son," as some did in Jesus' day (Matt. 13:55). They never called him the son of Adam, as does fleshly Mormon theology. Nor do demons attribute the fatherhood of Jesus to a German soldier, as the German rationalists have. Such blasphemy is unthinkable among the demons.

Notice how the demons addressed Jesus. A demon who possessed a man in Capernaum cried out, "What do you we want with us, Jesus of Nazareth? Have you came to destroy us? I know who you are – the Holy One of God!" (Mark 1:24). "The Holy One" is a sacred name used to describe the Son of God (Psa. 16:10; Acts 2:27; 3:14; 13:35 et al.). Although many modernists, liberal theologians and cultists do not believe that Jesus Christ is the Son of God, demons do. "Whenever the evil spirits saw him, they fell down before him and cried out, 'You are the Son of God'" (Mark 3:11). They did not say, "You are a son of God" (like Jehovah's Witnesses). Demons know that Jesus is the Holy One of God, the only begotten Son of God. That is why they fell down in His presence.

One thing demons don't fall for is the popular line that Jesus was a good man but not God. Isn't it amazing that the religious belief of demons is stronger than that of many people today – even religious groups? They do not accept the patronizing nonsense that Jesus was just a good teacher, a good man, but not the divine Son of God. Demons know better! But will their faith save them? Not on your life. Certainly not on theirs! Like the unregenerated men they once were, demons have a "form of godliness" but are "denying its power" by their evil works (2 Tim. 3:5).

The belief of demons does not lead them to repent of their wicked works. Without repentance, all will perish (Luke 13:3,5). They obeyed Jesus, when He commanded them to come out, not because they *wanted* to but because they *had* to. They yielded to His sovereign power. The faith of demons is a powerful testimony to the utter futility of the doctrine of "salvation by faith alone." If all a person must do to be saved is to believe in Christ and confess that faith, every demon in hell would be – and should be – saved! For they believe that Jesus is the Christ, confess it and shudder! And "shudder" is what everyone should do who professes to believe in Jesus Christ but does not do the things which He, as Lord, requires. Listen to Jesus: "Why do you call me, 'Lord, Lord,' and do not do what I say?" (Luke 6:46). Our Lord Jesus Christ has commanded repentance (Luke 13:3,5). Have all who profess faith in Christ repented of sin, turned away from the ways of the world? Jesus required a public declaration of allegiance to Him (Matt. 10:32). Have all who believed in Jesus done that? Jesus decreed that believers should be baptized in order to be saved (Mark 16:16). Have all who claim faith in Jesus obeyed in baptism? Jesus demanded that His followers live a life of faithfulness, even unto death (Rev. 2:10). Have all who said they believe in Jesus been living a life of faithfulness to Him? It takes more than faith in Jesus to be saved; it takes obedience to Jesus as Lord as well. As the hymnist, J. H. Samms wrote, "What He says, we will do; Where He sends, we will go; Never fear, only trust and obey."

DEMONS BELIEVE IN HELL

Believe it or not, Ripley, demons believe in the existence of a place of eternal punishment. Once more we are impressed with the credence of these creatures. They believe in God. They believe that Jesus Christ is the Son of God. They believe in the existence of hell.

The average person does not believe in a place called hell. They do not fear it. They do not think that they will go there. Not so with the demons! Hear the testimony of

Scripture. When Jesus came into the region of the Gadarenes, two demon-possessed men met Him. "What do you want with us, Son of God?" they shouted. "Have you come here to torture us before the appointed time?" (Matt. 8:29).

Torture? Torment? What is this? Isn't hell just the fevered imagination of an overworked mind? Isn't hell just a curse word? Isn't the only hell we'll suffer right here on earth? An unbelieving world had better listen to the testimony of the hell-bound demons!

When the rich man of Luke 16 died, the Bible says he was buried (that is, his body was buried). But "in hell" – where his spirit was – "he was in torment" (Luke 16:22, 23). He cried, "Have pity on me . . . because I am in agony in this fire" (Luke 16:24). The demons know that hell is a place of torment.

What does this phrase, "before the appointed time" (Matt. 8:29), mean? Simply this. Hell is a very real, a very dreadful place. Jesus said that it was "prepared for the devil and his angels" (Matt. 25:41). It is a place of everlasting fire and punishment (Matt. 25:46). The devil, along with his angels and demons, knows that someday they will be cast into this dreadful place. They will suffer torment day and night for ever and ever (Rev. 20:10). Who wouldn't shudder! Who wouldn't tremble at the thought that this might be the day!

Demons do not brush off the Bible's teaching on hell by saying, "Oh, that's just your interpretation" or "Hell is figurative language" or "God is too good to let anyone go to hell" or "I believe in the total annihilation of the dead." Because they swore allegiance to Satan long ago they have bought their one-way ticket to hell. They realize, with horror, that there will literally be "hell to pay" someday.

This may explain several things. For one, why Satan is so fierce and rapacious in his attacks on Christianity. He doesn't want to go to hell alone. He seeks to devour Christians (1 Pet. 5:8) – not just their bodies but their souls as well. He is going to take as many with him as he can.

This helps us understand why he works so long and hard to destroy us. Another thing it explains is why Satan and his evil forces attack the Bible so viciously, calling it a collection of fairy tales, causing men to doubt its inspiration and authority. Why, especially, does Satan attack the books of Genesis and Revelation? Because in Genesis his eventual doom is announced (Gen. 3:15) and in Revelation his final fate is sealed (Rev. 20:10). Hence, the awesome attacks on both the people of God and the Word of God. You and I should understand this. When Satan and his helpers were cast out of heaven, John heard a voice saying, "Therefore rejoice, you heavens and you who dwell in them! But woe to the earth and the sea, because the devil has gone down to you! He is filled with fury, because he knows that his time is short" (Rev. 12:12). The devil and his demons are working "overtime" because their time is short and because they know they are soon to be tormented in hell.

31 DEMONS IN THE OLD TESTAMENT (1)

DEMONS AND THE OCCULT

The appearance and activity of demons in the Old Testament is primarily twofold. First, we will consider the matter of men consulting spirits; then, men worshiping demons. In both instances, it is obvious that men voluntarily chose to be involved with the spirit world. This stands in stark contrast with the activity of demons in the Gospel accounts. There we find demons invading the bodies and personalities of unwilling subjects. It can be said with reasonable assurance that in the Gospel accounts demons sought men whereas in the Old Testament men sought demons.

Let us first consider the matter of men consulting spirits in the Old Testament. This really involves what is called the "occult." The term "occult" comes from the Latin *occultus*, a form of the verb *occulere* meaning "to cover or hide." The occult world, then, is the world of things that are hidden, secret, dark and mysterious. The Bible says that such things belong only to the Lord: "The secret things belong to the Lord our God, but the things revealed belong to us and to our children forever, that we may follow all the words of this law" (Deut. 29:29). In spite of this stern warning, men dare to enter the secretive world of the occult.

Occult practices in the Old Testament can be divided into at least three categories, all involving demons or unclean spirits. They are:

1. Consulting the dead.
2. Foretelling the future.
3. The practice of magic.

CONSULTING THE DEAD

There are three terms used in the Old Testament to describe this deplorable practice.

King James Version	New International Version
familiar spirits	mediums
wizards	spiritists
necromancers	those who consult the dead

All such practices, and even more, were strictly forbidden by God. "Let no one be found among you who sacrifices his son or daughter in the fire, who practices divination or sorcery, interprets omens, engages in witchcraft, or casts spells, or who is a medium, or spiritist or who consults the dead. Anyone who does these things is detestable to the Lord, and because of these detestable practices the Lord your God will drive out those nations before you. You must be blameless before the Lord your God" (Deut. 18:10-13).

1. Familiar spirits (mediums)

One who is said to have a "familiar spirit" was a medium or go-between. Loved ones who wanted to talk to their dead friends or family members ("familiar" comes from "family") would go to a medium. The medium, for a price, would seek to contact the spirits of the departed friend or family member. By going into a "trance," the medium would open up himself or herself to a temporary possession of a spirit who would then speak through the medium's vocal cords to the friend or relative who was seeking a message. According to Isaiah the prophet, the voice of the familiar spirit would seem to come out of the ground. In pronouncing a woe on Ariel, a city where David once lived, God said, "And thou shalt be brought down, and shalt speak out of the ground, and thy speech shall be low out of the dust, and thy voice shall be, as one that hath a familiar spirit, out of the ground, and thy speech shall whisper out of the dust" (Isa. 29:4 KJV). This confirms the truth of the Hebrew word for spirit, *owb*. This word meant to mumble, a hollow sound as coming from a jar, waterskin or bottle, hence a ventriloquist. The word is used of familiar spirits and necromancers.

Demons have the ability to impersonate the dead by speaking through the medium's vocal cords. Listen to this chilling testimony from a former spiritist, Ben Alexander:

> Demons . . . are able to produce different voices as they take control of the vocal cords of the medium. Once my wife, Miranda, went to a seance before she became a Christian. At this seance (we have a tape recording of it) a spirit had taken control of a female medium's voice and was speaking through the woman in a masculine voice and giving my wife information pertaining to astrology. After the spirit had finished speaking, the spirit asked my wife if there were any questions. My wife said, "Yes, how is it you are able to speak through that woman in a completely different voice, a masculine voice?" At that time my wife was most anxious to be a medium herself and was inquiring why the spirits were not able to use her vocal cords. She had been going to seances, known as "developing classes," in order to become a spirit medium – which is the goal of every spiritualist. The spirit entity speaking through the woman in a different voice, said to my wife, "Don't be stereotyped. Everybody wants us to take control of their vocal cords. We, in the spirit world, are not so much interested in taking control of your vocal cords as we are in taking control of your thoughts. Then, when we have control of your thoughts, we can give our philosophical messages from the spirit world to help you." Suddenly the whole thing fell into focus. The desire of these demons was to take control mainly of our minds. Then, when they had control of our minds, they literally had control of our bodies, souls and actions ("Demon Possession," *Exposing Satan's Power, Newsletter* Vol. VI, No.2, April, 1978).

The practice of consulting the dead through a familiar spirit or medium was strictly forbidden by God. Israel was warned, "Do not turn to mediums or seek out spiritists, for you will be defiled by them. I am the Lord your God" (Lev. 19:31). God called the practice "abominable" and "detestable" (Deut. 18:12). God wanted His people to seek Him, not the dead, in their times of trouble and loneliness. "When men tell you to consult mediums and spiritists, who whisper and mutter, should not a people inquire of their God? Why consult the dead on behalf of the living? To the law and to the testimony! If they do not speak according to this word, they have no light of dawn" (Isa. 8:19, 20).

Because this practice was so base and vile, God decreed that any Israelite who sought the services of mediums and spiritists would be personally dealt with by God Himself. "I will set my face against the person who turns to mediums and spiritists to prostitute himself by following them, and I will cut him off from his people" (Lev. 20:6). But He expected the nation of Israel to carry out the sentence: "A man or woman who is a medium or spiritist among you must be put to death. You are to stone them; their blood will be on their own heads" (Lev. 20:27). Surely our God would not have placed so severe a penalty on this practice if it was just a game or a fraud! God takes the practice of spiritualism seriously and so should we.

When Saul was king of Israel, he did a good thing by having the mediums and spiritists expelled from the land (1 Sam. 28:3). But after his friend and confidant, Samuel, died, Saul – in a moment of terror and weakness when surrounded by the Philistines – commissioned his attendants to find a medium through which he could inquire of his former advisor, Samuel (1 Sam. 28:7). They informed Saul that a woman living in Endor was still engaged in the forbidden practice of consulting spirits. The Bible does not call her a "witch" – she was a medium. The spirit of Samuel was brought up. Scholars have argued for centuries whether it was Samuel or not and whether it was the woman or the Lord who brought Samuel up. Saul did not care about such matters. He knew it was Samuel and fell to the ground (1 Sam. 28:14). Samuel brought Saul a terrifying message: "The Lord will hand over both Israel and you to the Philistines, and tomorrow you and your sons will be with me" (1 Sam. 28:19). Saul was going to die because he consulted a medium instead of the Lord. That is precisely what happened. "Saul died because he was unfaithful to the Lord; he did not keep the word of the Lord and even consulted a medium for guidance, and did not inquire of the Lord. So the Lord put him to death and turned the kingdom over to David son of Jesse" (1 Chron. 10:13,14).

In a paper entitled "Hades, or the Unseen," Moses Lard had these comments concerning the account of Saul, Samuel and the spiritist of Endor:

> In what light are we to view the narrative in question – as literal, or as not? This, as a preliminary, merits a first word. We reply, without going at length into its vindication, that the narrative is, in our judgment, wholly and strictly literal. Saul was real; so was the woman. Her character was known, and place of residence, to the servants of Saul. These were both given. Saul disguises himself and visits her at night. The reason for this is given. The interview is natural – in brief, the whole scene, its persons, incidents, and drapery; its antecedents and results – all are told in the simplest narrative style; and many of them are corroborated by other parts of the sacred history. We hence feel compelled to regard the whole as a literal statement of what actually and truly took place. Indeed, if the narrative is not literal, or is to be taken in some mythological sense, then it seems to me that the whole framework of sacred history stands without a trustworthy basis. I do not see on what ground we can vindicate as true the story of Messiah's resurrection, if the case of Saul and the Endor woman are to be set down as fabulous, or as parabolic, which frequently comes to the same thing....
>
> But there is another point in the case in hand which we must not omit to notice. It is found in the following from Samuel: "Tomorrow shalt thou and thy sons be with me." This language can not be construed as referring simply to death. Its meaning is not: Tomorrow you shall be with me in

> the unseen abode of the spirits of the dead. That there is such an abode, necromancy, the case of Samuel, and the language now in hand take for granted. They assume it as a known reality, and proceed to regard it as a matter of course. Many truths are thus assumed and treated by the Bible; and in deciding several important points, we are compelled to allow the circumstance great weight (*Lard's Quarterly*, Vol. II, pp. 271,272, April 1865).

Nor was Saul the only king who trafficked with familiar spirits. Wicked Manasseh – who sacrificed his own sons in the fire – "practiced sorcery and divination, and consulted mediums and spiritists. He did much evil in the eyes of the Lord, provoking him to anger" (2 Kings 21:6; 2 Chron. 33:6). Manasseh's grandson, however, was a different story. Young Josiah led Israel in a revival of spiritual reform: "Josiah got rid of the mediums and spiritists, the household gods, the idols and all the other detestable things seen in Judah and Jerusalem" (2 Kings 23:24).

2. Wizards (spiritists)

A similar source the demons used were the "wizards" or "spiritists." You have probably already noted that nearly every time "familiar spirits" are mentioned in the Old Testament, "wizards" are connected with them. For example, Leviticus 20:27, KJV: "A man also or woman that hath a familiar spirit, or that is a wizard, shall surely be put to death." Other references where the two are mentioned in the same breath are Lev. 19:31; 20:6; Deut. 18:11; 1 Sam. 28:3, 9; 2 Kings 21:6; 23:24; 2 Chron. 33:6; Isa. 8:19; 18:3.

The Hebrew word for "wizard" means "one who knows." This is the same meaning for demons, "the knowing ones." Wizards (spiritists) were people that demons used to convey their message to those who consulted them through such mediums or go-betweens. Virtually everything we have said about the familiar spirits and mediums could be said about the wizards and spiritists. Just as there are different names for ministers (preachers, evangelists) and elders (bishops, pastors), so there are different names in the Bible for these practitioners of evil.

3. Necromancers (those who consult the dead)

This is another term that is practically synonymous with the aforementioned. The practice of necromancy – consulting the dead – received God's stern denunciation (Deut. 18:10-12).

The forbidden practice of consulting the dead continues today. Many seek to contact the dead via spiritualists and trance mediums. Merrill Unger divides spiritist phenomena today into five categories:

> 1. Physical phenomena (levitations, apports, and telekinesis);
> 2. Psychic phenomena (spiritistic visions, automatic writing, speaking in a trance, materializations, table lifting, tumbler moving, excursions of the psyche);
> 3. Metaphysical phenomena (apparitions, ghosts);
> 4. Magic phenomena (magic persecution, magic defense);
> 5. Cultic phenomena (spiritistic cults, spiritism among Christians)
>
> (*Demons in the World Today*, p. 38).

To which Fred Dickason adds,

> The dynamic behind these phenomena is demonic. Demons with their great power and intelligence accomplish many sense-defying effects. Behind the supposed communication with the dead are deceiving spirits who through the mediums under their control impersonate the dead. Through their large number and pooling of their great intelligence they may supply much information, even detailed personal matters; for they have long been observers of the human scene (*Angels: Elect and Evil*, p. 200).

FORETELLING THE FUTURE

The second major group involves those who sought the help of the spirit world in foretelling the future. Included in this listing would be diviners and soothsayers. The terms "diviners" and "soothsayers" are very similar (like "familiar spirits" and "wizards"). The word "divine" comes from the Latin *divinare*, meaning "to foresee." Today we call them "fortune tellers." Regardless of what it is called, divining is forbidden in Scripture (Deut. 18:10).

1. Diviners

Those who practiced divination sought to obtain secret knowledge – especially knowledge of the future – by consulting spirits (i.e., demons, "the knowing ones"). For example, the Moabites and Midianites attempted in vain to bribe Balaam, a seer, to divine against Israel. (Num. 22:7). But in Balaam's second oracle we find these words; "There is no sorcery against Jacob, no divination against Israel" (Num. 23:23). God is more powerful than the force behind divination – the devil and the demons.

The nation of Israel themselves, however, engaged in the prohibited practice of divination under King Hoshea. "They practiced divination and sorcery and sold themselves to do evil in the eyes of the Lord, provoking him to anger" (2 Kings 17:17). Even the prophets of Israel stooped to use divination, seeking the counsel of unclean spirits rather than the Holy Spirit of God. "Then the Lord said to me, 'The prophets are prophesying lies in my name. I have not sent them or appointed them or spoken to them. They are prophesying to you false visions, divinations, idolatries and the delusions of their own minds'" (Jer. 14:14).

During the reign of Zedekiah, King of Judah, God told Jeremiah that He would punish the nation that listened to advice from diviners, mediums and sorcerers (Jer. 27:9). When Israel was in exile, God warned them about taking up the practice of divination when they returned to their homeland (Ezek. 12:24). But even during the exile, God had to caution the people concerning false prophets who were speaking by divination. "Their visions are false and their divinations a lie. They say, 'The Lord declares,' when the Lord has not sent them; yet they expect their words to be fulfilled. Have you not seen false visions and uttered lying divinations when you say, 'The Lord declares,' though I have not spoken?" (Ezek. 13:6, 7). The King of Babylon used omens, lots and divination against Jerusalem (Ezek. 21:21-23). The New International Version has "examine the liver" in place of "divination." This is known as "hepatoscopy." The liver of an animal was considered to be the seat of life. The demon to whom the animal was sacrificed was supposed to yield knowledge.

In the New Testament, divination is mentioned in Acts 16:16. A young girl had a "spirit of divination" by which she brought her masters considerable financial gain through "soothsaying." As stated earlier, divining and soothsaying are almost one and the same. Paul cast out the demon by which she was foretelling the future (Acts 16:18).

2. Soothsaying

Soothsayers (fortune-tellers) were engaged in the profitable business of contacting the spirit world for messages about the future. King Nebuchadnezzar had soothsayers, or diviners, who could foretell the future and interpret dreams – although they were stumped by his dream of the statue of gold, silver, bronze, iron and clay (Dan. 2:27; 4:7). None of them (or the magicians, enchanters and astrologers) could interpret that dream. Only Daniel, who possessed the spirit of the true God, could do that.

Belshazzar was another pagan Babylonian ruler who resorted to soothsayers (Dan. 5:7,11) but they were baffled by the mysterious handwriting on the wall. Again, only Daniel, possessor of the true ability to interpret dreams, could do so. God is greater.

Judah and Jerusalem picked up the evil exercise of soothsaying from the godless Philistines. "Therefore thou hast forsaken thy people the house of Jacob, because they be replenished from the east, and are soothsayers like the Philistines" (Isa. 2:6).

The slave girl in Philippi (Acts 16:16) made her owners a good living from soothsaying. The spirit that possessed her not only foretold the future but recognized Paul and Silas as true ministers of God, something the demons always did when encountered by Jesus Christ in the Gospels (Matt. 8:29; Mark 5:7).

Through the inspired prophet Micah, God did a little "fortune telling" of His own! He predicted that when the One born in Bethlehem came to rule Israel, soothsaying (along with witchcraft) would be conquered (Mic. 5:2, 12). This truth is certainly seen in Christ's triumph over the demon world in His day and the continued success of the apostles in casting out demons in their day (Mark 16:17,20; Col. 2:15; Acts 16:16-18 et al.).

Today there are many who continue to dabble in divination and experiment with soothsaying. There are fortune tellers, palm readers, astrologers and those who interpret dreams and visions. There are those who practice cartomancy (reading cards, like Tarot cards), psychometry (clairvoyance). Some use crystal balls, some use the supposedly "harmless" Ouija board. All of these are controlled by the spirit world and are strictly "off limits" for true believers.

THE USE OF MAGIC

Our third group to consider among those who dealt with demons in the Old Testament is that grouping which includes witches and sorcerers, both of whom used magic and spells through the power of demons.

1. Witchcraft

Witchcraft and sorcery are nearly the same in Scripture. In John Wyclif's translation of Acts 8:9, Simon the Sorcerer is called Simon the Witch. The Revised Standard Version has "sorcerer" in place of "witch" in such passages as Exodus 22:18 and Deuteronomy 18:10. The etymological meaning of "witch" is the same as demon – "one who knows." Witchcraft cannot be separated from demonology.

Traditionally, witches have been pictured as females; ugly old hags with black peaked hats, stringy hair and warts on long, crooked noses. This is a far cry from the Biblical picture of witches. They could be either male or female, just as there were sorcerers and sorceresses (Isa. 57:3). Jezebel was a striking woman – physically speaking – but the Bible says she practiced witchcraft. "'How can there be peace,' Jehu replied, 'as long as all the idolatry and witchcraft of your mother Jezebel abound?'" (2 Kings 9:22).

Our custom of Halloween has glamorized witches but God's Word calls witchcraft a sin. "For rebellion is as the sin of witchcraft, and stubborness is as iniquity and idolatry" (1 Sam. 15:23). It is certainly nothing to dabble in or by which to be entertained. God called it "sin" and instructed His people of old that they were not to "suffer a witch to live" (Exod. 22:18). That is pretty "strong medicine" for something that most people suffer or allow. Witchcraft is called an "abomination" to God (Deut. 18:10). It was practiced by the cruel and evil Ninevites. Nineveh was called the "mistress of witchcrafts" (Nahum 3:4 KJV). Israel's King Manasseh sank to using witches (2 Chron. 33:6) and was called "evil" for doing so. God predicted that His Bethlehem-born Son would triumph over the magicians and witches when He came to earth (Micah 5:12). When the Ephesians burned their valuable books on magic, a great triumph was certainly realized (Acts 19:19).

In Galatians 5:19,20, witchcraft is listed as one of the "works of the flesh." Those who practice such things will not be allowed into heaven.

Witches often used (and continue to use) drugs in their incantations. In fact, the Greek word for "sorcerers" in Revelation 21:8 is *pharmakeia*, one who used drugs, potions, spells and enchantments. The word is also found in Revelation 22:15 where a list of those who will be barred from heaven is given. Sorcerers are mentioned right alongside whoremongers, murders and idolaters.

W. E. Vine comments on *pharmakeia*:

> In sorcery, the use of drugs, whether simple or potent, was generally accompanied by incantations and appeals to occult powers, with the provision of various charms, amulets, etc., professedly to keep the applicant or patient from the attention and power of demons, but actually to impress the applicant with the mysterious resources and powers of the sorcerer (*Expository Dictionary of Old and New Testament Words*, Vol. 4, p. 52).

How subtle and sly is Satan!

2. Sorcery

Sorcerers were also in league with Satan and his demons. Paul made no bones about it, calling Elymas the Sorcerer a "child of the devil" (Acts 13:10). Sorcerers and sorceresses (Isa. 57:3) contacted the spirits for help in their magic, incantations and spells. Sorcery was widespread in Biblical times. Pharaoh had his magicians and sorcerers who could even duplicate the first three miracles of Moses. They, through demonic powers, were able to turn their staves into snakes (Exod. 7:11). However, Aaron's rod swallowed up their rods (Exod. 7:12). They were able to bring up frogs on the land of Egypt (Exod. 8:7). But they were not able to duplicate the miracle of the lice (Exod. 8:18). Admitting defeat they exclaimed, "This is the finger of God" (Exod. 8:19). God is greater!

In the days of Daniel, sorcerers interpreted dreams by the powers of demons (Dan. 2:2). Sorcerers were always regarded in Scripture as evil, no matter how successful or unsuccessful they were in interpreting dreams. They did not operate under the Spirit of God but by the unclean spirits of Satan. The Babylonians were told that they would suffer personal family tragedies because of the obsession with sorcery: "Both of these will overtake you in a moment, on a single day: loss of children and widowhood. They will come upon you in full measure, in spite of your many sorceries and all your potent spells" (Isa. 47:9). The Babylonians had been involved in sorcery for many years. "Keep on, then, with your magic spells and with your many sorceries, which you have labored at since childhood" (Isa. 47:12).

Even God's chosen people, the nation of Israel, were plagued with the problem of sorcery. Through the prophet Malachi, God told them He would come in judgment upon them because of their involvement in this forbidden practice. "So I will come near to you for judgment. I will be quick to testify against sorcerers, adulterers and perjurers . . ." (Mal. 3:5). When they were in captivity to the Babylonians, He warned them not to hearken to the demon-inspired counsel of prophets, diviners, interpreters of dreams, mediums or sorcerers (Jer. 27:9).

There are several sorcerers mentioned by name in the New Testament. Two of them appear to be the magicians who competed against Moses (2 Tim. 3:8). These two were in contact with demonic powers to enable them to perform miracles by means of magical arts. Paul also encountered a sorcerer on the island of Cyprus during his first missionary journey. This man also opposed the work of God. Paul was filled with the Holy Spirit and called Elymas the Sorcerer a "child of the devil, and an enemy of everything that is right" (Acts 13:10). Elymas was stricken with blindness, an appropriate punishment for his dabbling in dark things. Peter encountered Simon the Sorcerer in Acts 8:9-24. He too, received an apostolic denunciation (Acts 8:20-23). Sorcery is of Satan. It is powerful but not as powerful as the things of God.

In the book of Revelation, those suffering the plague of

the sixth trumpet stubbornly refused to repent but continued in their worship of demons and practice of sorcery (Rev. 9:20,21). What a grip the demons have on those who traffic with them! Spiritual Babylon – probably a veiled reference to the Roman Church – is described as becoming a home and a haunt for demons and evil spirits, a place where sorcery is practiced (Rev. 18:2, 23). Certainly, many "signs and wonders" were performed by demonic means (Rev. 13:13; 16:14), just as Jesus and Paul predicted (Matt. 24:24; 2 Thess. 2:9).

Our world today is besmirched and fouled by the presence of those practicing witchcraft and sorcery. The powers of darkness are summoned in Satanic and demonic incantations, spells, amulets, curses and other wicked forms. Often drugs are involved in such activity. It is not surprising to find much – if not all of this and more – in the twisted and depraved religion of "Satanism." Obviously, the child of God should have nothing to do with any of the things mentioned in this chapter.

32 DEMONS IN THE OLD TESTAMENT (2)

DEMON WORSHIP

There are several names for demons in the Old Testament. These names indicate that demons and idol worship are one and the same. That being the case, there are hundreds of references to demons in the Bible! Fred Dickason categorizes for us the names for demons in the Old Testament:

NAMES FOR DEMONS IN THE OLD TESTAMENT

1. Shedhim (Deut. 32:17; Ps. 106:37)

Always in the plural, this word has the idea of rulers or lords. It speaks of idols as lords, since the Hebrew regarded images as visible symbols of invisible demons. So the Israelites committing idolatry were said to have "sacrificed to demons" (*shedhim*, Deut. 32:17).

2. Sherim (Lev. 17:7)

The Hebrews were to sacrifice at the altar of the tabernacle and not to sacrifice in the desert to "he-goats" (LXX, *daimonia*). Jeroboam I appointed worship for the serim (2 Ch. 11:15), and Josiah "broke down the high places of the gates (*sherim*)," which is to be read *seirim* (2 Ki. 22:8). These goat-like conceptions represented demon-satyrs. *Isaiah's* reference to them dancing in the desolated Babylon is translated in the Septuagint by *daimonia* (Isa. 13:21; 34:14).

3. 'elilim (Ps. 96:5, LXX 95:5)

This passage identifies demons with idols and suggests demonism as the dynamic of idolatry. The plural word conveys emptiness, the nothingness of idols. The demons behind them are the real existences.

4. Gad (Isa. 65:11)

Those that forsake Jehovah "set a table for Fortune" (NASB, LXX, *daimonion*). The demon god Fortune was worshiped by the Babylonians. This idolatry was elsewhere called the worship of Baal, or Bel.

5. Qeter (Ps. 91:6; LXX 90:6)

The "destruction *(qeter)* that wasteth at noonday" was regarded as an evil spirit (*Angels: Elect and Evil*, p. 152).

DEMONS — THE DYNAMIC BEHIND IDOLATRY

What does all this suggest? It suggests that the idols in the Old Testament (and the New Testament for that matter) were only *visible symbols of the invisible source* behind them – demons, who sought men to worship them instead of God! This fact should really not be surprising to discover. Satan has always been busy trying to get mankind to worship anyone or anything except God. At Mount Sinai he succeeded in getting Israel to worship a golden calf. "They have been quick to turn away from what I commanded them and have made themselves an idol cast in the shape of a calf. They have bowed down to it and sacrificed to it and have said, 'These are your gods, O Israel, who brought you up out of Egypt.'" (Exod. 32:8). Satan even went so far as to tempt the very Son of God to fall down and worship him. "'All this will I give you,' he said, 'if you will bow down and worship me.'" (Matt. 4:9). Why, then, should we think it strange that Satan's cohorts, the demons, would be behind idol worship? It all falls into place in Satan's evil scheme to wrest worship from God and Christ.

From the very outset of human history, demons have been the evil force behind idolatry. Millions of people in unevangelized countries continue to worship demons, knowingly or unknowingly. It is all a part of ancient history, going way back to the beginning of things. In the book of Genesis, for instance, idols and images are not long in coming on the scene. Terah, the father of the illustrious Abraham, was an idolater. Joshua reminded the Israelites, "Long ago your forefathers, including Terah the father of Abraham and Nahor, lived beyond the River and worshiped other gods" (Josh. 24:2). Though Abraham himself was not an idolater, the besetting sin of the Israelites, his descendants, would be idolatry. Time and time again they forsook the true worship of God and went after idols. This both hurt and angered God for the relationship He wanted to have with His people was a covenant relationship, somewhat akin to marriage (Isa. 54:5; Jer. 3:14). He regarded the worship of false gods, idols and images as religious adultery. The penalty for such was death (Exod. 22:20).

Even Rachel, the beloved wife of Jacob, was attached to her father's images. "When Laban had gone to shear his sheep, Rachel stole her father's household gods" (Gen. 31:19). When Laban caught up with Jacob he asked him why he had taken the images. Unaware of what his wife had done, Jacob responded, "If you find anyone who has your gods, he shall not live" (Gen. 31:32). He urged Laban to search the camp. When Laban entered Rachel's tent, he found nothing. "Rachel had taken the household gods and put them inside her camel's saddle and was sitting on them" (Gen. 31:34).

These two stories serve to indicate the early beginnings of idolatry in Israel's history. From the very outset of things, demons were vying with God for the devotion of His people. How clever they were and are.

GOAT IDOLS

Moses, in the book of Leviticus, cites several instances of demon worship in the history of Israel. For example, Leviticus 17:7. "They must no longer offer any of their sacrifices to the goat idols to whom they prostitute themselves. This is to be a lasting ordinance for them and for the generations to come." The footnote for "goat idols" in the New International Version is "demons." The Hebrew word here is *seirim*, a shaggy he-goat.

Demon worship involved the worship of animals, especially goats. Satan himself appeared to Eve in the form of a serpent (Gen. 3:1). Through the centuries he has deceived mankind by getting them to worship the creation rather than the Creator. "Although they claimed to be wise, they became fools and exchanged the glory of the immortal God for images made to look like mortal man and birds and animals and reptiles" (Rom. 1:22, 23).

The goat, in particular, became the object of man's diverted and perverted worship. Goats are mentioned 130 times in Scripture. The wicked are likened unto goats on the day of Judgment (Matt. 25:31-33). They will be cast into the lake of fire along with the devil and his angels (Matt. 25:41). The goat's head is the symbol of modern Satanism and is featured in Satanic vestments and literature.

OTHER REFERENCES TO DEMON WORSHIP

In the Song of Moses, he worthily recounts the up-and-down history of the Israelites. After recounting how God had blessed Israel, he makes this observation: "Jeshurun grew fat and kicked; filled with food, he became heavy and sleek. He abandoned the God who made him and rejected the Rock his savior. They made him jealous with their foreign gods and angered him with their detestable idols. They sacrificed to demons, which are not God – gods they had not known, gods that recently appeared, gods your fathers did not fear. You deserted the Rock, who fathered you; you forgot the God who gave you birth" (Deut. 32:15-18). Moses knew that the dynamic behind idols was demonic in nature.

The book of Psalms contains a number of references to demon worship. Besides those that Dickason mentions in the Septuagint, there is Psalm 106. This psalm details the awful practice of sacrificing children to demons, an abominable practice in Canaanite religion. "They did not destroy the peoples as the Lord had commanded them, but they mingled with the nations and adopted their customs. They worshiped their idols, which became a snare to them. They sacrificed their sons and their daughters to demons. They shed innocent blood, the blood of their sons and daughters, whom they sacrificed to the idols of Canaan, and the land was desecrated by their blood" (Psa. 106:34-38). Satan is a murderer (John 8:44). He is the destroyer (Rev. 9:11). His demons also seek to kill and destroy, even little children (Mark 9:22). Those who are drawn to modern Satanism should take heed. It exacts a terrible toll – human sacrifice. It is all a part of the demonic scheme.

Demon worship does not end in the Old Testament. Paul warned the church in Corinth about participating in demon worship. He drew on Old Testament Israel for an example: "Consider the people of Israel: Do not those who eat the sacrifices participate in the altar? Do I mean then that a sacrifice offered to an idol is anything, or that an idol is anything? No, but the sacrifices of pagans are offered to demons, not to God, and I do not want you to be participants with demons. You cannot drink the cup of the Lord and the cup of demons too; you cannot have a part in both the Lord's table and the table of demons. Are we trying to arouse the Lord's jealousy? Are we stronger than he?" (1 Cor. 10:18-22).

Nor does demon worship end with the epistles. Revelation 9:20,21 speaks of those who "did not stop worshiping demons" and links demon worship with its evil partners: murder, magic arts, and sexual immorality.

It bears repeating: all references to idolatry in the Bible are actually references to demons. The idols and images themselves were nothing but mere statues of wood or silver or gold. The real power in idolatry was the dark force behind the practice: demons. The idols were nothing; the demons behind them were (and are) very real. Let us not be "partakers with demons."

EVIL SPIRITS FROM THE LORD

Of special interest is the fact that on several different occasions, God allowed or permitted evil spirits, demons, to trouble people. Evil spirits, like Satan himself, can do nothing without God's permission (Job 1:12). God uses them to accomplish His sovereign will in the affairs of men and the world.

There are at least three different individuals in the Old Testament who experienced visits from evil spirits that came from the presence of the Lord. All were men of position and all were humbled by God in this strange manner.

1. Abimelech

The first man was Abimelech, a worthless son of a good man, Gideon. After his father's death, he talked 70 of his brothers into helping him become king of Shechem. As soon as he became king, he murdered them in cold blood (Judges 9:1-5). Only one brother, Jotham, escaped the carnage. After three years, "God sent an evil spirit between Abimelech and the citizens of Shechem, who acted treacherously against Abimelech. God did this in order that the crime against Jerub-Baal's seventy sons, the shedding of their blood, might be avenged on their brother Abimelech and on the citizens of Shechem, who had helped him murder his brothers" (Judg. 9:23,24). Truly, God moves in mysterious ways, His wonders to perform! The Shechemites are thoroughly routed, Abimelech dies an ignominious death and vengeance belongs to the Lord (Judg. 9:49, 54, 56).

2. Saul

The second man to be so visited was King Saul. "Now the Spirit of the Lord had departed from Saul, and an evil spirit from the Lord tormented him" (1 Sam. 16:14). Even Saul's attendants understood that the evil spirit had come from the Lord (1 Sam. 16:15). They suggest that Saul find someone to play the harp whenever the spirit comes upon him (1 Sam. 16:16). Saul agrees and David is found to appease the evil spirit with his music. "Whenever the spirit from God came upon Saul, David would take his harp and play. Then relief would come to Saul; he would feel better, and the evil spirit would leave him" (1 Sam. 16:23). Truly, "music soothes the savage beast." Later, the evil spirit returns but this time with a different twist. "The next day an evil spirit from God came forcefully upon Saul. He was prophesying in his house, while David was playing the harp, as he usually did. Saul had a spear in his hand and he hurled it, saying to himself, 'I'll pin David to the wall.' But David eluded him twice" (1 Sam. 18:10,11). Evil spirits are often behind false prophecies and murderous assaults. The evil spirits motivated Saul in a similar fashion a third time (1 Sam. 19:9). How can we explain these strange happenings? Some see the evil spirit coming on Saul as "judicial punishment from God because of certain tendencies in the king's character" (*The New Bible Commentary*, p. 272).

3. Ahab

The third man was also a king, Ahab. Here is the background: Jehoshaphat, king of Judah, had come to Ahab, king of Israel, with a plan to merge their armies against the Syrians in order to recover Ramoth Gilead. Together, they inquire of false prophets, who assure them of victory (1 Kings 22:6). But Micaiah, a true prophet of God, foretells disaster (1 Kings 22:17). He shares a strange vision with Ahab: "I saw the Lord sitting on his throne with all the host of heaven standing around him on his right and on his left. And the Lord said, 'Who will lure Ahab into attacking Ramoth Gilead and going to his death there?' One suggested this, and another that. Finally, a spirit came forward, stood before the Lord and said, 'I will lure him.' 'By what means?' the Lord asked. 'I will go out and be a lying spirit in the mouths of all his prophets,' he said. 'You will succeed in luring him,' said the Lord. 'Go and do it.'" (1 Kings 22:19-22).

Micaiah then tells Ahab, "So now the Lord has put a lying spirit in the mouths of all these prophets of yours. The Lord has decreed disaster for you" (1 Kings 22:23). The upshot of the story is Micaiah gets a slap in the face but Ahab gets an arrow in the heart. Adam Clarke comments,

> Never was a man more circumstantially and fairly warned; he had counsels from the God of truth, and counsels from the spirit of falsity; he obstinately forsook the former and followed the latter. He was shown by this parable how everything was going on, and that all was under the control and direction of God, and that still it was possible for him to make that God his friend whom by his continual transgressions he had made his enemy; but he would not: his blood was therefore upon his own head (*Clarke's Commentary*, Vol. II, p. 476).

These accounts are in the Bible to show us that even evil spirits are under God's control and He can do with them as He pleases. Clarke adds,

> Is it requisite again to remind the reader that the Scriptures repeatedly represent God as doing what, in the course of his providence, he only permits or suffers to be done? Nothing can be done in heaven, in earth, or hell, but either by his immediate energy or permission (*Ibid*., p. 476).

33 DEMONS IN THE GOSPELS (1)

There is more "column space" given to the activity of demons in the gospels of Matthew, Mark and Luke than anywhere else in the entire Bible. Why? Why this unusual devotion to such a despicable topic? And why this sudden surge of demonic activity? Up to this point in the Bible, demons pretty much confined themselves to those who sought them out; i.e., those who either worshiped demons or consulted the spirits. In the Old Testament, men seek demons. In the gospels, demons seek men!

When we open the pages of the New Testament, it is as though we have opened Pandora's box. It is as though all hell is assailing the people of Christ's day: Perhaps Satan – sensing the nearness of that predicted act which will "crush his head" (Gen. 3:15) – sets loose myriads of his malignant minions to counteract the work of Christ. Therefore, we are not surprised to see demons attacking people left and right, with violent endeavor, with maniacal fury. It is as though Satan called all the demons in the Abyss to a hurried conference. "Hey, fellows. You think this place is bad? Well, God has now sent His own Son to redeem mankind. Then, at the end of time, we are going to be thrown into a place that will make this place look like a Sunday School. Do you want that?" A chorus of howls goes up: "No!" "Then get out there and do your dead-evil best to stop it!" Dramatics aside, the assault that demons made on men, women, children and even animals in Jesus' day is terrible to behold.

WHY WERE DEMONS ALLOWED TO ENTER MEN?

Wayne Jackson does a good job of answering this perplexing question.

> Since demons were obviously under the control of God ultimately (Lk. 10:17ff.), why were they allowed to enter into and to afflict those ancient folks? Apparently, demon possession was divinely permitted by God in order that the supreme authority of Christ might be made manifest. As the Lord revealed his control over nature (Mk. 4:30), disease (Mk. 1:12), material things (Jn. 2:9), and even death (Jn. 11:44), so also must the Son of God demonstrate his power over the spirit realm. His power over unclean spirits heralded his approaching reign – "If I by the finger of God cast out demons, then is the kingdom of God come upon you" (Lk. 11:20). (*Christian Courier*, Vol. XX, No. 2, June 1984).

Even the followers of Jesus would be permitted to expel demons (Luke 10:17).

Victor Hoven adds:

> In the time of Jesus they were more active than at any other time, and it seems to have been divinely permitted on account of the contest between Christ and Satan. Jesus' expulsion of them showed publicly His power over him whose works He came to destroy (1 John 3:8). To that end our Lord regarded the expulsion of demons as a triumph over Satan (Matt. 12:28, 29; Lk. 10:17, 18). (*Outlines of Biblical Doctrine*, pp. 41, 42).

Alexander Campbell, in his "Address on Demonology," took the position that demons were the spirits of wicked dead men whom God, in harmony with His divine purpose, permitted to escape the Hadean realm in order that the supreme power and authority of Jesus Christ might be manifest. Surely this position would not be out of order. Consider how God allowed or permitted Satan himself to afflict one of His servants, the patriarch Job (Job 1:6-12; 2:1-6). God did not allow Satan to take the life of Job and, as far as we can ascertain, no demon ever took the life of a human victim. Not that they didn't try. Oh, how wickedly they tried – even to the point of casting children into water and fire in vain attempts to drown or burn them (Mark 9:22). The only loss of life because of demon possession seems to be the herd of about 2,000 swine that thundered down a cliff and drowned in the Sea of Galilee (Mark 5:13).

WHY JOHN IS "SILENT" ON DEMONS

Have you wondered why the apostle John doesn't mention much about demons in his gospel? Merrill F. Unger explains,

> It is perhaps not without significance that almost all the cases of demon possession are recorded as occurring among the rude and half-Gentile populations of Galilee. John, dealing mainly with the ministry in Judaea and Jerusalem, where the population seemed to have been more cultured and refined, does not mention an actual case of possession or expulsion, but emphatically recognizes the existence of the phenomenon (John 7:20; 8:48; 10:20). It was, it would seem, natural for the Satanic method to assume the special form in numerous instances of possession in an age of such unprecedented and brutal sensuality as that which preceded the Messiah's Advent, and to continue until the cleansing power of Christianity was felt. This is why the phenomenon still occurs in rude and Satan dominated, so-called "heathen" lands (*Biblical Demonology*, p. 94).

CASE #1: THE SYNAGOGUE DEMONIAC

There are at least seven separate incidents in the Gospels where Jesus encountered individual people who were possessed with demons. In every case Christ triumphed over the devil by casting out the demons. Truly, Jesus is the "Doctor Who Never Lost a Case."

The first account took place in a Jewish synagogue in

Capernaum, just after Jesus began His Galilean ministry. The account is found in Mark 1:21-28 and Luke 4:31-37. Capernaum was where most of Christ's mighty miracles were performed (Matt. 11:20-23). Although the Son of God had personally confronted Satan in the temptations in the wilderness (Matt. 4:1-11), this is our Lord's first recorded meeting with the wicked world of unclean spirits.

It should be noted that the encounter took place when Jesus was teaching the Word of God. "They went to Capernaum, and when the Sabbath came, Jesus went into the synagogue and began to teach. The people were amazed at his teaching, because he taught them as one who had authority, not as the teachers of the law" (Mark 1:21, 22). It is at this point that demons begin their assault on the work of Christ. "Just then a man in their synagogue who was possessed by an evil spirit cried out . . ." (Mark 1:23).

Is it possible that this was Satan's response to the preaching of truth? It is entirely possible, if not probable. Satan always tries to snatch away the Word that has been sown in the hearts of hearers (Matt. 13:16). Indeed, one is led to wonder if many of the distractions that take place when the Seed is being sown are not direct attempts of demons to "snatch away the word." Anyone who has tried to share God's Word with sinners – whether in the privacy of a home or in a public church assembly – knows the feelings of despair and frustration because of "infernal interruptions" and "devilish distractions." How we need to pray for the blessing of the Holy Spirit when we are sowing the Seed of the Kingdom!

What was there in the teaching of Christ that caused the demon to cry out, "What do you want with us, Jesus of Nazareth? Have you came to destroy us? I know who you are – the Holy One of God!" (Mark 1:24). The text yields no clues as to what Jesus was teaching. But we know that Christ spoke the truth, was the truth (John 14:6), and wherever truth is voiced, Satan, the prince of error, will rear his ugly head in opposition.

Demons, of course, have nothing to do with Christ. He is good, they are evil. He is pure, they are unclean. He is from God, they are from the devil. Righteousness cannot have fellowship with unrighteousness; light cannot have communion with darkness; Christ cannot have concord with Belial (2 Cor. 6:14,15). Yet at the same time, they are drawn to Him in some unexplainable kind of fascination. The power and authority of Christ is so great that even demons confess that He is the Holy One of God. But they want to be left alone: "Let us alone; what have we to do with thee, thou Jesus of Nazareth?" (Luke 4:34 KJV). But Christ does not leave them alone. They have encountered Him and He meets them head on and, as always, triumphs over evil and error. God is greater than all the unholy opposition that the devil and Hades can offer.

The unholy spirits know who Jesus is: "the Holy One of God." How do they know? Remember, demons are "knowing ones." Where do they get this knowledge? It is folly to think that the devil would dispatch them on such a mission without informing them of their opponent. Surely he gave them a thorough "briefing" on Jesus, the Son of God. There are other explanations as well. If demons are indeed the spirits of the wicked dead, then perhaps some of them heard the Son of God in their own lifetime. Some may have heard the good news about Jesus through the apostles, evangelists or Christians. The Bible also says that Christ, after being put to death in the flesh, went in the spirit and preached to the spirits in prison (1 Pet. 3:18, 19). We know that Jesus did not go to the place of suffering in Hades (Tartarus). He went to Paradise as He said He would (Luke 23:43). It must have been from this vantage point that He addressed the spirits of the wicked, like Abraham was able to do (Luke 16:25). The message was not one of invitation but of vindication. The Bible does not teach that men receive a second chance after death (Heb. 9:27) but it does teach that Christ was vindicated in the spirit (1 Tim. 3:16). Whatever the case, demons knew Jesus to be the Holy One of God, an inspired term descriptive of the

Messiah (Psa. 16:10; Acts 2:27; 3:14; 13:35; 1 John 2:20). This was not heart surrender on their part, just head knowledge. Like many people, the demons will miss heaven by 18 inches – the distance from the heart to the head.

The thing that concerned this demon in the synagogue was this: "Have you come to destroy us?" The answer is an emphatic "Yes!" Jesus came to destroy the works of the devil. "The reason the Son of God appeared was to destroy the devil's work" (1 John 3:8). Jesus manifested His power over the devil by casting out the demons of Beelzebub. Their expulsion spelled Satan's defeat.

It should also be noted that when the demon cried out to Jesus, he used the man's tongue. It was not the poor demoniac who was actually addressing Jesus – it was the demon that had possessed him. Our hearts certainly go out to those unfortunate people whom demons had possessed. They were not their own anymore. How terrible it must have been to be invaded by these uninvited, unwelcome guests! But Christ rebuked him – the demon, not the man – with these words, "Be quiet!. . . Come out of him!" (Mark 1:25). Herbert Lockyer observes:

> Christ rebuked not the man, but the demon possessing him, and said, "Hold thy peace," which actually means "Be gagged, or muzzled," and is the same word He uses when calming the winds and waves (Mark 4:39). He gave the evil spirit a short, direct order. Speaking sharply He said, "Silence! Come out." It was the harsh word such an unclean, tormenting demon deserved. Obedient to the command of silence, the demon did not speak any more, although it did cry with a loud voice, an inarticulate cry of rage and pain. The demon had been the strong one in the man; now a stronger Man, superior in might to the prince of demons, destroys his works. The Devil, however, chafed over losing his hold on one he possessed, does all the harm he can; so in departing from the poor man his emissary threw him down and tore him with terrible convulsions. The victim was hurled with a convulsive leap into the midst of the astonished congregation and he was left prostrate but unhurt. There is no contradiction between Luke, who says

> that the evil spirit hurt him not, and Mark's description of the demon as having torn him. The man suffered no permanent injury, although cast to the ground (*All the Miracles of the Bible*, p. 170).

Lockyer also adds an interesting thought concerning the fact that the demon opposed the work of Christ in a synagogue, a house of worship. The Bible teaches that the main work of demons today is through false doctrine (1 Tim. 4:1-3; 1 John 4:1-3).

> Have we anything today answering to the demon in the synagogue? Has history repeated itself? We think it has. When, in buildings erected for the preaching of the inspired infallible Scriptures, preachers discredit the reliability of the Bible, repudiate the miracles, flout the virgin birth, the atoning blood, and the physical resurrection of Christ, what are they with all their education and polish but demons in the synagogue? As they do not represent the Spirit of truth, some other spirit must possess them (*All the Miracles of the Bible*, p. 169).

The first demonic attempt to thwart the work of Christ ends in abject failure for the hosts of darkness. The evil spirit comes out of the man. No one saw the spirit leave (spirits cannot be seen) but the observers note that the man was no longer demon-possessed. They are amazed and recognize the awesome authority of Christ: "What is this? A new teaching – and with authority! He even gives orders to evil spirits and they obey him" (Mark 1:27). The news about this event spreads quickly over the region of Galilee. The battle is on!

CASE #2: MARY MAGDALENE

Sometime during Christ's Galilean ministry, our Lord cast demons out of Mary Magdalene. In reality, Mary Magdalene was just one of several women whom Jesus helped in this way. Luke tells us who was traveling with Jesus at this time and gives us some background information on them. "After this, Jesus traveled about from one town to another, proclaiming the good news of the kingdom of God. The Twelve were with him, and also some women who had been cured of evil spirits and diseases: Mary (called Magdalene) from whom seven demons had come out; Joanna the wife of Cuza, the manager of Herod's household; Susanna; and many others. These women were helping to support them out of their own means" (Luke 8:1-3). Mark also records the fact that Jesus cast out seven demons from Mary Magdalene: "When Jesus rose early on the first day of the week, he appeared first to Mary Magdalene, out of whom he had driven seven demons" (Mark 16:9). We are not informed as to exactly when during the Galilean ministry this took place – only that it happened.

Jesus once referred to seven unclean spirits who were more wicked than the original demon who once possessed a man (Matt. 12:45; Luke 11:26). Cases of "multiple possession" often took place. It would be bad enough to be possessed by just one demon. Imagine being possessed by seven! In the case of Legion there were "many" (Mark 5:9). This poor man is probably the worst case in all of the Bible. A "legion" was a unit of Roman soldiers, about 6,000 strong! No wonder the poor man roamed the countryside and cut himself with sharp stones. No wonder the herd of about 2,000 swine catapulted into the sea!

There is no good reason to believe that Mary Magdalene is the notorious sinful woman who washed the feet of Jesus with her tears at the house of Simon the Pharisee (Luke 7:36-50). Yet the tradition is still heard today. Is it possible that this tradition is perpetuated by demons? If so, talk about revenge! Demons do disseminate false doctrine (1 Tim. 4:1). We would not put it past them, heartless creatures that they are. One thing for sure: it is a "doctrine of demons" to assert, as some so wickedly and viciously do, that Mary Magdalene was a lover of Jesus. Others contend that she, along with Mary and Martha, were actually the wives of Jesus, that they were a part of His "harem." The cult of Mormonism, in order to justify its doctrine of polygamy, taught that Jesus was not only a married man but a polygamist as well! Brigham Young declared, "Jesus Christ was a polygamist; Mary and Martha, the sisters of Lazarus, were his plural wives, and Mary Magdalene was another. Also, the bridal feast of Cana in Galilee, where Jesus turned the water into wine, was on the occasion of one of his own marriages" (*The Chaos of Cults*, Jan Karel Van Baalen, p. 176). The Mormon "apostle" Orson Hyde blasphemously stated, "We say it was Jesus Christ who was married (at Cana, to Martha and Mary), whereby he could see his own seed before he was crucified" (*Ibid.*, p. 176). Talk about a doctrine of demons!

The truth of the matter is that Mary Magdalene was so grateful that Jesus had helped her by casting out the demons, she, along with other women whom Jesus had helped, supported Jesus and His disciples out of her own means (Luke 8:3). The Bible knows nothing of the blasphemous, demon-inspired doctrine that Mary Magdalene was a lover and wife of Jesus Christ. Demons and men have besmirched the reputation of this good woman. God honored the lady from the little village of Magdala by allowing her to be the first to receive the news of the resurrection of Christ (John 20:1-18).

34 DEMONS IN THE GOSPELS (2)

CASE# 3: THE BLIND AND MUTE DEMONIAC

The third account of our Lord's special ministry to those possessed with demons is found in two gospels: Matthew 12:22-27 and Luke 11:14-23. It is the case of the blind and mute man. Demons could inflict people with physical as well as emotional problems. Not every sick person had a demon but several demoniacs were sick as a result of their possession. Besides blindness and muteness, demons were responsible for deafness (Mark 9:25), curvature of the spine (Luke 13:11), convulsions or epilepsy (Luke 4:33; 9:37; Mark 1:23; 9:17) and suicidal mania (Mark 5:6; 9:17; Luke 9:37).

This particular incident took place in Galilee. Luke records that the man was mute, he could not speak (Luke 11:14). Matthew adds that the demoniac was blind as well (Matt. 12:22). In his pitiable condition, he had to be brought to Jesus. He could not see to walk, he could not speak to ask for help. Evidently he had some friends who still cared for him. Like the man "borne of four," he was brought to Jesus. The evil spirits who had afflicted him did not want him to be helped but his friends did. What a pathetic sight he must have been. Sightless, he could not see for himself; mute, he could not speak for himself. Demons had robbed him of two of man's most important senses: sight and speech. Today, demons seek to rob men of spiritual sight. "The god of this age has blinded the minds of unbelievers, so that they cannot see the light of the gospel of the glory of Christ, who is the image of God" (2 Cor. 4:4). At Satan's bidding they also oppress believers with fear to keep them from sharing this glorious gospel. "For God did not give us a spirit of timidity, but a spirit of power, of love and of self-discipline" (2 Tim. 1:7.) If God has not paralyzed believers with fear, then who but the devil and his demons?

Jesus healed this pathetic creature. He cast out the source of the man's blindness and muteness – the demon. After the demon departed, the man was able to both see and speak (Luke 11:14; Matt. 12:22). What a thrill that must have been for him, to be able to see and speak once again. We do not realize how precious the five senses are until we have lost one of them. But not everyone was thrilled – not on your life! Naturally, the demons and Satan were not overjoyed. There were others present who did not find this an occasion for joy – the Pharisees (Matt. 12:24). While all the onlookers were marveling over this display of divine power, saying, "Could this be the Son of David?" (Matt. 12:23), the Pharisees (who had come from Jerusalem to stir up trouble, Mark 3:22), seized upon this occasion to blasphemously charge Jesus with casting out demons by the power of Beelzebub.

CHARGES OF CASTING OUT DEMONS BY BEELZEBUB

Mark joins Matthew and Luke in recording this wicked assertion (Mark 3:20-30). It is noteworthy that the religious opponents of Jesus did not deny that Christ cast out the demon. The man could now see and talk and this was crushing proof that something great and out of the ordinary had happened. His healing could not be denied. The enemies of Christ therefore resorted to making the accusation that Jesus was in league with Beelzebub – a corruption of Baalzebub, "the god of the fly." A fly is a busy and filthy creature. So is Satan, "the prince of the power of the air" (Eph. 2:2). Jesus Christ, therefore, was charged with casting out demons by the prince of demons, Satan!

J. W. McGarvey, in his harmony of the Four Gospels, examines the four arguments Jesus used to prove how ludicrous, ridiculous, and blasphemous this accusation was.

1. How can Satan cast out Satan? Why would the devil want to dismantle his own evil empire? Satan could do this but would he cooperate with Christ to do such a self-defeating thing? Would Satan rob himself of his greatest achievement, namely, his triumph over the souls and bodies of men? "If Satan drives out Satan, he is divided against himself. How then can his kingdom stand?" (Matt. 12:26).

2. If Jesus cast out demons by Beelzebub, then by what power did their sons cast out demons? Jesus added, "So then, they will be your judges" (Luke 11:19). McGarvey states,

> The sons of the Pharisees were not their children, but their disciples (2 Kings 2:3; Acts 19:13,14). Josephus mentions three exorcists (Ant. 8:2,5 and Wars 7:6,3), and there is abundant mention of them in later rabbinical books. Our Lord's reference to them was merely for the purpose of presenting an *argumentum ad hominem*, and in no way implies that they exerised any real power over the demons; nor could they have done so in any marked degree, else the similar work of Christ would not have created such an astonishment. The argument therefore is this, I have already shown you that it is against reason that Satan casts out Satan; I now show you that it is against experience. The only instances of dispossession which you can cite are those of your own disciples. Do they act by the power of Satan? They therefore shall be your judges as to whether you have spoken rightly in saying that Satan casts out Satan (*Fourfold Gospel*, p. 301).

3. Jesus cast out demons by the "finger" or Spirit of God (Matt. 12:28; Luke 11:20). The phrase "the finger of God" shows the awesome power of God. The heavens, the moon and the stars, are the work of God's fingers (Psa. 8:3). The demon-backed magicians in Egypt were forced to admit, after the plague of lice which they could not duplicate, that this was "the finger of God" (Exod. 8:19). Again we cite McGarvey:

> Jesus here draws a conclusion from the two arguments presented. Since he does not cast out by Satan, he must cast out by the power of God, and therefore his actions demonstrated the potential arrival of the kingdom of God. The occasional accidental deliverance of exorcists might be evidence of the flow and ebb of a spiritual battle, but the steady, daily conquests of Christ over the powers of evil presented to the people the triumphant progress of an invading kingdom. It is an argument against the idea that there was a collusion between Christ and Satan (*Ibid.*, p. 302).

Christ's ability to cast out demons not only showed the power of God but also that the kingdom was approaching. "But if I drive out demons by the finger of God, then the kingdom of God has come to you" (Luke 11:20).

4. The illustration of the strong man (Matt. 12:29; Mark 3:27; Luke 11:21, 22).

> Satan is the strong man, his house the body of the demoniac, and his goods the evil spirit within the man. Jesus had entered his house, and robbed him of his goods; and this proved that, instead of being in league with Satan, he had overpowered Satan. Thus Jesus put to shame the Pharisees, and caused the divinity of his miracle to stand out in clearer light than ever. The power of Jesus to dispossess the demon was one of his most convincing credentials, and its meaning now stood forth in its true light (*Ibid.*, p. 302).

THE UNPARDONABLE SIN

It was on this occasion – the healing of the blind and mute demoniac which resulted in the charge of Jesus casting out demons by Beelzebub – that Jesus gave his famous teaching on what is often called "The Unpardonable Sin." This teaching was directed to the Pharisees who had maliciously charged Him with not only casting out demons by the power of Satan but by being possessed of a demon as well! "And the teachers of the law who came down from

Jerusalem said, 'He is possessed by Beelzebub! By the prince of demons he is driving out demons'" (Mark 3:22). This was blasphemy of the rankest sort and could not be tolerated, even for a moment. Jesus plainly taught that He cast out demons by the Spirit of God (Matt. 12:28). His enemies claimed that He cast out demons by the power of the devil. To persist in saying that Jesus cast out demons by Satan was to blaspheme or speak against the Holy Spirit of God. "The unpardonable sin" is to attribute the works of the Spirit to Satan. This is what the Pharisees were doing. The Pharisees were the object of Jesus' teaching. He said this because they were saying, "He has an evil spirit" (Mark 3:30). Blasphemy of the Holy Spirit, "the unpardonable sin," is to say that Jesus was possessed of a demon and that he cast out demons by the prince of demons, Satan.

The devil is cunning and crafty (Gen. 3:1). He is a great deceiver (Gen. 3:4, 5; Rev. 20:8, 10). Today he deceives many sincere, conscientious Christians into thinking that they have somehow committed "the unpardonable sin." A fleeting, momentary evil thought about the Spirit-directed work of Christ can in no way be called the "unpardonable sin." No one need fear that they have committed the "unpardonable" sin who grieves over such thoughts and seeks pardon. It is the person who perseveres in reviling Christ, without any qualm of conscience (like the Jerusalem scribes) who is committing such a sin. The Greek tense for "they were saying" (Mark 3:30) is the imperfect tense. It means "they kept saying or persisted in saying." Stephen accused the Jewish Sanhedrin of his day with these telling words: "You stiffnecked people, with uncircumcised hearts and ears! You are just like your fathers. You always resist the Holy Spirit!" (Acts 7:51).

To oppose the work of the Holy Spirit day after day, year after year, decade after decade, is to harden one's heart, to sear one's conscience, until the Holy Spirit's prodding can no longer be felt. Blasphemy of the Holy Spirit is a state, not an act.

The Bible clearly teaches that the blood of Jesus is able to cleanse from all sin (1 John 1:7). Those who are willing to confess their sins – including the sins of blasphemous thoughts, words or deeds – will be forgiven of all sin and unrighteousness (1 John 1:9). Hymenaeus and Alexander, two members of the early church, were blood-red guilty of blasphemy but Paul had hopes that they might learn not to do it any longer (1 Tim. 1:20). Paul himself was once a blasphemer but received forgiveness (1 Tim. 1:13). God is not willing that any should perish but that all should reach repentance (2 Pet. 3:9). Satan knows this and therefore works to deceive tender-hearted Christians into thinking that they can never be forgiven because of some thought they once had about the Holy Spirit.

CASE #4: THE GADARENE DEMONIAC, "THE TERROR OF GADARA"

The fourth instance of our Lord's ministry to demoniacs is that of the man from Gadara, the chief city of Peraea, five miles southeast of the Sea of Galilee. The terms Gadarene, Gerasene and Gergesene are all found in Scripture. "The place where the Gospel incident occurred may have been referred to sometimes as the country of the Gergesenes, a purely local name; or of the Gadarenes, from the nearest city; or of the Gerasenes, from the most important city of the district" (*Zondervan's Pictorial Bible Dictionary*, p. 308). Gadara was a part of the "Decapolis" (Mark 5:20), a district of ten cities southeast of Galilee. They were Scythopolis, Damascus, Hippos, Philadelphia, *Gadara*, Pella, Dion, *Gerasa*, Kanatha, and Raphana.

Perhaps we would be more proper in referring this account as the Gadarene Demoniacs (plural) because, according to Matthew's account, there were two such possessed men who met Christ at the edge of Galilee's shoreline. "When he arrived at the other side in the region of the Gadarenes, two demon-possessed men coming from the tombs met him" (Matt. 8:28). Mark (Mark 5:2) and Luke (Luke 8:27) mention only one man. Why? Probably because the one man's case was so arresting. There is no contradiction in Scripture here. As Matthew Henry observed, "If there were two, then there was one." This man was to be most pitied. From the composite accounts (Matt. 8:28-34; Mark 5:1-20; Luke 8:26-40) we learn the following about this sufferer:

1. *The Gadarene demoniac was homeless.* Later, after he was freed of his burden, the man was told to "Go home to your family and tell them how much the Lord has done for you, and how he has had mercy on you" (Mark 5:19). At this point in time, however, he was reduced to living in the local cemetery. He had not lived in a house for a long time (Luke 8:27). Demons, the spirits of the wicked dead, have some morbid delight in returning to burial sites.

2. *His case of demonic possession was growing worse.* At one time the townfolks could subdue him with fetters and chains. But his condition had grown so bad that he could actually break his bonds! "This man lived in the tombs, and no one could bind him any more, not even with a chain. For he had often been chained hand and foot, but he tore the chains apart and broke the irons on his feet. No one was strong enough to subdue him" (Mark 5:3,4). Demons possess superhuman strength. Both demoniacs "were so violent that no one could pass that way" (Matt. 8:28). Demons are responsible for much of the violence that occurs today. How else can we explain the absolutely inhuman things that people do to one another, including family members?

3. *He was restless.* Demons, even when succeeding in taking possession of a person, are restless: Jesus taught that they are constantly "seeking rest, finding none" (Matt. 12:43). One wonders about our restless generation. "Night and day" the demoniac would roam among the tombs and hills of Gadara (Mark 5:5). The poor man had not a moment to call his own, to lie down and rest. To not be able to get rest is a terrible thing. How utterly miserable the man must

have been. Hell is a place devoid of rest (Rev. 14:11). No wonder demons begged Jesus not to send them there!

4. *He was in perpetual anguish.* Mark tells us that the demoniac would "cry out" the livelong day (Mark 5:5). How pathetic his cries must have been. Our hearts go out to him. Jesus' certainly did. McGarvey comments, "The natural spirit of the man seeking to throw off the dominion of the demons would cry out in agony, and the demons themselves, in their own misery, would use him as a vehicle to express their own grief. It would be hard to imagine a more horrible state" (*The Fourfold Gospel*, p. 345).

5. *He was suicidal.* Our friend was so tortured by his unwelcome guests that he would often "cut himself with stones" (Mark 5:5). This does not appear to be the kind of cutting that Job did to himself (Job 2:8). That ancient sufferer scraped himself with bits of broken pottery to lance his boils. The Gadarene demoniac may have been trying to kill himself. We do know that demons do the devil's work and the devil is "a murderer from the beginning" (John 8:44). Demons tried to kill a young boy by throwing him into the water and fire (Mark 9:22). One of the most horrible things happening today are the lyrics to some rock music songs which actually suggest that young people take their lives. This "music" must be demonic in origin.

6. *He was naked.* Doctor Luke notes that "for a long time this man had not worn clothes" (Luke 8:27). Was it simply because of his open sores? We think not. Nor does it appear that the man was some cheap exhibitionist. Both the unholy angels and unclean spirits use nakedness to separate believers from their relationship with Christ (Rom. 8:35, 38). Who can doubt for a moment that the floodtide of hard-core pornography in our world today is not inspired by the devil and his demons? Nudity in public places, unheard of just a few years ago, is now commonplace, even in small communities. What a triumph for the forces of wickedness! When Christ comes into a sinner's life, they

will be found "dressed" (Mark 5:15). When Satan controls, the opposite will be true.

7. *He was insane.* Who wouldn't be, considering all he had gone through! Possessed by a host of unclean spirits, he truly was not his own self anymore. But Luke, a physician, records that after the healing work of Jesus, the man was found "sitting at the feet of Jesus, dressed and in his right mind" (Luke 8:35). He had been out of his mind; now he again possessed his mental faculties. How wonderful is our Lord! How relieved the Gadarene must have felt – to have peace of mind once more.

There are some additional interesting insights in this story. First, the Bible says that the men came to meet Jesus on His arrival (Matt. 12:28; Mark 5:2; Luke 8:27). In spite of their shocking condition, the demon-possessed men still had enough will and volition to seek Christ for help. Demons do not have total possession of a person's body and mind. "When he saw Jesus from a distance, he ran and fell on his knees in front of him" (Mark 5:6). This was the man acting on his own. What he had left in him, he offered to Jesus. Demons, though recognizing Jesus as the Son of God, do not worship Him. Their master is Satan.

When the Bible says that the demoniac cried out to Jesus, we are not to believe that this was the man speaking of his own free will. The demons within him had control of his tongue. Though the man's voice is heard, the message is from the demons: "'What do you want with us, son of God?' they shouted. 'Have you come to torture us before the appointed time?'" (Matt. 8:29). Only after the demons have been cast out can the man speak to Jesus of his own will. The man begged Jesus' permission to accompany Him on His way (Mark 5:18; Luke 8:38). Even when Jesus asked him his name it was the demons who answered, "My name is Legion, for we are many" (Mark 5:9). But Christ has greater power than the devil. He commanded the demons to leave the man. They begged Him not to send them into the Abyss, the proper abode of demons (Luke 8:31). Preferring embodiment in pigs, they asked Jesus to send them into a nearby herd of swine. The result was instantaneous and incredible. The herd of swine went "hog-wild" – racing pell-mell down a steep slope, drowning in the Sea of Galilee (Matt. 8:33; Mark 5:13; Luke 8:38). All it took was one word from Jesus: "Go!" (Matt. 8:32). Such is the power of our Lord over demonic forces.

The Bible does not say what happened to the unclean spirits. Did they perish along with the swine? Such is doubtful since the spirit of a man – good or bad – does not die. Were they returned to the Abyss, the proper abode of wicked spirits? Did they continue to roam about, seeking rest? The text yields no clues. But the Bible does say what happened to the man, "Legion." The former demoniac, so long a prisoner against his will, was completely healed. "The people went out to see what had happened. When they came to Jesus, they found the man from whom the demons had gone out, sitting at Jesus' feet, dressed and in his right mind; and they were afraid" (Luke 8:35). He was calm, clothed, collected. He begged Jesus to allow him to become one of His disciples and travel with Him (Mark 5:18; Luke 8:38). But Jesus told him, "Go home to your family and tell them how much the Lord has done for you, and how he has had mercy on you" (Mark 5:19). Home! What beautiful words! Family! How long had it been since he had seen them or they him? What a reunion it must have been. And what an evangelist the former demoniac became: "So the man went away and began to tell in the Decapolis how much Jesus had done for him. And all the people were amazed" (Mark 5:20). Jesus changes lives – even the world's worst demoniac.

35 DEMONS IN THE GOSPELS (3)

CASE #5: THE MUTE DEMONIAC

The fifth account of Christ's ministry to demoniacs in the gospels is that of the mute man in Matthew 9:32-34. This incident probably took place in Capernaum, just after Jesus had healed two men who begged Him to restore their sight (Matt. 9:27-31). The mute man, on the other hand, could make no request of Jesus. How terrible it must be to not be able to voice one's concerns. At least the man must have had some sympathetic friends for the Bible says he was "brought to Jesus" (Matt. 9:32). The reason the man could not talk was because he was possessed with a demon. The man's tongue and vocal cords were bound by an unclean spirit.

"And when the demon was driven out, the man who had been dumb spoke" (Matt. 9:33). It would be interesting to know what his first words were. Did he sing, did hc shout, did he dance and leap about like the man in Acts 3? Did he thank Jesus for helping him or did he go away unthankful like the nine lepers? We shall not know on this earth for the Scriptures do not say. But they do tell us about the reaction of the crowd: "The crowd was amazed and said, 'Nothing like this has ever been seen in Israel'" (Matt. 9:33). Although demons could cause temporary physical problems, like muteness, Christ could cast out the source of such problems – the demons themselves. With the demons gone, people were restored to good health, hence the terms "healed" and "cured" appear from time to time in describing the casting out of demons (Luke 8:2).

The reaction of the Pharisees stands in stark contrast with that of the admiring crowd. "It is by the prince of demons that he drives out demons" (Matt. 9:34). This blasphemous charge was made several times against Jesus. His answer to the charge can be found in Matthew 12:25-32; Mark 3:23-30; and Luke 11:17-22.

CASE #6 : THE SYRIAN-PHOENICIAN WOMAN'S DEMON-POSSESSED DAUGHTER

The case of the Syrian-Phoenician woman's daughter (Matt. 15:22-28; Mark 7:25-30) is unique in the instances of demon expulsion by Jesus. In this particular case, Jesus did not deal directly with the one who was demon-possessed. Like the centurion's son who was healed at a distance (Matt. 8:5-13), the Syrian-Phoenician woman's daughter was delivered of a demon.

The foreign woman came to Jesus when He was near Tyre and Sidon, His only departure from Israel. A woman from that vicinity heard about His being in the area and went to Him with her request. "Lord, Son of David, have mercy on me! My daughter is suffering terribly from demon possession" (Matt. 15:22). We are not told in what way the demon was affecting the girl. Demon possession affected people in a variety of ways. We only know that the girl was "little" (Mark 7:24) and that the case was "grievous" (Matt. 15:22 KJV). The mother, pagan idolater that she undoubtedly was (Phoenicians worshipped the mother-goddess Ashtoreth), requested Jesus to help her. For a time, Jesus would not. But her faith so impressed Him that He at last granted her request. He told her, "The demon has left your daughter" (Mark 7:29). The persistent mother went home and "found her child lying on the bed, and the demon gone" (Mark 7:30). Matthew adds, "Her daughter was healed from that very hour" (Matt. 15:28), i.e., from the hour that Jesus spoke the word. What power there is in the voice of Christ! In this case, a demon obeyed His voice even though Jesus was not there to personally confront the demon and cast him out.

CASE # 7: THE EPILEPTIC BOY

A seventh account of Jesus helping demoniacs is that of the epileptic boy (Matt. 17:14-20; Mark 9:14-29; Luke 9:37-43). This event occurred just after Christ descended from the mount of Transfiguration in the vicinity of Caesarea Philippi. A large crowd of people had gathered at the foot of the mountain. In the crowd was a man whose son was possessed with a demon. He had asked the disciples to cast out the demon but they were not able to (Matt. 17:16; Mark 9:18; Luke 9:40). The boy was his only child (Luke 9:38).

We learn several things about this poor lad:

1. *The demon had impaired the boy's speech.* "Teacher, I brought you my son, who is possessed by a spirit that has robbed him of speech" (Mark 9:17). What a blessing it is to be young and able to talk and sing and shout! Conversely, what a sad thing it is to see a young child who cannot articulate his feelings.

2. *He suffered greatly from epilepsy.* "'Lord, have mercy on my son' he said. 'He is an epileptic and is suffering greatly'" (Matt. 17:15). The seizures must have been quite severe. Doctor Luke notes, "A spirit seizes him and he suddenly screams; it throws him into convulsions so that he foams at the mouth. It scarcely ever leaves him and is destroying him" (Luke 9:39). This does not mean that everyone who suffered from epilepsy was possessed with a demon, only that demons sometimes afflicted people in this manner.

3. *The lad was also deaf.* "When Jesus saw that a crowd was running to the scene, he rebuked the evil spirit. 'You deaf and dumb spirit,' he said, 'I command you, come out of him and never enter him again'" (Mark 9:25). Not content with robbing the boy of speech, the demon had also wickedly impaired his hearing. Little wonder Mark calls

him a "foul" spirit (Mark 9:25 KJV). The demons do not possess a single shred of compassion for their victims.

4. *The demon was slowly killing the boy.* The demon-inspired epileptic seizures were slowly but surely taking their toll on the young lad. Mark records that he "pineth away" (Mark 9:18 KJV). Luke's account says, "It scarcely ever leaves him and is destroying him" (Luke 9:39).

5. *Not content with slow death, the demon had even tried to kill the boy.* From the lad's "childhood" the demon had "often thrown him into fire or water to kill him" (Mark 9:21, 22). We can only imagine the terrible scars on the little boy's body. But the emotional scars on his spirit must have been even worse. This is to say nothing of the boy's distraught father. His face must have been the saddest of men. No painter could aptly paint the anguish on his face as he talked to Jesus.

It is difficult for us to imagine the untold hours of suffering this father and son had endured at the hands of this evil spirit. The disciples of Jesus undoubtedly wanted to help them but were unable to (Matt. 17:16). After hearing the father affirm his faith in His ability to help him, Jesus rebuked the spirit. "The spirit shrieked, convulsed him violently and came out. The boy looked so much like a corpse that many said, 'He's dead.' But Jesus took him by the hand and lifted him to his feet, and he stood up" (Mark 9:26, 27). Demons, no matter how obscene and obstinate, must ultimately yield to the authority of Christ.

After the casting out of this particularly vile demon, Jesus' disciples asked Him privately, "Why couldn't we drive it out?" (Mark 9:28). Evidently they had attempted but failed. Jesus replied, "This kind can come out only by prayer" (Mark 9:29). Some translations add "and fasting." All demons are wicked but some are "more wicked" (Luke 11:26) than others, necessitating more prayer and fasting.

CASE #8: THE WOMAN WITH THE "SPIRIT OF INFIRMITY"

There is yet another account of Christ's ministry to those afflicted by demons – the woman who had a spirit of infirmity (Luke 13:10-17). This woman does not appear to be demon possessed at the time of her encounter with Christ but it does seem apparent that she was suffering from a long standing demon-inflicted infirmity. Luke tells us that she "had been crippled by a spirit for eighteen years. She was bent over and could not straighten up at all" (Luke 13:11). This may have been an extreme case of curvature of the spine. When the Lord saw her, He asked her to come forward. "Woman, you are set free from your infirmity" (Luke 13:12). The Bible does not say that He ordered the spirit to come out of her; just that she had been loosed from the infirmity that the demon had inflicted upon her. "Then he put his hands on her, and immediately she straightened up and praised God" (Luke 13:13).

This was not just an "ordinary" healing of an "ordinary" infirmity. The woman had been cruelly crippled by a demon. She had remained in this pathetic condition for 18 long years. Jesus declared, "Should not this woman, a daughter of Abraham, whom Satan has kept bound for eighteen long years, be set free on the Sabbath day from what bound her?" (Luke 13:16). An evil spirit sent from Satan was responsible for this deplorable deed. McGarvey notes, "In attributing the infirmity to Satan he acknowledges the action of the demon as Satan's agent. Diseases were not infrequently ascribed to Satan and the demons – Acts 10:38; 2 Cor. 12:7" (*Fourfold Gospel*, p. 483).

The healing of this woman appears to be a case where Jesus was helping a person who was oppressed by rather than possessed of a demon. The demon had done his dirty work and apparently was gone. Jesus then healed her of the demon-inflicted malady. This was a part of our Lord's compassionate ministry. "God anointed Jesus of Nazareth with the Holy Ghost and with power: who went about doing good, and healing all that were oppressed of the devil; for God was with him" (Acts 10:38 KJV).

DEMONS CAST OUT EN MASSE

In addition to the personal encounters Christ had with individual demoniacs, there are several instances where our Lord cast out demons on a mass scale. Using J. W. McGarvey's "Harmony of the Four Gospels" we will consider these accounts in as near chronological order as we can.

1. The first account of Christ's casting out demons en masse was in Capernaum, just after Jesus had cast out a demon in the Jewish synagogue and healed Peter's mother-in-law of a fever (Matt. 8:14-17; Mark 1:29-34; Luke 4:38-41). As the sun was setting on that eventful day, many who were sick and many who were possessed with demons were brought to the house where Jesus was staying. A clear distinction is made between the diseased and the demoniacs. Christ is said to have "healed" the sick but to have driven out the demons. "And Jesus healed many who had various diseases. He also drove out many demons, but he would not let the demons speak because they knew who he was" (Mark 1:34). McGarvey notes,

> Those who are disposed to frequent spiritual seances and to seek information from mediums should remember that the Son of God permitted his disciples to receive no information from such sources. He forbade demons to speak in the presence of his own, even on the most important of all topics (*The Fourfold Gospel*, p. 171).

2. As Jesus continued on His first preaching circuit of Galilee, He preached in Jewish synagogues and drove out demons (Mark 1:39). We have already noted the casting out of the demon in the synagogue in Capernaum (Mark 1:21-28). Did demons come out in full force when Jesus entered

such places to teach the Word of God? It seems to be the case. In any event, "Jesus went throughout Galilee, teaching in their synagogues, preaching the good news of the kingdom, and healing every disease and sickness among the people. News about him spread all over Syria, and people brought to him all who were ill with various diseases, those suffering severe pain, the demon possessed, the epileptics, and the paralytics, and he healed them all" (Matt. 4:23, 24). Again, note the distinction between diseases and demon-possession.

3. Later in the Galilean ministry, Jesus healed many by the Sea of Galilee (Mark 3:7-12). People were coming to Him from Judea, Jerusalem, Idumea and the regions across Jordan and around Tyre and Sidon. Those with diseases were pushing forward to touch Him (Mark 3:10) and demoniacs were falling down before Him: "Whenever the evil spirits saw him, they fell down before him and cried out, 'You are the Son of God.' But he gave them strict orders not to tell who he was" (Mark 3:11, 12). As McGarvey observed, "This was not the right time, nor were they the right witnesses to make him known" (*The Fourfold Gospel*, p. 219).

4. Just prior to the famous "Sermon on the Mount," a great multitude came to see this great miracle worker (Matt. 5:1,2; Luke 6:17-20). Some of them came to hear Jesus speak (Luke 6:18). Still others came to have demons cast out: "Those troubled by evil spirits were cured, and the people all tried to touch him, because power was coming from him and healing them all" (Luke 6:18,19). But the greatest blessing remained to be given – the wonderful, healing message: "Blessed are you . . . ."

5. Much later in the life of Jesus, after John the Baptist had been put into prison, two disciples came from John asking Jesus if He really was the Messiah (Luke 7:18-20). The timing could not have been better for that question. "At that very time Jesus cured many who had diseases, sicknesses and evil spirits, and gave sight to many who were blind" (Luke 7:21). Jesus sent the messengers back

with a message to the effect that signs like these should certainly be proof of His Messiahship (Luke 7:22,23).

6. During the Perean ministry, Jesus received a warning that Herod was seeking to kill Him. This was our Lord's response: "Go tell that fox, I will drive out demons and heal people today and tomorrow, and on the third day I will reach my goal" (Luke 13:32). Jesus was still casting out demons.

Casting out demons was a very important phase of Christ's ministry on earth. "The reason the Son of God appeared was to destroy the devil's work" (1 John 3:8). As far as can be determined from Scripture, Jesus never met a demon-possessed person that He could not or did not help. He "went about doing good, and healing all that were oppressed of the devil" (Acts 10:38 KJV). His casting out demons signaled the coming of His kingdom. "But if I drive out demons by the finger of God, then the kingdom of God has come to you" (Luke 11:20). Although it is not clearly stated as such in Scripture, the reason that God permitted wicked spirits to indwell some people was in order that the supreme authority of Christ might be clearly manifested. We do know that was the case with some sicknesses. Of the man who was born blind, Jesus said, "Neither this man nor his parents sinned, but this happened so that the work of God might be displayed in his life" (John 9:3). And of His good friend Lazarus, our Lord declared,"This sickness will not end in death. No, it is for God's glory so that God's Son may be glorified through it" (John 11:4). It is not improbable that the same could be said for those whom God allowed to be afflicted with demons.

THE DISCIPLES AND DEMONS

Jesus was not the only one to cast out demons in the gospels. A number of His followers were empowered to drive out demons. Among them were:

1. *The Twelve apostles.* The accounts are found in Matthew 10:1,8; Mark 6:7, 13; and Luke 9:1. All three accounts include the commission to cast out demons and distinction is made between this and healing the sick. "He called his twelve disciples to him and gave them authority to drive out evil spirits and to heal every disease and sickness . . . . Heal the sick, raise the dead, cleanse those who have leprosy, drive out demons'" (Matt. 10:1, 8). "When Jesus had called the Twelve together, he gave them power and authority to drive out demons and to cure diseases" (Luke 9:1).

Mark's account informs us that this is precisely what they were able to do. "They drove out many demons and anointed many sick people with oil and healed them" (Mark 6:13). The authority that Christ gave them enabled them to conquer the spirit world.

In the Great Commission, Mark also includes the charge to drive out demons that was given to the apostles. "And these signs will accompany those who believe: In my name they will drive out demons . . ." (Mark 16:17). The apostles, who had just been rebuked for their unbelief (Mark 16:14), at last became "those who believe." Once convinced that Jesus really was the Christ, they "went out and preached everywhere, and the Lord worked with them and confirmed his word by the signs that accompanied it" (Mark 16:20). What signs? The signs that Jesus had promised the apostles in verses 17 and 18, including casting out demons. These signs (as were all miracles) were intended to "confirm the word" (Heb. 2:4). The apostles' ability to drive out demons was a sign to the world that they were authentic spokesmen for God.

The only failure that Jesus' followers had in casting out demons is recorded in Matthew 17:14-20 and Mark 9:14-29. While Jesus was on the mount of transfiguration with Peter, James and John, an obviously distraught man brought his son to the waiting disciples of Jesus. He wanted them to cast out a demon that was slowly killing his son but the disciples could not. Later, after Jesus had cast out the demon, they asked Him in private the reason for their failure. Matthew's account says, "Because you have so little faith" (Matt. 17:20). Mark records Jesus' answer: "This kind can come out only by prayer" (Mark 9:29). Some translations add "and fasting." Evidently the disciples did not realize the degrees of wickedness that exist among demons and had not approached the attempt to cast him out with enough spiritual preparation (i.e., faith, prayer and fasting).

2. *The 70 disciples.* Jesus also commissioned 70 other followers to cast out demons. Although the actual charge to do so is not found in Luke's account, we must assume that they had been so commissioned as were the 12 (Matt. 10:1,8; Mark 6:7; Luke 9:1). They returned from their mission with joy and told Jesus. "Lord, even the demons submit to us in your name" (Luke 10:17). The reason demons obeyed these disciples is because they (the disciples) believed in the name of Jesus. Jewish exorcists who tried to use the name of Jesus as a new incantation met with miserable failure (Acts 19:13-16). They were not true believers in Christ. Jesus Himself said that on the Day of Judgment some would try to claim that they had driven out demons in His name (Matt. 7:22). But such people never obeyed the will of God (Matt. 7:21). It takes more than repeating the name of Jesus to get to heaven. "Why do you call me, 'Lord, Lord,' and do not do what I say?" (Luke 6:46).

In response to the overjoyed disciples, Jesus replied, "I saw Satan fall like lightning from heaven" (Luke 10:18). Some see this as a pronouncement from Jesus that the overthrow of Satan's kingdom was now in progress: even believers in Jesus could defeat the hosts of Satan. Others see it as a reference to the original fall of Satan (Isa. 14:12; Jude 6). He then reminded them, "I have given you authority to trample on snakes and scorpions and to overcome all the power of the enemy; nothing will harm you. However, do not rejoice that the spirits submit to you, but rejoice that your names are written in heaven" (Luke

10:19,20). As B. W. Johnson so wisely points out, even Judas once had this power in Christ's name! Those who are caught up in the so-called "deliverance ministry" today need to heed these words. We should not be so caught up in demonism that we fail to be caught up into glory. The salvation of our souls is more important than having demons submit to us. If we could somehow cause every unclean spirit in the world to submit to us and lose our souls in the end, would it be worth it? What shall a man give in exchange for his soul – obsession with exploring and conquering the spirit world?

3. *The unknown disciple.* Both Mark (Mark 9:38-41) and Luke (Luke 9:49, 50) record this interesting story. One of the apostles, John, told Jesus that they had seen a man driving out demons in the name of Jesus. The apostles told the man to stop what he was doing because "he was not one of us." Though John and his companions meant well, Jesus rebuked them. John did not always have the best spirit about him. He and his brother once wanted to destroy an entire village because they had refused Jesus simple hospitality. Peter once cut off a man's ear because He was approaching his Master. Yes, the disciples needed a lesson in hospitality themselves! They remind us of young Joshua who once tried to get Moses to forbid two men, Eldad and Medad, who were not of the 70 elders, from prophesying. Moses rebuked Joshua, "Are you jealous for my sake? I wish that all the Lord's people were prophets and that the Lord would put his Spirit on them!" (Num. 11:29).

Jesus told His jealous disciples, "Do not stop him, for whoever is not against you is for you" (Luke 9:50). Mark's account reads, "'Do not stop him,' Jesus said. 'No one who does a miracle in my name can in the next moment say anything bad about me, for whoever is not against us is for us.'" (Mark 9:38; Luke 9:49). Why didn't this work for the Jewish exorcists (Acts 19:13-16)? Because they were not true believers in the Messiah. Was this man? Evidently, for Jesus said not to stop him in his good work. Apparently, the man was a believer in Jesus even though he was not a traveler with Him. This story is a powerful illustration against the sectarian spirit that sometimes surfaces in our hearts. Ryle observes,

> He neither praises nor blames him for following an independent course, and not working with his disciples. He simply declares that he must not be forbidden, and that those who work the same kind of work that we do should be regarded, not as enemies, but allies. Thousands, in every period of church history, have spent their lives in copying John's mistake. They have labored to stop every man who will not work for Christ in their way from working for Christ at all (*The People's New Testament*, p. 194).

36 DEMONS IN THE BOOK OF ACTS

The book of Acts recounts the acts of the apostles of Christ. Some have contended that the book should actually be called the "Acts of the Holy Spirit" for, indeed, many acts of the Holy Spirit are found in the book. Perhaps we could settle for a compromise and call it the "Acts of the Holy Spirit Through the Apostles." At any rate, the acts of the Spirit-directed apostles are seen from time to time in head-on conflicts with the world of unclean spirits. The battle between God's Holy Spirit and Satan's unholy spirits continues.

Demons did not cease to exist with the ascension of Christ into heaven. In fact, just before He ascended into heaven, Jesus commissioned His apostles to continue the work of driving out demons (Mark 16:15-17). The inspired record states that this happened: "Then the disciples went out and preached everywhere, and the Lord worked with them and confirmed his word by the signs that accompanied it" (Mark 16:20). What signs? The signs Jesus promised them – speaking in tongues, not being harmed by poison or snakes, healing the sick and casting out demons. Clearly, the Bible teaches that demons continued to exist after the ascension of Christ.

DEMONIACS IN AND AROUND JERUSALEM

The first encounter the apostles had with demons in the book of Acts is found in Acts 5:12-16. Following the deaths of Ananias and Sapphira, the apostles performed many miraculous signs and wonders among the people (Acts

5:12). They were held in high esteem because of these powerful deeds (Acts 5:13). Many people were turning to Christ as a result. The church was growing by leaps and bounds (Acts 5:14). As word of these things spread through Jerusalem, a great number of sick people were brought out into the streets and laid on their pallets "so that at least Peter's shadow might fall on some of them as he passed by" (Acts 5:15). Evidently they (or their relatives) had faith that even this vague contact might bring healing.

News of the healing power of the apostles soon spread to the towns around Jerusalem. Soon folks from all around were bringing their sick to be healed. Luke also adds that they brought "those tormented by evil spirits" (Acts 5:16). Both the sick and the demon-afflicted were cured: "all of them were healed" (Acts 5:16). Peter and the other apostles were able to do what their Lord had empowered them to do – drive out demons (Mark 16:17).

DEMONS CAST OUT IN SAMARIA

Samaria was an area targeted by our Lord for evangelism (Acts 1:8). Following the death of Stephen and the persecution of the church in Jerusalem, Philip went to a city in Samaria and proclaimed Christ (Acts 8:5). Philip was an honest man, full of the Holy Spirit and wisdom (Acts 6:3). The apostles had ordained men like Philip and Stephen (Acts 6:6), enabling them to perform miracles (Acts 6:8). When Philip arrived in Samaria, he was able to perform miracles (Acts 8:6). The miracles caused the people to pay attention to what he preached. "When the crowds heard Philip and saw the miraculous signs he did, they all paid close attention to what he said" (Acts 8:6). This was the Biblical purpose of miracles (Heb. 2:4).

Now notice the effect on evil spirits this Spirit-filled man had: "With shrieks, evil spirits came out of many, and many paralytics and cripples were healed. So there was great joy in that city" (Acts 8:7,8). The shrieks emitted by the unclean spirits were not shrieks of joy but cries of rage, hatred and despair. But there was "dancing in the streets" by former demoniacs, their friends and loved ones. What joy there must have been in that city that night! When Jesus comes, there is "joy in the camp."

THE CASE OF SIMON THE SORCERER

The third occurrence of demons in Acts is that of a man who made his living by contacting the spirit world, Simon the Sorcerer (Acts 8:9-24). In this particular city in Samaria lived a sorcerer, Simon by name. A sorcerer is one who practices the magic arts: drug-related spells and incantations, charms, amulets, etc. Sorcery was forbidden in the Old Testament (Isa. 47:9; Mal. 3:5) and is called a "work of the flesh" in the New Testament (Gal. 5:19,20, translated "witchcraft" in the NIV). Simon was also a braggart, boasting that he was someone great and, indeed, everyone in the city thought he really was. Of him they testified, "This man is the divine power known as the Great Power" (Acts 8:10). For a long time he had held these people spellbound with his forbidden magical practices.

Then Philip came to town, preaching "the good news of the kingdom of God and the name of Jesus Christ" (Acts 8:12), and a great revival took place. Men and women were baptized (Acts 8:12). And (miracle of miracles) "Simon himself believed and was baptized" (Acts 8:13). Was he saved? Why should we doubt his conversion? Did not our Lord promise, "He that believes and is baptized shall be saved" (Mark 16:16)? Is this not what Simon did? Did the Lord forgive him of his sins or not? Why should we doubt the promise of our dear Lord?

For a time, Simon "continued" (Acts 8:13 KJV) with Philip, amazed by the miracle-working powers of this Spirit-filled man. Later, when Peter and John arrive from Jerusalem to impart the miracle-working power of the Holy Spirit on these new Christians, Simon does a very terrible thing – he offers to buy this gift so that he can impart the Holy Spirit to people (Acts 8:18, 19). From this offer we get the word "simony" meaning "the buying or selling of a church office." The old desire to be a Great One had cropped up in Simon's heart once more. Peter turns to Simon and tells him that his heart is not right with God and that he should repent and pray for forgiveness (Acts 8:20-23). The record ends with Simon asking Peter to pray for him but we are left in the dark as to what happened to him.

THE CASE OF ELYMAS THE SORCERER

Another sorcerer who came in conflict with an apostle was Elymas, a sorcerer in the city of Paphos, on the island of Cyprus (Acts 13:4-12). Not only was he a sorcerer, he was a false prophet as well (Acts 13:6). Demons are the dynamic behind false prophets (Matt. 24:24; 1 Tim. 4:1; 1 John 4:1; 2 Thess. 2:9-11). This man was deeply involved with the spirit world.

No sooner had Paul and Barnabas set off on their first missionary journey than they run into this vessel of Satan. The Holy Spirit of God separated them for this great work (Acts 13:2) and the unholy spirit world of Satan meets them head on! Elymas, also called Bar-Jesus, was an attendant to the governor of Cyprus, Sergius Paulus. This man, extremely intelligent and interested in the Word of God, sent for Paul and Barnabas (Acts 13:7). What an opportunity this was! To be able to share Christ with a leader such as Sergius Paulus. Satan and his demons do all they can to hinder the gospel. Elymas "opposed them and tried to turn the proconsul from the faith" (Acts 13:8). Is this not the work of the devil? Does he not try to snatch away the seed? "Those along the path are the ones who hear, and then the devil comes and takes away the word from their hearts, so that they cannot believe and be saved" (Luke 8:12). This is precisely what Elymas, the man in league with spirits, was trying to do.

But God is greater than Satan. Paul is filled with the Holy Spirit. He looks Elymas right in the eye and declares, "You are a child of the devil and an enemy of everything that is right! You are full of all kinds of deceit and trickery. Will you never stop perverting the right ways of the Lord? Now the hand of the Lord is against you. You are going to be blind, and for a time you will be unable to see the light of the sun" (Acts 13:10,11). How appropriate! A man who has been trying to keep a sincere seeker of truth from seeing the light of God's Word is now going to be unable to see the light! Such irony! A mist and darkness came over Elymas and he staggered about, seeking someone to lead him by the hand. Paul, unencumbered, then led Sergius Paulus to Christ (Acts 13:12). The powers of darkness are great but the power of truth and light is far greater.

THE SLAVE GIRL WITH THE "SPIRIT OF DIVINATION"

The fifth instance of demon activity in Acts is found in Acts 16. Responding to the "Macedonian call," Paul and his traveling companions find themselves in Philippi, a Roman colony and leading city of the district of Macedonia (Acts 16:12). One day, on their way to a prayer meeting, they are met by a slave girl who had a "spirit of divination" (Acts 16:16 KJV). Divination, discovering the future by consulting the spirits of the dead, was an evil practice, forbidden in Scripture (Num. 22:7; 23:23; Deut. 18:10, et al). The New International Version says, "a slave girl who had a spirit by which she predicted the future." Fortune-telling was and is a very lucrative business. She earned a good deal of money for her owners. This is why they were so upset when Paul cast the demon out of her (Acts 16:19).

The girl begins to follow Paul and his entourage, shouting, "These men are servants of the Most High God, who are telling you the way to be saved" (Acts 16:17). Donald G. Hunt comments,

> Demons also spoke the truth when crying out concerning Jesus (Mark 1:23,24), but Jesus cast them out and quieted them (Mark 1:25, 34) even as Paul does to this soothsaying girl (v. 18). Just as Jesus was displeased with demons giving Him publicity, so Paul is "grieved" with the same (v. 18). In print we have what the demons say, but print does not convey the tone nor the attitude with which they speak. Paul considers this poor advertising, much like a known prostitute following an evangelistic party through city streets saying, "These be the men of the most high God who are preaching the gospel at 38th and Adams every night." (*Simple, Stimulating Studies in the Great Book of Acts*, p. 152).

Note that Paul turns and speaks to the spirit, not the girl (Acts 16:18). He realized that a demon was using the poor girl's vocal cords and tongue. Note, too, that he commands the demon to come forth "in the name of Jesus Christ" (Acts 16:18). At the name of Jesus, the spirit leaves the girl. No longer was the slave girl controlled by the unclean spirit; now she could come under the control of the Holy Spirit, should she so choose.

DEMONS IN EPHESUS CAST OUT BY PAUL'S HANDKERCHIEFS AND APRONS

The sixth instance of demons in Acts is a most extraordinary one. Arriving in Ephesus, Paul teaches for two years in the lecture hall of Tyrannus. During this period of time, a truly amazing thing happens. "God did extraordinary miracles through Paul. Handkerchiefs and aprons that had touched him were taken to the sick, and their illnesses were cured and the evil spirits left them" (Acts 19:11, 12). Did this really happen? We have no reason to believe otherwise. A woman who had been hemorrhaging for 12 years once touched the hem of Jesus' garment and was healed (Matt. 9:20, 21). In Gennesaret, great crowds of people begged Jesus to let the sick touch the edge of His cloak. All who touched Him were healed

(Matt. 14:34-36). Sick people were laid in the streets of Jerusalem so that Peter's shadow might fall on them (Acts 5:15). Both the diseased and the demon-possessed were healed.

The text does not say that these personal items were sent by Paul; only that they were taken. B. W. Johnson notes, "If miracles are wrought, it is always God's work, and he can work them as he wills. In this case, in order to magnify the name of his preacher, he let his power go with the articles that were carried from Paul to the sick. The Lord, in his wisdom, can make use of any instrument he chooses" (*The People's New Testament*, p. 500). Not only were the sick in Ephesus healed in this unusual manner, evil spirits left people as well. What power our Sovereign God has! Demons – who once caused a man to go unclothed (Mark 5:5) – are now expelled by articles of clothing.

THE EPHESIAN DEMONIAC AND THE SEVEN SONS OF SCEVA

The seventh and final account of demonic activity in the book of Acts is found in Acts 19:13-20. News of these aforementioned extraordinary miracles reached the ears of some Jewish "exorcists" who were living in Ephesus. A Jewish chief priest, Sceva by name, had seven sons who dabbled in the black arts. J. W. McGarvey's comments are interesting:

> These exorcists, as their title indicates, pretended to the power of casting out demons; and they appeared to the people to succeed often enough to keep up some reputation. Doubtless the fact that they were seven brothers added to the mystery of their pretensions, just as a fortuneteller at the present day who is the seventh daughter of the seventh daughter is more highly credited than others of her class. They employed for the purpose incantations over the demoniacs, in which they uttered certain unmeaning words that they claimed to have derived from Solomon, and they

> naturally supposed that the secret of Paul's power was something of the same kind; so they watched him as he cast out demons, to see if they could discover his talismanic word. They were not long in observing that in every instance he used the name of Jesus; and they concluded that the charm was in that word; so two of them put the matter to a test by getting a demoniac into a room where they would be unobserved if they met with a failure, and intending, if they succeeded, to go before the public as rivals of Paul (*New Commentary on Acts of Apostles*, Vol. II, p. 156).

The experiment was doomed from the start. The sons of Sceva did not have personal faith in the Lord Jesus Christ. They merely thought there might be something magical in pronouncing His name. When they tried their ploy on the demoniac, they said, "In the name of Jesus, whom Paul preaches, I command you to come out" (Acts 19:13). To their dismay and horror, the demon replied, "Jesus I know and Paul I know about, but who are you?" (Acts 19:15). Demons are not dumbbells. They know who Jesus is and who His faithful proclaimers are. The demon then caused the man in whom he dwelled to leap upon the brothers. What had started out to be an experiment turned into a nightmare for them. The demoniac proceeded to give them such a beating that they burst out of the house, "naked and bleeding," and fled down the street. What a sight it must have been! Seven bloodied brothers running from one wild-eyed man.

The result of this exposure was a mighty revival in wicked Ephesus. "When this became known to the Jews and Greeks living in Ephesus, they were all seized with fear, and the name of the Lord Jesus was held in high honor. Many of those who believed now came and openly confessed their evil deeds. A number who had practiced sorcery brought their scrolls together and burned them publicly. When they calculated the value of the scrolls, the total came to fifty thousand drachmas. In this way the word of the Lord spread widely and grew in power" (Acts 19:17-19). Observe that traffic with the spirit world (sorcery) is here called "evil deeds." Satan has tricked many today into thinking that such things either do not exist or that they are harmless. Observe, also, that because of this great exposure, the Word of God grows mightily and prevails. This is highly significant for this is the last mention in the New Testament of demons possessing people in this manner. From this point on, all references to unclean spirits will be of a different nature: "seducing spirits and doctrines of demons"(1 Tim. 4:1). Satan is not through using his demons. Not on your life. Subtle deceiver that he is, he simply switches his strategy. Demonizing men's bodies hasn't worked so well. Jesus and His apostles have triumphed over every one. Now he tries operating on men's spirits.

37 DEMONS IN THE EPISTLES(1)

Demons are mentioned in over half of the New Testament epistles (Gal., 2 Thess., 1 Cor., Rom., Jas., Eph., Phil., Col., 1 Tim., 1 Pet., and 1 John). Their appearance in the epistles stands in sharp contrast with the gospel accounts. Satan is a master of craftiness (Gen. 3:1; 2 Cor. 11:3). He now seems to change his strategy 180 degrees. In the gospels – and even in Acts – demonic activity is largely efforts to attack the physical person of people. We read of people, even children, being invaded and harmed physically. Demons caused deafness, dumbness (muteness), blindness, convulsions (epilepsy), long-standing infirmities, self-inflicted wounds, perhaps suicidal mania. The emotional state of these people was under attack as well. As someone has said, the body and the mind catch each other's diseases. Physical suffering causes mental anguish and vice versa.

From Acts 19:20 on, however, the picture seems to change. No longer do we read of incidents of demonic possession like in Jesus' day. This is not to say that demons no longer possessed men or no longer do so today. It is just to say that there are no more recorded instances of such in the New Testament. The balance of New Testament documents reveal a subtle shift in Satan's strategy. No longer does he seem as interested in attacking people's bodies. He tried that time and time again and failed in each effort. Jesus and the apostles were able to overcome his evil demonizing power. Christ had come to destroy the works of the devil (1 John 3:8) and He had done so. At the cross, the focal point of all history, He "disarmed the powers and authorities, he made a public spectacle of them, triumphing over them by the cross" (Col. 2:15). Ousted spirits spelled the doom of Satan. Now he goes to work on the spirits of men with equal ferocity. He unleashes his forces of evil to deceive the hearts of men.

The devil has practiced deception from the very beginning. He deceived himself into thinking that he was greater than he really was (1 Tim. 3:6). He deceived his fellow angels into thinking they could usurp authority in heaven (Rev. 12:9). He deceived Eve into thinking she could partake of forbidden fruit without incurring God's displeasure (1 Tim. 2:14). The Bible calls Satan a great deceiver (Rev. 20: 3,8, 10). In the epistles, the inspired writers declare that his main methods of "devouring" men today is through demonic deception – spirits who seduce men into following "doctrines of demons" that are taught by false teachers. Such age-old practices as spiritualism, sorcery, witchcraft, demon worship, etc., continue but the main emphasis seems to be false doctrine. Having failed to thwart the work of Christ by attacking men's bodies, Satan turns his guns on the spiritual side of man.

WITCHCRAFT: A WORK OF THE FLESH

Paul warns about "the works of the flesh" and includes "witchcraft" among them (Gal. 5:19,20). "Witchcraft" comes from the Greek word *pharmakeia* and is also translated "sorcery." A sorcerer or witch was in league with evil spirits. They used magic, drugs, incantations and spells. The Bible calls it a "sin" (1 Sam. 15:23) and condemns all such activity, by whatever name (Exod. 22:18; Deut. 18:10-14; 1 Sam. 28:3,9; 2 Kings 23:24; Isa. 8:19; Acts 19:18, 19).

Two things should be noted about witchcraft: (1) it is called a "work of the flesh." You cannot live according to the dictates of the flesh and still be pleasing to God (Rom. 8:7, 8). The mind of the flesh is enmity against God. Those who live after the flesh will die in their sins. We are to put to death the deeds of the flesh (Rom. 8:13). It would be impossible for a Christian to dabble in fleshly things like witchcraft and still be pleasing to God. (2) Those who practice such things "will not inherit the kingdom of God." This is the ultimate penalty for trafficking with the spirit world. If a person is so interested in the spirit world, that is where they will go – forever! The Abyss – and later, hell – will be small comfort for such involvement.

DEMONS SEEK TO SEPARATE BELIEVERS FROM CHRIST

In his letter to the church at Rome, Paul indicates that there are forces who want to "separate us from the love of Christ" (Rom. 8:35). These forces promote trouble, hardship, persecution, famine, nakedness, danger, even the sword. But Paul writes that we are "more than conquerors through him who loved us" (Rom. 8:37) and then states this truth: "For I am convinced that neither death nor life, neither angels nor demons, neither the present nor the future, nor any powers, neither height nor depth, nor anything else in all creation, will be able to separate us from the love of God that is in Christ Jesus our Lord" (Rom. 8:38, 39).

The King James Version has "principalities" in place of "demons." *Arche* Is the Greek word and is defined by W. E. Vine thusly: "Supramundane beings who exercise rule." The footnote to "demons" in the New International Version is "heavenly rulers." This may be referring to fallen angels but it is not likely. Paul is using a number of contrasts: death/life; present/future; height/depth. Included in these contrasts is angels/demons. It does not appear that angels and demons are one and the same. When Paul stood before the Sanhedrin, strife broke out between the Sadducees and the Pharisees when he spoke of the resurrection of the dead. Luke adds this parenthetical insertion: "(The Sadducees say that there is no resurrection, and that there are neither angels nor spirits, but the Pharisees acknowledge them all)" (Acts 23:8). Some of the Pharisees, taking sides with Paul for once, said, "What if a spirit or an angel has spoken to him?" (Acts 23:9). People in Biblical times understood the distinction between angels and demons. But there is no distinction between the evil objectives and goals of fallen angels and unclean spirits – both seek to separate believers from the object of their faith, Jesus Christ! They will resort to every evil trick in their book to obtain this objective. The believer can take heart, however, in Paul's strong affirmation that nothing in all creation is able to separate us from the love God has for us in Christ Jesus our Lord! How we need to believe this and live each day in the strength our loving God supplies!

DECEIVING SPIRITS IN THESSALONICA

Another reference to demonic activity in the epistles is Paul's reference to deceiving spirits in the young church in Thessalonica. Paul wrote, "That ye be not soon shaken in mind, or be troubled, neither by spirit, nor by word, nor by letter as from us, as that the day of Christ is at hand. Let no man deceive you by any means . . ." (2 Thess. 2:2, 3 KJV). Evidently Satan had commissioned some evil spirit to give these young Christians a prophecy – either orally or by a forged letter – that the day of the Lord had already come. Only the devil could think of a thing so wicked. Only demons could have pulled it off. Satan is a master at perverting and twisting the pure Word of God (Gen. 3:1-5). This he did, through demonic interference, in sending an untrue prophecy to these new Christians. Apparently the infant church did not yet have "discerners of spirits," thus necessitating this second and special letter from Paul.

The balance of the second chapter of 2 Thessalonians is a warning from Paul that Satan will someday be at work through the "man of sin" who will deceive people through demon-wrought miracles. "And then the lawless one will be revealed, whom the Lord Jesus will overthrow with the breath of his mouth and destroy by the splendor of his coming. The coming of the lawless one will be in accordance with the work of Satan displayed in all kinds of counterfeit miracles, signs and wonders, and in every sort of evil that deceives those who are perishing. They perish because they refused to love the truth and so be saved" (2 Thess. 2:8-11).

God wanted Christians in that day to beware of miracles. Miracles, in themselves, do not necessarily prove that the one who performed the miracle is from God. Pagan magicians in Egypt could perform miracles (Exod. 7:11, 12). Jesus warned of false prophets who would do the same (Matt. 24:24). A careful examination with the Scripture text in one hand and a reputable church history textbook in the other will reveal that the "falling away" and "man of sin" are inseparably connected with the Roman Catholic system. Wilbur Fields writes,

> . . . the Roman church is almost built on claims of miracles. Every time a dead man is proclaimed a "saint," there must be evidence (?) brought forth that he (or she) did at least two miracles. The shrines of Romanism (such as the one at Lourdes, France) attract thousands of pilgrims, many of whom go away saying they are healed. We read about Catholics who have spontaneously bleeding wounds (stigmata) in the places where Christ was wounded on the cross. We are told that the bread and wine miraculously change into the very flesh and blood of Christ during the mass. But why say more? Remember the apostle of Jesus Christ, Paul, warned us about "powers and signs and lying wonders" (*Thinking Through Thessalonians*, p. 206).

To these could be added, the supposed miracles of bleeding or weeping statues (usually proven to be fraudulent), seeing the face of Jesus in such mundane things as a tortilla, the celebrated shroud of Turin, etc. We must be careful that we are not swept away by these deceptive miracles wrought by demons, lest we should "believe a lie" (2 Thess. 2:11).

DEMON WORSHIP IN CORINTH

Demon worship is nothing new. It is mentioned several times in the Bible (Lev. 17:7; Deut. 32:17; Psa. 106:37; Rev. 9:20). Satan has always wanted men to worship himself rather than God. He even tried to tempt Jesus to do this (Matt. 4:9). We should not be astounded, then, that he attempts – and succeeds – in getting men to worship him and his hellish helpers, the demons.

Demons are the dynamic behind idolatry. An idol or image, of course, is nothing. The power behind the idol is something else. Idols were only the visible symbol of the invisible source behind them that sought men to worship them – demons. "They worshiped their idols, which became a snare to them. They sacrificed their sons and their daughters to demons" (Psa. 106: 36, 37).

Paul told Christians in Corinth to "flee from idolatry" (1 Cor. 10:14). He advised them to consider the people of ancient Israel (1 Cor. 10:18). He wrote, "Do I mean then that a sacrifice offered to an idol is anything, or that an idol is anything? No. But the sacrifices of pagans are offered to demons, not to God, and I do not want you to be participants with demons. You cannot drink the cup of the Lord and the cup of demons too; you cannot have a part in both the Lord's table and the table of demons. Are we trying to arouse the Lord's jealousy? Are we stronger than he?" (1 Cor. 10:19-22). Paul knew that the real power and dynamic behind idolatry was demons and he sounded this grave warning to them. Demon worship was alive and well in Paul's time. It continues to thrive in many countries today. No man can commune with Christ at the blessed table of our Lord who is dabbling with demons. Any Christian who is involved with the spirit world should repent and abandon the practice before partaking of the Lord's Supper.

"DISCERNERS OF SPIRITS" IN CORINTH

In the days of the early church, God gifted certain individuals with the ability to distinguish between those men who were speaking by the Spirit of God and those imposters who were speaking by the spirit of Satan. The first Christians did not possess complete copies of the Word of God as we have today. For example, the church in Thessalonica, as nearly as we can determine, received the first inspired documents of Scripture around A. D. 52 or 53. In this letter they were told, "Quench not the Spirit. Despise not prophesyings. Prove all things; hold fast that which is good" (1 Thess. 5:19-21 KJV). God would inspire men, known as "prophets," to speak for Him. All well and good. But Satan is God's "ape." He counterfeits the true, the genuine. So he would motivate men, through his spirits, to speak in "God's" name. As a result the early church found itself in a quandary. How could they know who was speaking by inspiration and who was speaking by deception? Some were throwing up their hands, quenching the Spirit's word, despising any prophecy, giving it all up, throwing in the towel. So Paul tells them to "prove" or "test" all things. Fine. But how? They could use what Scriptures they had – the Old Testament – just like the noble Bereans did when they "searched the Scriptures" to see if the message they had heard was accurate (Acts 17:11). But copies of the Scriptures were scarce. What then? Here is where "discerners of spirits" helped.

Those who were given the ability to "distinguish between spirits" (1 Cor. 12:10), were a valuable asset to the church as a whole. God gifted these people with perceptive powers that enabled them to distinguish between truth and error. They could determine whether a doctrine was demonic or divine in nature and origin, whether the prophet was from God or Satan. Demons, as we will soon see, influence the teachings of certain men (1 Tim. 4:1-3; 1 John 4:1-3). Those who had the gift of discernment were a great help to the church in those uncertain days. Today we do not have men so gifted. We can "try the spirits" with the help of the complete revelation of God's Word. That which is perfect is come; that which is in part is done away (1 Cor. 13:10). The Bible, God's perfect Word, is the yardstick by which we can measure all teachings, oral or written. We test all things by these questions: "What does the Bible say?" "What did Jesus say?" "What did the apostles teach?"

DEMONS "BELIEVE AND TREMBLE"

Demons were present in James' day. He wrote. "You believe that there is one God. Good! Even the demons believe that – and shudder" (Jas. 2:19). The demonic beings that he referred to were as real as the human beings he mentions in the same chapter: Abraham, Isaac, and Rahab.

Demons are not fools. They believe in the existence of God. Fools say in their heart, "There is no God" (Psa. 14:1; 53:1). Demons also believe that Jesus is the Christ, the Holy One of God, the Son of God. Many times they confessed His deity (Mark 1:24; 3:11 et al).

Then why do they "shudder?" Because they know that Christ, being superior to them, will ultimately banish them to the place of eternal torment. They cried, "Have you come here to torture us before the appointed time?" (Matt. 8:29). They begged Him not to send them into the Abyss (Luke 8:31). The Abyss is the unseen abode of the wicked dead where the demons on the loose rightfully belong. No wonder they tremble and shudder before the Son of God.

Perhaps this is why the demons work with such frenzy and fervor. They, like Satan, know their time is short (Rev. 12:12). As time and eternity come closer together, we can expect an increase in demonic activity in the world – especially in spiritual things since that seems to be their present target.

38 DEMONS IN THE EPISTLES (2)

THE INVISIBLE WAR

Twice in his letter to the Ephesians, the apostle Paul connects our spiritual battle to unseen forces. Demons, unclean spirits, are also unseen forces that the Christian must reckon with. Reminding believers of their preconversion state, Paul wrote, "As for you, you were dead in your transgressions and sins, in which you used to live when you followed the ways of the world and of the ruler of the kingdom of the air, the spirit who is now at work in those who are disobedient" (Eph. 2:1, 2). What is Paul saying here? He is saying that these people were once under the control of Satan and the demons; that this same spirit continues to control the lives of those who disobey God.

Satan, of course, is the "ruler of the kingdom of the air." The Jews of Jesus' day knew that the devil was the "prince of demons" (Matt. 9:34; 12:24; Mark 3:22). Christ called Satan the "prince of this world" (John 16:11). The apostle John testified that "the whole world is under the control of the evil one" (1 John 5:19). How does Satan do this? How has he corralled mankind?

The Bible teaches that Satan is extremely active in seeking to destroy the souls of men. When the devil presented himself before God in the days of Job, God asked him, "Where have you come from?" (Job 1:7). His reply: "From roaming through the earth and going back and forth in it" (Job 1:7; 2:2). From our Lord's teaching on demons, we know that Satan is not the only one who roams the earth. Jesus said that the unclean spirits wander through arid places, seeking rest, that is to say, human embodiment (Matt. 12:43). The devil and his demons are our unseen enemies – powers of the air.

Weymouth's translation of Ephesians 2:2 is interesting: "The prince of the powers of the air, the spirits that are now at work in the hearts of the sons of disobedience." Merrill F. Unger comments,

> It seems evident from Scripture that the activity of demons is so intimately and inseparably bound up with their prince-leader that their work and his is identified rather than differentiated. Thus the earthly ministry of our Lord is described as going about "doing good, and healing all that were oppressed of the devil" (Acts 10:38). It is obvious, even from a cursory examination of the facts, that this so-called oppression of the "devil" was largely the work of his emissaries and servants, the demons. Doubtless, very crucial cases of temptation (Matt. 4:1; Luke 22:3; 22:31) are the direct task of Satan himself, but since he is neither omnipresent, omnipotent, nor omniscient, the greater part of this colossal activity must be thought of as delegated to demons (*Biblical Demonology*, p. 69).

In view of all this, Paul warns the Christian about "The Invisible War" in Ephesians 6:11-13. "Put on the full armor of God so that you can take your stand against the devil's schemes. For our struggle is not against flesh and blood, but against rulers, against the authorities, against the rulers of this dark world and against the spiritual forces of evil in the heavenly realms. Therefore put on the full armor of God, so that when the day of evil comes, you may be able to stand your ground, and after you have done everything, to stand." What else can Paul be referring to if not the wicked angels and evil spirits? Most commentators see the "rulers and authorities" ("principalities and powers," KJV) as varying ranks of Satan's fallen angels (see Rom. 8:38; 1 Cor. 15:24; Eph. 1:21; 3:10; Col. 1:16; 2:10, 15). Satan himself, of course, is the ruler of this world (John 12:31; 14:30; 16:11), the god of this world (2 Cor. 4:4). He is behind all the wickedness in the world, especially of those who have abused authority. The "spiritual forces of evil in the heavenly realms" are probably referring to demons although it could include the unholy angels as well. Both unholy angels and demons seek to separate believers from Christ (Rom. 8:38).

What a battle is being waged for the souls of men! "The Invisible War" continues. Kenny Boles says,

> The battle of the ages takes place in the "heavenly places." We cannot see or hear the battle, but we can certainly feel it going on within us, and around us. The demons of hell throw themselves into the battle with total abandon, knowing they have nothing more to lose. We must face our foe with total conviction, knowing we have everything to gain (*Thirteen Lessons on Ephesians*, p. 100).

In order to fortify ourselves against:

RULERS
AUTHORITIES
POWERS OF THE DARK WORLD
AND SPIRITUAL FORCES OF EVIL IN THE HEAVENLY REALMS

Paul advises us to put on the "full armor of God," which includes:

THE BELT OF TRUTH
THE BREASTPLATE OF RIGHTEOUSNESS
FEET SHOD WITH THE PREPARATION
OF THE GOSPEL OF PEACE (KJV)
THE SHIELD OF FAITH
THE HELMET OF SALVATION
AND THE SWORD OF THE SPIRIT,
WHICH IS THE WORD OF GOD
AND TO PRAY IN THE SPIRIT ON ALL OCCASIONS.

Truth, righteousness, the gospel, faith, salvation, the Bible and prayer are our weapons of warfare in this ongoing spiritual struggle with Satan, his angels and demons, "The Invisible War." Truly, it is the "war to end all wars." And if we take our stand, we will win!

THINGS UNDER THE EARTH

Another reference to the spirit world in the epistles is Paul's comment to the Philippians concerning "things under the earth." Here is the statement in full. "Therefore God exalted him to the highest place and gave him the name that is above every name, that at the name of Jesus every knee should bow, in heaven and on earth and under the earth, and every tongue confess that Jesus Christ is Lord, to the glory of God the Father" (Phil. 2:10, 11).

The Twelve were commissioned to cast out demons "in the name of Jesus" (Mark 16:17). When the 70 returned from their mission, they were ecstatic. "Lord, even the demons submit to us in your name" (Luke 10:17). The apostle Paul cast a demon out of a young girl "in the name of Jesus Christ" (Acts 16:18), but when the sons of Sceva tried to do the same thing, using the precious name of Jesus like some talismanic word, they themselves were severely beaten by a demoniac (Acts 19:13-16).

Did demons confess the name of Jesus when our Lord was upon the earth? Yes, many times (Mark 1:24; 3:11; 5:7; et al). Did demons "bow the knee" to Jesus? When the Gadarene demoniac saw Jesus, "he ran and fell on his knees in front of him" (Mark 5:6). Sometimes it is difficult to determine from the text what a demoniac was doing or saying on his own as opposed to what the demon within was doing or saying. One thing for sure: on the Day of Judgment, every knee will bow and every tongue will confess. Won't that be something? Lifelong atheists and antichrists, bowing before Jesus and confessing His name! Even Satan will experience this ultimate humility before being cast into hell.

Every knee should bow before Jesus and every tongue should confess that Jesus Christ is Lord. God has sworn by Himself that this will take place (Isa. 45:23). Paul repeats this solemn statement (Rom. 14:11). Whom does this include?

1. It includes *angelic beings*: everything "in heaven." All the angels at one time bowed before Jesus. Then came the great angelic rebellion. The angels that kept not their first estate were cast out of heaven (Jude 6; Rev. 12:8). The holy angels continued to worship and serve the Lord. But all angels will eventually bow before Jesus and confess His holy name. Not that this will somehow "redeem" the angels that sinned. They will be cast into hell, along with their master, Satan (Matt. 25:41).

2. It includes *human beings*: everything "on earth." We were created in His image (Gen. 1:26), "predestined to be conformed to the likeness of his Son" (Rom. 8:29). Some have submitted to the Lordship of Christ and are striving to be like Him. The majority of mankind, however, has chosen to "do their own thing." Jesus wants us to confess Him to our salvation (Matt. 10:32; Rom. 10:9, 10) but many have refused. What will happen to men who refuse to acknowledge Christ in this life? "For we will all stand before God's judgment seat. It is written: 'As surely as I live,' says the Lord, 'Every knee will bow before me; every tongue will confess to God.' So then, each one of us will give an account of himself to God" (Rom. 14:10-12). This will not be confession unto salvation but confession unto condemnation.

3. It includes *demonic beings*: everything "under the earth." The Abyss, the unseen abode of the wicked dead, comes from the Greek word *abussos* meaning "bottomless." The King James Version translates this word "the bottomless pit." W. E. Vine defines it as follows:

> It describes an immeasurable depth, the underworld, the lower regions, the abyss of Sheol. In Rom. 10:7, quoted from Deut. 30:13, the abyss (the abode of the lost dead) is substituted for the sea (the change in the quotation is due to

> the facts of the Death and Resurrection of Christ); the A. V. has "deep" here and in Luke 8:31; the reference is to the lower regions as the abode of demons, out of which they can be let loose, Rev. 11:7; 17:8; it is found seven times in the Apocalypse, 9:1, 2, 11; 11:7; 17:8; 20:1, 3; in 9:1, 2 the R.V. has "the pit of the abyss." (*Vine's Expository Dictionary of Old and New Testament Words*, Vol. 1, p. 142).

Demons, whose proper abode is in the Abyss – a dark and forlorn place deep in the bowels of the earth – will some day stand before God, bow the knee to Christ, confess His divine name and then be cast into that place they have dreaded for centuries (Matt. 8:29).

THE COSMIC TRIUMPH

Paul declares that the cross of Christ vanquished forever the powers of the demonic world. "And having disarmed the powers and authorities, he made a public spectacle of them, triumphing over them by the cross" (Col. 2:15). Some link this verse to the "parade from paradise," when Christ ascended into heaven, "leading captivity captive" (Eph. 4:8). That may be. The verse may also be referring to the spell of doom sounded to Satan and his helpers (John 12:31; Heb. 2:14).

William Barclay comments on this verse as follows:

> One other great picture flashes on the screen of Paul's mind. Jesus has stripped the powers and authorities and made them his captives . . . . Jesus conquered them for ever. He stripped them; the word used is the word for stripping the weapons and the armour from a defeated foe. Once and for all Jesus broke their power. He put them to open shame and led them captive in his triumphant train. The picture is that of the triumph of a Roman general. When a Roman general had won a really notable victory, he was allowed to march his victorious armies and the leaders and the peoples he had vanquished. They were openly branded as his spoils. Paul thinks of Jesus as a conqueror enjoying a kind of

> cosmic triumph, and in his triumphal procession are the powers of evil, beaten forever, for every one to see (*The Letters to the Philippians, Colossians, and Thessalonians*, p. 143).

The cross routed the powers of evil. C. Fred Dickason comments,

> The cross also disarmed demonic control of the believer in Christ. When Christ had stripped evil forces of their power, "He made a public display of them, having triumphed over them" (Col. 2:15, NASB). Not only does the cross cancel man's debt to God, but through it the powers that held men captive are themselves openly defeated and led in triumphal march. Christ thoroughly routed and publicly embarrassed Satan and demons so that men would never have to fear or follow them again (*Angels: Elect and Evil*, pp. 211, 212).

One of the purposes of Jesus' coming to earth was to defeat the work of Satan. "The reason the Son of God appeared was to destroy the devil's work" (1 John 3:8). This was accomplished in His work on the cross. Not only did He forgive men's sins through His shed blood, He freed men from the powers of evil. The cross of Christ brought a cosmic triumph!

DOCTRINES OF DEMONS AND SEDUCING SPIRITS

The primary work of demons in apostolic times is clearly revealed in 1 Timothy 4:1, "The Spirit clearly says that in later times some will abandon the faith and follow deceiving spirits and things taught by demons." Could anything be more plain? The demons, abandoning their futile efforts to stop the work of Christ by attacking men's bodies, now turn their evil energies toward seducing the spirits of men. How do they do this? The next verse yields the answer. "Such teachings come through hypocritical liars, whose consciences have been seared as with a hot iron" (1 Tim. 4:2). What is God saying here? He is telling us that unprincipled men and women, who have sold their souls to Satan, are actually being used by spirits to carry out their wicked work.

Does this mean that the blatant false teachers of our day are actually pawns of demons? It would appear so. The "doctrines of demons" were in fact being taught by reprobates. What a hellish thing! Human beings – who knew they were teaching falsehood – teaching other human beings – who were not aware that such teaching was demonic in origin. The results were equally shocking; some were abandoning the faith. For example, Hymenaeus and Philetus left the truth and were teaching that the resurrection (the keystone to the Christian faith) had already taken place (2 Tim. 2:17, 18). Paul said their teaching was spreading "like gangrene" and that they were destroying the faith of believers. This blasphemous teaching could only be the work of demons. Paul personally delivered Hymenaeus and Alexander (another false teacher) to the source of their ruinous teaching – Satan – that they might learn not to engage in blasphemous teaching any more (1 Tim. 1:20).

Where do blasphemous teachings come from? What is the originating source of such doctrines as celibacy and abstaining from certain meats? The Holy Spirit tells us these doctrines which admittedly, are taught by men in the Catholic system, actually emanate from "deceiving spirits" (1 Tim. 4:1, 3). Don DeWelt comments,

> Are we to understand that those who fall away from the truth do so because they are influenced by supernatural evil powers? We believe it is even so. Satan has his power, and his preachers, and in this sense he is a counterpart, as well as a counterfeit of the true. The "seducing spirits" are from beneath, and are in contact with the "lying teachers." The teaching of such men proceeds from and through "demons." The tragedy is not that we have such hypocrites, for they have always been with us, but that multitudes will give heed to their Satan-inspired doctrines (*Paul's Letters to Timothy and Titus*, p. 78).

THE SPIRITS IN PRISON

Peter mentions "the spirits in prison" in his first epistle (1 Pet. 3:19). Here is the fuller text: "For Christ died for sins once for all, the righteous for the unrighteous, to bring you to God. He was put to death in the body but made alive by the Spirit, through whom also he went and preached to the spirits in prison who disobeyed long ago when God waited patiently in the days of Noah while the ark was being built" (1 Pet. 3:18-20). The American Standard Version (1901) seems to make more sense. Christ, "being put to death in the flesh, but made alive in the spirit; in which also he went and preached unto the spirits in prison . . . ."

The context indicates that the spirits of men who were in prison were those who lived in Noah's day (v. 20). They were exceedingly wicked, "every inclination of the thoughts of his heart was only evil all the time" (Gen. 6:5). In fact, they were so wicked that God determined to wipe them from the face of the earth (Gen. 6:7), which thing He did in the great flood. The bodies of these wicked people perished in the flood (Gen. 7:21-23). But what of their spirits? The Bible teaches that the spirits of the wicked dead go to a place of awful suffering and torment (Luke 16:22, 23). Hades, the unseen abode of the dead, had two compartments in Jesus' day. It was divided by a great chasm (Luke 16:26). One place, Paradise, was where Christ's spirit went when He died. He promised the penitent thief, "I tell you the truth, today you will be with me in paradise" (Luke 23:43). Paradise is a place of comfort and rest (Luke 16:25), very much like heaven. Tartarus (2 Pet. 2:4) is the place of anguish and suffering (Luke 16:24). This is where the spirits of the wicked dead from Noah's day were incarcerated.

We do not believe that Jesus went to this place of suffering. That His spirit went to Hades at death cannot be denied (Acts 2:27; Rom. 10:7; Eph. 4:9, 10). That He went to Tartarus and suffered could and should be denied. Jesus said He was going to Paradise (Luke 23:43) and that is where His spirit went at death. The suffering that Christ accomplished was on the cross, not in Hades. Furthermore, we do not believe that Christ visited the compartment of suffering in His three-day stay in Hades. Such would violate Jesus' own teaching on Hades and the great gulf: "And besides all this, between us and you a great chasm has been fixed, so that those who want to go from here to you cannot, nor can anyone cross over from there to us" (Luke 16:26).

How, then, did Jesus, in the spirit, preach to the spirits in prison (i.e., Tartarus)? Is it unthinkable to say that He spoke to them in the same way that Abraham spoke to the lost rich man? Abraham, according to Luke 16:25, 26, 29, 31, addressed the rich man in Tartarus from his vantage point in Paradise. Could not Jesus have addressed the spirits in prison in the same way?

Why would Jesus want to preach to the spirits in prison? What did He preach to them? The Bible does not say. We do not believe that our Lord preached the gospel to them, that He offered an *invitation* to be saved. There is no second chance after death (Heb. 9:27). But we do believe that His message may have been one of *vindication*. Christ was justified or vindicated in the spirit (1 Tim. 3:16).

TESTING THE SPIRITS

The last reference to demons in the epistles that will be considered is John's command to "test the spirits." "Dear friends, do not believe every spirit, but test the spirits to see whether they are from God, because many false prophets have gone out into the world" (1 John 4:1).

A group known as the "Gnostics" were claiming to have superior knowledge in spiritual matters (the Greek *gnosis* means "to know"). They were troubling the Christians of John's day with their false teaching about the person of Christ. This teaching they were promulgating was coming from demons. Demons, ("knowing ones") are far too intelligent and crafty to attack the deity of Jesus Christ.

They know that He is the Son of God and often confessed the same (Mark 1:24; Matt. 5:29). So what did these "knowing ones" do? They inspired a group of men who were claiming superior knowledge to attack the humanity of Christ – to say that Jesus Christ never actually appeared in the flesh! "This is how you can recognize the Spirit of God: Every spirit that acknowledges that Jesus Christ has come in the flesh is from God but every spirit that does not acknowledge Jesus is not from God. This is the spirit of the antichrist, which you have heard is coming and even now is already in the world" (1 John 4:2, 3).

The demons love to "spiritualize" Jesus. The Bible view of Jesus that He is God in the flesh (Isa. 7:20; 9:6; John 1:1, 14; Phil. 2:6, 7; 1 Tim. 3:16). The spirits deceive men into thinking He did not take on flesh. If there was no incarnation, there could be no suffering in the flesh on the cross. If there was no death on the cross, there would be no atonement. "Without the shedding of blood there is no forgiveness" (Heb. 9:22). No incarnation? No atonement! No atonement? No forgiveness of sins! Any church, preacher or person who does not believe in the incarnation of Christ is "antichrist" and should be shunned at all costs.

John tells us to "test the spirits." How can we do this? A spirit does not have flesh and bones (Luke 24:39). How can we test these nefarious, nebulous beings? If we can't see them, how in the world can we test them? It is true that a spirit cannot be seen nor heard. But their oracles can be seen and heard. John connects these deceiving spirits with false prophets (1 John 4:1). Spirits do not have flesh and bones but their mouthpieces, the false prophets, do. Demons assail the person and work of Christ through those false teachers who deny that Jesus was the incarnate son of God. The way Christians could "test the spirits" was by asking specific questions about the person and work of Jesus Christ to those who were casting doubt on His incarnation, atonement, resurrection, etc. The early church had "discerners of spirits" (1 Cor. 12:10). They could immediately identify doctrines of demons. Today we have the perfect, completed Word of God by which we can measure all doctrines, oral or written. We are to continue steadfastly in the apostles' doctrine (Acts 2:42). When you are familiar with the apostles' doctrine, you will be able to recognize the demon's doctrines. Our Federal Bureau of Investigation has a unique way of training people to recognize counterfeit money. Trainees handle only genuine bills. That way, when a piece of counterfeit money comes into their hands, it is instantly recognized. Why? Because it does not have the distinctive marks of the genuine. God's Word is truth (John 17:17). When we are conversant with truth, error will be readily recognized. "We are from God, and whoever knows God listens to us; but whoever is not from God does not listen to us. This is how we recognize the Spirit of truth and the spirit of falsehood" (1 John 4:6).

In his second epistle, John sounds a similar warning concerning teachers who have been deceived by demons. He tells his readers how they can recognize them and what to do about them. The advice is good for us today. "Many deceivers, who do not acknowledge Jesus Christ as coming in the flesh, have gone out into the world. Any such person is the deceiver and the antichrist. Watch out that you do not lose what you have worked for, but that you may be rewarded fully. Anyone who runs ahead and does not continue in the teaching of Christ does not have God; whoever continues in the teaching has both the Father and the Son. If anyone comes to you and does not bring this teaching, do not take him into your house or welcome him. Anyone who welcomes him shares in his wicked work" (2 John 7-11). Such teachers are themselves deceived by demons. How can they help but deceive others? They are the true "antichrist" – forget the sensational ideas modern writers and filmmakers have about "the Antichrist." Also be careful that you don't lose your eternal reward by being sucked in by the cults. Stay with the Word of God. Continue in the apostles' doctrine. Those who will not agree with the Biblical view of the person and work of Christ must be rejected. Do not welcome them into your home or send them on their way with support, whether verbal or financial. The work they are engaged in is wicked, demonic, of the devil. Demons are alive and well on planet earth. Our streets and sidewalks should have warning signs: *"Caution: spirits at work!"*

39 DEMONS IN THE BOOK OF REVELATION

Demons are a Biblical topic from beginning to end. We find them in the first book of the Bible – Genesis –the dark and evil force behind idolatry. We are not surprised to discover their unholy presence in the Apocalypse, or Revelation. It is a matter of fact that demons meet their predicted doom in this book (cf. Matt. 8:29; Mark 5:7; Luke 8;:28; Rev. 14:10; 20:10). More than that, the presence and activity of demons is seen both in transpired history and, possibly, events yet to come. Merril F. Unger writes, "The prominent demonology of the Apocalypse strongly implies a powerful demonic influence and inhabitation" (*Biblical Demonology*, p. 81).

There are a number of passages in Revelation that refer to demons or demon-related practices (Rev. 9:1-21; 16:13, 14; 18:2, 23; 21:8; and 22:15).

INTERPRETING REVELATION

The problem we face, as always, is how to interpret Revelation. There are about as many interpretations to this book as Baskin-Robbins has flavors of ice cream.

> In the main the various types of exposition of the Revelation reduce themselves to four. The *preterist* view regards the prophecies as wholly concerned with the circumstances of John's day, having no reference whatever to future ages. The *historicist* interpretation construes the visions as a preview of history from the time of the writer to the end of the world. The *futurist* explanation places the

> relevance of the visions entirely at the end of the age, largely divorcing them from the prophet's time. The *poetic* view considers all hard and fast canons of interpretation to be illegitimate; the prophet simply describes, by means of his powers of artistry, the sure triumph of God over all evil powers.
>
> Liberal scholars largely endorse the Preterist view and repudiate the predictive elements of the book; many, however, accept as valid the principles of God's moral government which lie at the root of the prophet's teaching. The Reformers generally adopted the Historicist view. They identified the persecuting power with papal Rome. Rigidly interpreted, however, this view seems to be contrary to the analogy of all other prophecy in the Bible. The Futurist view was that of the earliest centuries of the Church and is widely held by evangelical Christians today. In its popular form, however, it is open to serious criticism, in that the historical setting of the book is almost wholly ignored. Indeed, it is often said that John wrote the Revelation not for his own age but for the Church of the end time. Hence the book is made to yield information and ideas such as the prophet had never dreamed of. Vagaries of this sort drive many readers to value the book solely from an aesthetic viewpoint, denying that it ever had a specific occasion in view (*The New Bible Commentary*, pp. 1168, 1169).

Great care should be taken in trying to interpret the passages on demons in Revelation. Scholars of the Restoration Movement, B. W. Johnson notably, have taken the Historicist viewpoint. This is the type of exposition the author was schooled in although he has considerable leanings toward the Poetic view. He likes the carefully worded statement of Adam Clarke, a Bible commentator of bygone years who leaned to the Historicist explanation. After commenting on Rev. 9:1-20, the able expositor wrote:

> These things may be intended, but it is going too far to say that this is the true interpretation. And yet to express any doubt on this subject is with some little else than heresy. If such men can see these things so clearly in such obscure prophecies, let them be thankful for their sight, and indulgent to those who still sit in darkness (*Clarke's Commentary*, Vol. VI, p. 1003).

With this in mind, let's look at the references to demons in the book of Revelation.

THE RISE OF ISLAM AND THE UNREPENTANT ROMAN CHURCH

The ninth chapter of Revelation opens with the fifth angel sounding his trumpet. A star falls from heaven. A key is given to the fallen star. It is the key to the Abyss (Rev. 9:1).

The star uses the key to open the Abyss. Smoke ascends from the Abyss, blotting out the sun. Emerging from the dense smoke are frightful locusts. Scorpion-like power is given to them (Rev. 9:2, 3).

The locusts are commanded not to hurt the grass, trees or any green thing on earth. They are allowed, however, to hurt those who do not have the seal of God on their foreheads. They cannot kill those people but are permitted to torment them for five months. Those tormented seek death but are not able to find it (Rev. 9:4-6).

The terrible looking locusts (Rev. 9:7-10) have a king over them. He is called the angel of the Abyss. His Hebrew name is Abaddon; the Greek, Apollyon (Rev. 9:11).

After the sixth angel sounds his trumpet, four angels who have been kept bound at the Euphrates river are released to kill a third of mankind (Rev. 9:14, 15). Those not killed stubbornly refuse to repent of their sins. They continue to worship demons, practice idolatry, commit murder, sorcery, fornication and theft (Rev. 9:20, 21).

What are we to make of this strange story? Most commentators who take the historical view of Revelation (like Matthew Henry, Adam Clarke, Albert Barnes, B. W. Johnson) see the rise of Islam in the fifth angel's trumpet and the unrepentant state of the Roman church in the sixth angel's trumpet.

The fallen star is thought to be Mohammed, "a leader, a military chieftain, a warrior" (Barnes), "the devil's turnkey"

(Henry). Christ, of course, holds the key to death and Hades (Rev. 1:18) but it appears that the key is here temporarily given to this fallen star to loose the evil forces in the Abyss. The star uses the key to open the Abyss, the proper abode of demons. The smoke that emerges is "false doctrine" (Clarke). Barnes states that the origin of the plague is demonic in nature. Demon locusts emerge to bring great trouble upon the earth. "The whole of this symbolical description of an overwhelming military force agrees very well with the troops of Mohammed" (Clarke). Barnes devotes several pages to this interpretation. The king of this "hellish squadron" (Henry) is thought to be Satan. It is either he or Christ who gives the demons their command. The Bible does not really make clear who the command comes from. The "five months," or 150 days, is taken to mean 150 years, a day often representing a year in some expositor's minds. Johnson's notes are interesting here:

> Though Mohammed's work began earlier, it was in A. D. 632 that the Arab hosts burst forth from their deserts to assail the world. Within a hundred years Palestine, Syria, Mesopotamia, Egypt, the north of Africa, and Spain had fallen beneath their sway. In 762, the capital of the Saracen Empire was placed at Bagdad and their rulers began to cherish peaceful ideas. In 781, the Caliph Haroun Al Rashid was their ruler. This is the golden age of the Saracen Empire. This is the era of the Arabian Nights. Bagdad was called the "City of Peace." How long is this from the time when the torment that had stricken half the world began? In A. D. 632, the Arabs assailed the nations, to which date one hundred and fifty years may be added. This would bring us to 782, the second year of Haroun Al Rashid's reign. Did the torment continue longer? Nay. He was engaged in friendly correspondence with the Christian rulers of Europe, and from this time the Saracens ceased their efforts to make the world Mohammedan. Their aggressive wars were forever ended (*The People's New Testament With Notes*, Vol. 2, pp. 450, 451).

The sixth angel's trumpet is seen by Clarke as the desolation brought upon the Greek Church by the Ottoman

Turks, who "entirely ruined that Church and the Greek empire." The church that remained was the Latin or Western church, "which was not at all corrected by the judgements which fell upon the eastern Church, but continued its senseless adoration of angels, saints, relics, etc., and does so to the present day." To which Johnson adds:

> This remarkable prophecy is still more exact. The reader cannot fail to note the particularity of its language. The four angels were prepared for a work that was to last last an hour, and a day, and a month, and a year, or as we have found, a period of three hundred and ninety-six years and four months, lacking a few days, from the time when they entered upon their work and crossed the Euphrates! Who can note this exact correspondence of the time with that predicted by the prophet and yet remain in doubt? (*A Vision of the Ages*, pp. 108, 109).

Johnson, like other historicists, sees the remaining Roman church as unrepentant. He asks six questions: Did they worship demons? Did they worship images? Did they engage in murder? Did they engage in sorcery? Did they commit fornication? Did they practice theft? Let's consider the charges found in Rev. 9:20, 21.

1. *Demon worship.* Barnes sees the worship of saints (departed spirits) in the Romish church as a "complete fulfillment" of this passage. "Homage rendered to the spirits of departed men, and substituted in the place of worship of the true God, would meet all that is properly implied here." He points us to the practice of praying to the saints, especially the virgin Mary. Demonolatry and Mariolatry are thus condemned.

2. *Idol worship.* Demons, of course, are the dark dynamic behind idolatry. Johnson cites the second general Council of Nicaea (787 A. D.) in which the worship of images was unanimously pronounced "agreeable to Scripture and reason."

3. *Murders.* Barnes documents the bloody story:

> . . .fifty millions of Christians have perished in these persecutions of the Waldenses, Albigenses, Bohemian Brethren, Wycliffites, and Protestants; that some fifteen millions of Indians perished in Cuba, Mexico, and South America, in the wars of the Spaniards, professedly to propagate the Catholic faith; that three millions and a half of Moors and Jews perished, by Catholic persecution and arms, in Spain; and that thus, probably, no less than sixty-eight millions and five hundred thousand human beings have been put to death by this one persecuting power (*Barnes' Notes on the New Testament*, p. 1633).

4. *Sorcery.* Henry calls to attention the charms, magical arts and rites of exorcism. Clarke and Johnson mention the bleeding images of Christ and Mary, children seeing apparitions, miraculous cures. "Hardly a month passes but the press records some pretended miracle. True, when examined, they are found to be tricks . . . but the superstitious masses receive them with unquestioning faith" (*A Vision of the Ages*, p. 110).

5. *Fornication.* Barnes comments, "It is as unnecessary as it would be improper to go into any detail on this point. Any one who is acquainted with the history of the Middle Ages – the period here supposed to be referred to – must be aware of the widespread licentiousness which then prevailed, especially among the clergy" (*Barnes' Notes on the New Testament*, p. 1633). Henry sees it as both "spiritual and carnal impurity."

6. *Theft.* Clarke sees this as the exactions and impositions made upon men for indulgences and pardons. Henry says that by these unjust means they have heaped together a vast deal of wealth, to the "injury and impoverishing" of families, cities and nations. Johnson mentions in particular Tetzel's indulgences in Germany.

SORCERY IN REVELATION

In addition to the mention of sorcery in Revelation 9:21, we find a number of companion references to this forbidden practice of the magical arts. In Revelation 18:23 Babylon (probably a veiled reference to Rome) has her doom announced. Included in a list of her sins is sorcery: ". . . for by thy sorceries were all nations deceived" (Rev. 18:23 KJV). Sorcery, like the dark power behind it, is a great deceiver.

In chapter 21, God lists those who will have their part in the lake of fire: "the fearful, and unbelieving, and the abominable, and murderers, and whoremongers, and sorcerers, and idolaters, and all liars" (Rev. 21:8 KJV). Hell is the price one must pay for practicing the magical arts.

The last chapter of Revelation also mentions sorcerers in a negative context. The Bible records those who will not be allowed into the holy city: "For without are dogs, and sorcerers, and whoremongers, and murderers, and idolaters, and whosoever loveth and maketh a lie" (Rev. 22:15 KJV).

ANTECEDENTS OF ARMAGEDDON

In the 16th chapter of Revelation, the sixth angel with the sixth bowl pours out his bowl upon the Euphrates river. The waters are dried up to prepare the way for the kings from the east (Rev. 16:12).

John then sees three frog-like evil spirits come out of the mouths of the dragon, the beast and the false prophet (Rev. 16:13). John identifies them as "spirits of demons" who will perform miraculous signs. They go out to the kings of the whole earth and gather them together for the battle of the great day of God (Rev. 16:14).

Unger describes this as the "last awful demon-energized, anti-God coalition at Armageddon" (*Biblical Demonology*, p. 69). Whatever it may be, demons are certainly the power behind this frightening scene.

At this point we cite Johnson at great length:

> The reader will observe that, before the seventh vial is poured out, there is an alliance of three powers described as the dragon, the beast, and the false prophet. From their mouths came three unclean spirits, like frogs, who go forth to the kings of the earth, rally their forces under the banners of the three allied powers, and march them to the battle of the great day of the Almighty. And the hosts join battle in a place called in the Hebrew tongue, Armageddon.
>
> I wish the reader to understand that in venturing upon this portion of Revelation, I do so as one who goes through a dim, mysterious and untraveled country. Thus far I have been writing of the past, and I have asked my reader to tread with me the solid ground of history . . . . But in this application we have now reached the year 1881. (Author's note: B. W. Johnson was writing these words in 1881, 36 years before the Bolshevik Revolution in 1917!) The gathering of the dragon, the beast, and the false prophet, belongs to the future. It is unfulfilled prophecy, and of the meaning of the unfulfilled prophecy we should always speak with modesty . . . .
>
> Yet, in the interpretation of this passage we are furnished with solid ground where we can place our feet. The dragon and the beast are symbols that have already been identified. All Protestant commentators are agreed that the dragon is a symbol of old, persecuting, imperial Rome, and that the beast represents the no less tyrannical and persecuting power of Papal Rome.
>
> Here a difficulty arises concerning one of these powers. Papal Rome still exists, but imperial Rome, once the mistress of the world, is gone forever. How then can the dragon appear in a conflict that is yet future? It cannot appear as imperial Rome, but it may appear as some great despotic power of kindred character, representing its work and spirit (*A Vision of the Ages*, pp. 178, 179).

Johnson, citing Milligan and other "judicious commentators," proceeds to Ezekiel 38 and 39 where he linguistically interprets Magog to be Russia, Meshech to be Moscow, etc. He states:

> I think that these facts clearly show that Ezekiel marks

> Russia as one of the powers destined to take part in the battle of Armageddon. In despotic form of government, in extent of dominions, in ambition, in military power, it more fitly represents imperial Rome than any other modern State, and since it is definitely described by Ezekiel, we are justified in regarding it as the revived imperial despotism symbolized by the dragon (*A Vision of the Ages*, p. 180).

Again, we stress that Johnson was writing this in 1881, 36 years before the Bolsheviks came to power in Russia. Certainly no "despotic" form of government today[1] rivals Russia in dominion, ambition and military power. If nothing else, Johnson is to be posthumously congratulated for his remarkable political perceptivity!

We continue to quote Johnson:

> Two of the powers that enter into the conflict can now be conjectured, viz: Russia, the great modern secular despotism, and the spiritual despotism of Rome, symbolized by the beast. These are not at present in union, but they will unite . . . . Papal Rome in the zenith of her power would have disdained an alliance with the eastern church, but in the humiliation brought upon her by the pouring out of the vials she will stretch out her hands for help . . . (*Ibid.*, p. 180).

Johnson here foresees a coming coalition between Russia and the Roman church or, as we would say today, Communism and Catholicism.

> The third power described as the false prophet, remains to be identified. The reader will note two facts: 1. The sixth vial treats the fall of the Turkish power. We have not yet passed to the seventh vial. The Sultan is the recognized "commander of the Faithful"; the head of Islam. The false prophet represents the Mohametan power; possibly not

---

[1]In the Fall of 1989, three years after the first edition of this book appeared (1986), cracks began to appear in the Iron Curtain. Today (1995), the collapse of Communism in the former Soviet Union and in Eastern Europe seems nearly complete.

> under the Sultan, but still existing. It is the religion of "The Prophet," as his disciples term Mohomet; of the false prophet, as the rest of the world suppose. 2. By turning to Ezekiel we find that it is stated that Persia, Ethiopia and Lybia with them, are joined in the conflict. These are the very countries that are peopled by Mohametans . . . .
>
> ...after the drying up of the Euphrates there will be a grand alliance of secular despotism led by Russia, spiritual despotism embodied in Papal Rome, and false religion as exemplified in Mohametanism. Their aim will be to check the progress of "political and religious freedom and the gospel of Christ (*Ibid.* pp. 180, 181).

Again we must pause to congratulate Johnson on his keen insight into the future.

Johnson now moves toward Armageddon:

> If this is a literal conflict of arms the place where it will take place is probably indicated. Possibly the conflict will be moral and spiritual, but if not, it is of interest to know where this great conflict will be fought. It is at a place. The place would therefore probably be found where the Hebrew tongue was spoken, and where the Jews were wont to bestow Hebrew names upon places. . . . The place named is not only Hebrew, but is a famous spot in Hebrew history. Armageddon means simply the Hill Megiddo. Upon the hill Megiddo was fought the battle in which King Josiah was slain. It was in the midst of the battle-ground of Israel. The plain of Esdraelon, the depression between Judea and Galilee, was tracked with armies. Philistines, Midianites, Syrians, Assyrians, and Egyptians contended with each other and with Israel. Upon this plain arose the hill of Megiddo. It may be that the last conflict before the fall of Babylon and the ushering in of the Millennium will be upon this ancient battle ground. If Ezekiel 37:8-17 is understood literally it signifies that Palestine shall be the theatre of this struggle, but of all these passages I am inclined to believe that they have a spiritual signification. The Israel of Ezekiel represents the church, the true Israel. Armageddon, the battle-ground of Israel, is used metaphorically to describe the great conflict of the Israel of God (Ibid., pp. 181, 182).

The antecedents of Armageddon – Communism, Catholicism and Islam – are inspired by the dark and evil forces of demonism. That is the gist of Rev. 16:13, 14. Their doctrines, whether political or religious, are false, inspired by demons. Their miracles, real or supposed, are the work of unclean spirits who seek to seduce the souls of men. The power and influence of demons will be great in the last days.

FALLEN BABYLON: A HAUNT FOR DEMONS

The 18th chapter of Revelation opens with an angel coming down from heaven. He has great power and authority. The earth is lit up by his glory and radiance (Rev. 18: 1).

He cries mightily with a loud voice, "Fallen! Fallen is Babylon the Great! She has become a home for demons and a haunt for every evil spirit . . ." (Rev. 18:2). The balance of the chapter contains the angel's dirge upon Babylon.

The historicists see Babylon as Papal Rome. Her fall, which had been predicted (Rev. 16:19; 17:16) now transpires. The picture is one of utter desolation. Even the historicists see this section of Scripture as one modeled on the doom songs of the Old Testament. Compare Isaiah 13:19-22, which is a doom song of ancient Babylon's fall from power and glory. Barnes comments:

> The idea is that of utter desolation; and the meaning here is, that spiritual Babylon – Papal Rome (chap. 19: 8) – will be reduced to a state of utter desolation resembling that of the real Babylon. It is not necessary to suppose this of the city of Rome itself – for that is not the object of the representation. It is the Papacy, represented under the image of the city, and having its seat there. That is to be destroyed as utterly as was Babylon of old (*Barnes' Notes on the Old Testament*, p. 1699).

The fall of Babylon will be so great that the demons will haunt the ruins where their power had once been so significant.

40 DO DEMONS EXIST TODAY?

Is the spirit world still active today? Do demons still exist? These questions can be answered in one word: "Yes." We believe that demons continue to do their evil work in the world.

Again, at the risk of boring the reader, we make our appeal to the Word of God. It matters little what you or I or anyone else says or thinks about the continuing existence of demons. If God in His Holy Word intimates that the spirit world is still at work, that should satisfy even the most skeptical mind. And God has much to say about the presence and power of demons in our world.

A BRIEF REVIEW OF BIBLICAL DEMONOLOGY

That demons existed in Old Testament times is not to be denied. Ample evidence can be found in the pages of the Old Testament to authenticate demonic presence and activity. Men consulted spirits (Exod. 22:18; Lev. 20:6; 1 Sam. 28:7) and worshiped demons (Lev. 17:7; Deut. 32:17; Psa. 106:37).

Nowhere in Scripture is the presence of demons felt more keenly than in the synoptic gospels. Matthew, Mark and Luke all record the powerful presence and wicked work of unclean spirits during the time of our Lord's earthly sojourn. Nor did demons cease their work during the days of the early church and the apostles. Before He ascended into heaven, Jesus charged the apostles to continue the work of driving out demons (Mark 16:20). The inspired record says they did (Mark 16:20). The book of

Acts cites several instances of demons being cast out by the followers of our Lord: Peter (Acts 5:16); Philip (Acts 8:7); and Paul (Acts 16:18). Sorcerers were still around. Simon (Acts 8:9-24) and Elymas (Acts 13:6-11) are two that are mentioned by name. Demons still possessed people (Acts 5:16; 8:7; 19:12, 16) and people still consulted the spirit world through diviners (Acts 16:16).

In the New Testament epistles we continue to read of their presence, power and perfidy. Such warnings as 1 Timothy 4:1-3 and 1 John 4:1-6 are not to be taken lightly by those of us who claim to continue steadfastly in the apostles' doctrine. Is Satan still alive and well on planet earth? Has he somehow obtained omnipresence so that he can be everywhere or does he continue to rely upon unclean spirits and fallen angels to carry out his wicked work? Are we to believe that he no longer has these hellish helpers? Such thinking would be absurd. Angels and demons still seek to disqualify us from the heavenly prize (Rom. 8:38) and our battle is still against unseen, unclean forces (Eph. 2:2; 6:12).

The last book of the Bible, Revelation or the Apocalypse, does not overlook the presence of demons. Revelation is largely a book of prophecy, written about things in the future, both near and far. We cannot take these references to demons lightly. John did not. By inspiration he recorded them (Rev. 9:20, 21; 16:14; 18:2).

POST-APOSTOLIC EVIDENCE

Although the evidence is not nearly as weighty as Biblical proof, the church fathers wrote of the existence and work of demons in their day. Justin Martyr, Tertullian, Cyprian, Origen, Clement of Alexandria, and Eusebius are but a few post-apostolic writers who verified the reality of demons in the days of the post-apostolic church.

Merrill F. Unger answers well the argument that demons no longer exist.

> That demon possession by no means ended with New Testament times is irrefutably proved by the witness of early Church history. The Epistle of Barnabas (13:19) represents the heart full of idolatry as the abode of demons. The Shepherd of Hermas (circa 120) contains considerable philosophy of demon possession. Justin Martyr views the phenomenon as due to inhabitation by the souls of the departed dead, and expulsions were almost as common to the contemporaries of Tertullian and Minucius as to the contemporaries of Jesus. Belief in demons and demon possession have persisted throughout the entire Christian era to the present day, and authenticated cases of expulsion have, from time to time, been adduced (*Biblical Demonology*, pp. 81, 82).

WHAT ABOUT ZECHARIAH'S PROPHECY?

Some people – even ministers of the Word – claim that demons no longer exist. How ironic. The devil would like nothing better than to get people – especially Christians – to believe that his hellish helpers are no longer around. Surely people in such an "enlightened" era as ours wouldn't continue to believe in the existence of demons, would they? To this we answer, "Yes." Just because some have distorted the idea of demons with their wild and fevered imaginations is no reason to jettison the Bible's teaching on demonology.

Many of these well-intentioned non-believers go to a prophecy in the Old Testament for support that demons no longer exist. "And it shall come to pass in that day, saith Jehovah of hosts, that I will cut off the names of the idols out of the land, and they shall no more be remembered; and also I will cause the prophets and the unclean spirit to pass out of the land" (Zech. 13:2 ASV).

"See?" non-believers say. "The Bible says that demons would pass out of the land."

Let's look closer at the context and meaning of Zechariah's prophecy. The prophet opens this chapter with a wonderful prediction about the long-awaited redemption of man: "In that day there shall be a fountain opened to the house of David and to the inhabitants of Jerusalem, for sin and for uncleanness" (Zech. 13:1). Nearly all Bible commentators are agreed that this is a prophecy about man's redemption through the shed blood of Jesus. What is the fountain? What else can it be but the riven side of our Lord (John 19:34)? William Cowper beautifully wrote,

There is a fountain filled with blood,
Drawn from Immanuel's veins;
And sinners, plunged beneath that flood,
Lose all their guilty stains.
E'er since by faith I saw the stream
Thy flowing wounds supply,
Redeeming love has been my theme
And shall be till I die.

To whom was this fountain opened? "To the house of David." The gospel was to go to "the Jew first" (Rom. 1:16). To whom else? "And to the inhabitants of Jerusalem." Were they not the first to hear the glorious message on Pentecost (Acts 2:5)? Why was this fountain to be opened? "For sin and for uncleanness." Why did Jesus shed His blood? "This is my blood of the covenant, which is poured out for many for the forgiveness of sins" (Matt. 26:28). What did Peter tell those noble Jews on the day of Pentecost? "Repent and be baptized, every one of you, in the name of Jesus Christ so that your sins may be forgiven. And you will receive the gift of the Holy Spirit" (Acts 2:38). Christ's blood, met in baptism (Rom. 6:3, 4), would wash away their sins. God's Holy Spirit would come into their lives, expelling the unclean and unholy presence of Satan.

Did idols and unclean spirits totally vanish from the scene on the day of Pentecost? While it is true that the presence and work of unclean spirits were greatly diminished after the death of Christ, we can in no way say they completely disappeared for the divine record states otherwise (see Acts 5:16; 8:7; 16:16; 19:12; 1 Cor. 10:20;

12:10; Eph. 2:2; 6:12; 2 Thess. 2:2; 1 Tim. 4:1; Jas. 2:19; 1 John 4:1; Rev. 9:20; 16:14; 18:2).

Furthermore, Zechariah said that the name of idols would be cut off in that day. And that false prophets would also pass out of the land. Did they? Have they? Idolatry was still rampant in Paul's day – even the worship of demons (1 Cor. 10:20). False prophets made their evil inroads – even into the church (2 Pet. 2:1 et al.). Are we to believe that only the demons ceased to exist? What did Zechariah mean? It seems reasonable to believe what he was predicting was a great moral reformation that would take place in the lives of those who turned to Christ for forgiveness. Those who had been bound by idolatry, false teaching and unclean spirits would no longer be "held in sin's dread sway." Idolatry, falsehood and unclean spirits have long existed on the earth and will continue to do so until Christ comes. But no longer would they reign in the hearts of true believers. Clarke notes, "Satan shall have neither a being in, nor power over, the hearts of sincere believers in Christ" (*Clarke's Commentary*, Vol. IV, p. 793).

Zechariah's prophecy does not prove that demons no longer exist – period. It does prove that no sinful or unclean power has dominion over the baptized believer in Jesus Christ!

This passage "exhibits the two grand doctrines of the gospel – justification and sanctification. The grace of the Spirit of Christ is needed for the latter, as the virtue of the blood of Christ is needed for the former . . . . Blood was needed for atonement . . . . the Spirit was required for sanctification . . . when Christ died the fountain was opened in reality . . . this cleansing was to be marked by moral reformation . . ." (*The New Bible Commentary*, p. 760).

TWO MODERN EXTREMES

Today we are faced with two extremes regarding the reality of present-day demons. One extreme takes the position that there are no demons today. What is their reasoning? Frankly, because it is neither *fashionable* nor *rational* to believe in such "superstitious" things. This group – many of whom accept the reality of demons in Biblical time – base their belief (or non-belief) in demons on pure rationale. "We are rational beings. It isn't rational that demons would continue to exist in our world today." Oh? How rational is our world today? It seems that there is an awful lot of irrational behavior going on in our society – abortion, child abuse, wife beating, murder of family members by family members, torture, dismemberment, pornography, drugs, alcoholism, perverted musical lyrics, violent and obscene books, movies and television programming. What, or more properly, who is responsible for such weird and wicked behavior?

The other extreme sees a demon under every bed. Those obsessed with demons see demons in everything imaginable, from scanning devices in your local supermarket and transistor chips to the Bilderbergers and the Trilateral Commission. While Satan's demons are behind much of the evil in our world, they are not the cause for everything that is new, different or difficult to comprehend (like the computer with which this book is being written).

Both of these extremes are to be avoided by the concerned child of God. The subject of Biblical demonology suffers at both ends of this spectrum.

THE CASE FOR DEMONS TODAY STATED

What, then, are we to believe? Do demons really exist today? Yes! How do we know? Because of two reasons: (1) the evidence in the Word of God; (2) the evidence in the world of Satan. The Bible knows nothing of the idea that demons suddenly dropped out of the picture. Demons, like the angels, have not been recalled by their master. Satan still relies on them to get his rotten work done. How do we know? The New Testament tells us so.

Paul warns about the fleshly work of witchcraft (Gal. 5:19, 20). A witch is "one who knows." They consult the "knowing ones," demons. Witchcraft and sorcery abound today. Paul also sounds the alarm on "counterfeit miracles" (2 Thess. 2:9-11). Are we still not plagued with supposed miracles such as weeping or bleeding statues, *stigmata*, faces of Jesus or Mary appearing in mundane places, and the modern tongues movement? Paul adds that both angels and demons continue to try and divorce believers from God and Christ (Rom 8:38).

James, the brother of our Lord, states that demons continue to believe in the deity of Christ and tremble (Jas. 2:19). Paul declares that the spirits now work in the hearts of the disobedient (Eph. 2:2, Weymouth) and that our spiritual battle with unseen entities continues as it has for ages (Eph. 6:12). He describes three groups that will one day bow the knee to Jesus and confess His holy name: angelic beings, human beings, demonic beings (Phil. 2:10). Would any deny the continued presence of angels? Would any be so foolish as to debate the ongoing presence of humans? Then why deny the reality of demons in our modern world?

Perhaps the greatest Scriptural evidence for the continuance of unclean spirits is the apostolic admonitions found in 1 Timothy 4:1-3 and 1 John 4:1-6. Here solemn warnings are sounded concerning false teachings that are the direct results of seducing spirits and deceiving demons. Why does falsehood have such a prominent place in the world today? Why has it made such deep inroads into the church? Jessie Penn-Lewis writes that it is urgent for the church in the 20th century to recognize the powers of darkness:

> For this the Christian Church must recognize that the existence of deceiving, lying spirits, is as real in the twentieth century as in the time of Christ, and their attitude to the human race unchanged. That their one ceaseless aim is to deceive every human being. That they are given up to wickedness all day long, and all night long, and that they are ceaselessly and actively pouring a stream of wickedness into the world, and are satisfied only when they succeed in their wicked plan to deceive and ruin men (*War on the Saints*, p. 33).

The second witness to the continuity of spirits is the veritable floodtide of abominable and inhuman things that are happening every day all around us. As the aged apostle wrote, "The whole world is under the control of the evil one" (1 John 5:19). How else can we explain the ungodly, unbelievable things that are going on? Take the Bible in one hand and a daily metropolitan newspaper in the other hand and you will have the twin evidences for the ongoing, continuing activity of demons in our world. Satanism. The cults. Witchcraft. Pornography. Drugs. Violence. Nudity. Illicit sex. Torture. Murder. Abortion. "Mercy" killings. Child abuse. Wife beatings. Parents killing children. Children killing parents. Mates killing mates. The list could go on and on.

To this we could add the testimonies of those who work on the mission field. And that of converted spiritists. These people know the awful reality of demons in our world. Whether we like it or not, there really are demons in our world today!

41 CAN A CHRISTIAN BE POSSESSED BY DEMONS?

Is it possible for a child of God, a baptized believer in Jesus Christ, to ever be possessed by the evil spirits of the devil? This question has caused a great deal of concern and consternation among some. The concern is real, even if the chances of such happening are not. It is for those who have been troubled over this question that this chapter is included. God wants us to know the answer to this troubling question. There are really three concerns that should be dealt with, two of which are often mistaken for demon possession. Those three concerns are:

1. Demon possession.
2. Demon obsession.
3. Demon oppression.

DEMON POSSESSION

First, the Bible teaches that a Christian, a baptized believer who has the Holy Spirit of God dwelling within, cannot be possessed by an unclean spirit of Satan. This is not to say that believers in Christ before their conversion to Christ were not possessed of demons. Before she began to follow Christ, Mary Magdalene was the victim of multiple demon possession. She was afflicted with seven demons which our Lord expelled (Mark 16:9; Luke 8:2). The man largely responsible for evangelizing the Decapolis was once terribly possessed by unclean spirits – a "Legion" of them (Mark 5:1-20). Even Simon the sorcerer "believed and was baptized" (Acts 8:13) and continued with the disciples for a time. That he backslid is evident; that he was taken over by demons once more is not. There is no indication in Scripture that anyone, once they became a Christian and lived according to the dictates of the Holy Spirit, was ever possessed by demons.

How can we be sure that Christians cannot be invaded by demons? To begin with, our Lord taught that in order for a power to take over a person's being, that power had to subdue the power present within that person (Matt. 12:29). Demons could enter people at will (but only with God's permission) because He who was greater, the Holy Spirit, was not yet given to men at large. Although demons represent a mighty power source, Satan, the Holy Spirit of God is far greater. "You, dear children, are from God and have overcome them, because the one who is in you is greater than the one who is in the world" (1 John 4:4). In the context, the people whom the children of God were able to overcome were the demon-inspired false teachers (1 John 4:1). The one who was in them was the Holy Spirit. Those who were in the world were the spirits of Satan. A child of God who has the Holy Spirit cannot be infiltrated by demons.

But what about Judas? What about Ananias and Sapphira? Weren't they believers? Didn't the devil get into their lives? Yes, he did. How was this possible?

Ananias and his wife Sapphira were members of the church in Jerusalem (Acts 4:31-5:1). Having obeyed the gospel, they must have received the Holy Spirit for He is promised to all who obey (Acts 2:38; 5:32). But the Holy Spirit can be grieved by the attitudes and actions of believers (Eph. 4:30). He can even be resisted (Acts 7:51). In fact, the Bible teaches that the work of the Holy Spirit can be quenched (1 Thess. 5:19). Just because they were Christians didn't mean Satan was going to leave them alone. When did he come to Jesus? Immediately after His baptism (Matt. 3:16; 4:1). There are two voices calling to us in the world: the voice of God and the voice of Satan. Which one will we listen to? heed? obey? This man and woman chose to listen to the temptation of Satan. They lied to the Holy

Spirit (Acts 5:3). The Holy Spirit's pleadings went to naught. He was resisted, He was lied to, He was grieved, He was quenched. Man has the power of choice. Just as Adam and Eve made a bad choice, so did another husband and wife, Ananias and Sapphira.

This story shows how important it is to be filled with the Holy Spirit (Eph. 5:18), to walk in the Spirit, to live in the Spirit (Gal. 5:26). Otherwise, we are fair game for the devil. Ananias and Sapphira had the Holy Spirit in their lives but did not live according to His wishes. Let every born-again believer take heed.

In the case of Judas, does not John 13:2 say that Satan put the idea to betray Jesus into his heart? And does not John 13:27 say that Satan entered Judas? Yes, to both questions. But what does this prove? Only that an unspiritual person is easy prey for the devil's ploys. Judas was not a "Christian," as we use the term today. True, he was chosen by Christ but only "that the scripture might be fulfilled" (John 17:12; 18:9; Psa. 109:8; Acts 1:20). Judas was an insensitive soul, a thief who often embezzled money from the treasury of the Lord and the apostles (John 12:6). Surely anyone in that woeful condition is fair game for the powers of darkness.

We like what Don DeWelt says about the impossibility of demons possessing believers:

> We need to be reminded that no mention is ever made of the presence of the Holy Spirit coinhabiting the same person with a demon or demons. There is no record of demon possession and Holy Spirit possession in the same person. We do not wish to minimize the power of the evil one nor ignore the attack on Christians by demons, but we emphasize once again: demons and the Holy Spirit do not live in the same person. If you have the Holy Spirit (and you do if you are a Christian, Romans 8:9), then you cannot be possessed by demons. You can be sorely vexed and tempted but not possessed (*The Power of The Holy Spirit*, Vol. 4, p. 449).

DEMON OBSESSION

Demonic possession is frighteningly real. Demon *obsession* can be just as frightening, even though the person is not actually possessed by unclean spirits. What do we mean by demon obsession? In demon possession, a person is actually taken over by a demon. In demon obsession, a person is only intrigued with the subject of demonology, Biblical or otherwise. Or, as Ben Alexander, a former spiritualist medium, says, "To be possessed means to be controlled by a demon. The person who is demon obsessed thinks he has a demon but in reality doesn't" (*Demon Possession*, p. 2).

There are a number of ungodly "feeders" that cause people to be obsessed with the subject of demonology. Without a doubt, Satan uses these modern mediums (pardon the pun) to aid his unholy cause. The Bible warns us not to be ignorant of his devices (2 Cor. 2:11).

1. One of these demonic devices is *novels* which glorify and glamorize the world of the occult. A cursory glance at today's bestsellers reveals an alarming number of books that feature the occult – demonism, exorcism, witchcraft, Satanism. Such literature, if we can even use that term here, is filled with explicit sex and violence – twin products of demonism. How can anyone possibly feed his mind on such books and not be adversely affected? "For as he thinketh in his heart, so is he" (Prov. 23:7 KJV). We are what we think. If we are subjecting ourselves to such trash, we will soon become obsessed with it. Thousands are obsessed with demons because of these best-selling novels. Children of the King will not feed on Stephen King!

2. Another Satanic device is *movies* and *television programs* that focus on occult practices. Many of these movies or television specials are taken from books on demonism such as Ira Levin's *Rosemary's Baby* and William Peter Blattey's *The Exorcist*. Hollywood is able to intensify the horror of the demon world with all kinds of clever and horrible artistry. Many people who view these films go

away thinking they are possessed by evil entities. Untold psychological damage has been done to the masses, especially children, who view such movies. The Bible says, "I will set before my eyes no vile thing. The deeds of faithless men I hate; they will not cling to me. Men of perverse heart shall be far from me, I will have nothing to do with evil" (Psa. 101:3, 4). That should be the believer's response to what Hollywood offers.

3. Certain *musical lyrics* are demonic in origin and cause demon obsession. It has been said that "Music soothes the savage beast." That is certainly true. Young David was able to soothe King Saul's troubled spirit with lovely music from his harp (1 Sam. 16:16-23). But music can also create savage beasts. That is because the source of "inspiration" behind it is demonic. Several of the recording artists in the rock music field are admittedly deeply involved with the spirit world. Their songs herald the prince of darkness, Satan. Drugs, sex, violence – even suicide – are the twisted themes of some rock songs. Drugs, sex, violence and suicidal mania cannot be separated from demonism. Just a fleeting glance at the music video industry is enough to convince any spiritual person that demons have invaded the dark, demented world of modern rock music.

4. There are several *table games* which should be avoided at all cost, especially by young people. Ben Alexander calls the Ouija Board, Parker Brother's best-selling "game," "the gateway to the occult." Alexander testifies,

> There is actually no power in the board or tripod itself, but the power is in the person who allows those of the spirit world to control him. The Ouija board is definitely the doorway to spiritualism and the occult practices. People start by playing with a Ouija board; then they begin experimenting with automatic writing (when the spirit uses a person's hands to write messages). Soon they are ushered into the very depths of the occult. Using the Ouija board is practicing a form of divination – the art of obtaining secret information from the spirit world – and could be called a type of seance ("Spiritualism: Satan's Tool," *The Lookout*, Jan. 20, 1980).

God's Word strictly forbids contact with the spirit world (Deut. 18:10-12; Lev. 19:31; 20:6, 27; 1 Chron. 10:13, 14; 2 Kings 21:6, 23:24; Isa. 8:19, 20, etc.). Another table game, "Dungeons and Dragons," has been called "America's most popular form of sorcery today." As many as 4 million people, mostly teenagers and young adults, play D & D. The "game," responsible for over two dozen killings and suicides, is inseparably linked with the vile world of demons and encourages simulated torture, strangulation, human sacrifice, assassination, sadism, curses of insanity and other forms of violence among its participants. Some people, unfortunately, are literally fulfilling these demonic fantasies.

5. The dark world of demons has even reached its evil fingers into the world of small children through *toys* and *television cartoons.* One day my wife and I were doing some shopping in a toy store in a large shopping mall. We could not believe the sinister figures on the "toy" shelves. Witches, wizards, lizards with darting tongues and evil eyes. Nearly naked "heroes" and "heroines," supposedly representing the forces of good. These are America's children's heroes? No wonder we have a growing problem with violence. Just a glance at the television screen on Saturday morning will reveal the inroads demonism has made in the "cartoons." Bugs Bunny and Porky Pig these are not! One minister bemoaned the fact that the children in his congregation bring their weird toys with them to Sunday School instead of their Bibles. And some people think we don't have a problem! The real problem is delinquent parents who are failing to monitor their children's selection of toys and cartoons.

In addition to such things as movies, television programs, music, plays, games and literature, Charles R. Swindoll warns of "actual occult practices":

> Those things which bring with them demonic contact: black magic, astrology, fetishes and talismans, fortune-telling, seance meetings, witchcraft, palmistry, spiritism, ESP (estra-sensory perception), pictures of witches and

occult propaganda, voodoo dolls, candles with occult significance, incense, excessive superstition, religious practices that highlight the emotional, cults, Satan worship, tarot cards, and related occult practices *(Satan . . . The Occult*, pp. 12, 13).

DEMON OPPRESSION

Third, there is demon *oppression*. What do we mean by this term? Christians are oppressed – harassed and harried – by the demons of Satan. They throw themselves against us with everything hell has to offer. They seek to hinder our spiritual growth and development. Even the great apostle Paul was hindered by Satan on several occasions (1 Thess. 2:18; Rom. 1:13; 15:22). He once wrote that he was "pressed on every side" (2 Cor. 4:8 ASV). He cautions us to remember that our battle is not against flesh and blood but against unseen and unclean powers (Eph. 6:12).

Time out for a personal testimony. Even in the writing of this book, I have sensed the opposition of spirits. There have been times when the desire was not there to write. Or there was confusion as to what to write. It was often difficult to concentrate or organize thoughts. Why? The devil and his crowd do not want their work exposed. It became necessary to wrestle in prayer, asking God for strength and help, praying in the Spirit for wisdom and power.

Many concerned Christians have experienced similar things. Take prayer for example. Every believer knows we should pray more often and with more fervency. We all could, too. We have more leisure time today than ever before. There are more pressing needs to pray about than ever before. So, why don't we pray? Because of demonic oppression. The devil doesn't want Christians to pray. He trembles at the sight of the weakest saint on his knees. The devil knows the power of prayer. He and his wicked cohorts will do everything in their power to prevent us from the "sweet hour of prayer."

Demonic oppression also diminishes our efforts to read and study God's Word. There are times when we just don't feel like reading the Bible. Who put that feeling there? Certainly not God. God wants us to read His Word. The devil and the demons, knowing what it says about them and what it can do for a sincere believer, stymie our efforts at Bible study. God's Word gives light and understanding (Psa. 119:130). That is the last thing in the world the world rulers of darkness want us to have. They love darkness and want to keep us in the dark (2 Cor. 4: 4). The believer must learn to discipline himself or herself when tempted not to read the Bible. Such oppression is from beneath the world.

Christians are also oppressed by the spirit world to not try and win people for Christ. How many times have Christians given in to this wicked oppression? We know that there are people that should be talked to about Christ. We know that they are lost without Him. We believe that we have the truth that can save them and set them free. But something holds us back. What is it? Fear. The Bible tells us that God has not given us that spirit of timidity (2 Tim. 1:7). Then who has? Satan and his spirits. Because of their wicked injection of fear into our lives, we often do not attempt to win people for Christ. What a tragedy!

Many teachers and preachers have experienced first-hand the dulling effects of demons. Sometimes it is extremely difficult to study or prepare a lesson or sermon. Sometimes there is just no desire to do so. Other times, there is a sense of hesitancy to really teach and preach the full counsel of God. Who is responsible for this drain of desire and zeal? You guessed it. The last thing on earth that demons want is for souls to hear a clear presentation of the gospel. They seek to discourage Bible teachers and preachers from making the proper preparation and the powerful presentation that the gospel deserves.

Entire families can be oppressed by the evil world of demons. They seek to separate family members from each other. Husband-wife relationships are often stormy. Parent-child relationships are adversely affected. Even the children have spats with one another. This, assuredly, is not God's plan for the home. His plan is wonderfully spelled out in such Scriptures as Ephesians 5:21-6:4. Satan ruined the first family on earth (Gen. 3:1-4:15) and he will not be satisfied until he ruins the last family unit on planet earth. His wicked workers, the demons, seek to oppress the Christian home by every means imaginable – including such "innocent" and "harmless" things as certain toys, games, books, music, literature and television programming.

SUMMARY

Spirit-filled Christians cannot be possessed by demons. Those things which can cause demon obsession should be stricken from our lives. Demon oppression can and does happen to Christians. That is why it is so important to put on the "full armor of God" and take our stand against the schemes of the devil (Eph. 6:10-18).

42 WHAT ABOUT "EXORCISM"?

What is exorcism? Did Christ and the apostles practice exorcism? What about those who claim to exorcise men of demons today? Can a Christian cast out demons?

EXORCISM DEFINED AND DISTINGUISHED

First, let us understand what exorcism was and is. Webster says to exorcise is to "expel by adjuration." Exorcism is "a spell or formula used in exorcising." Etymologically, the word means to cast out evil spirits by means of incantations, conjurations, spells or other means of magical rites. In this sense, Jesus was *not* an exorcist. Our Lord did not resort to such means in driving out demons. He testified that He did so "by the Spirit of God" (Matt. 12:28).

Nor did the disciples of Jesus drive out demons by means of exorcism. They were commissioned to cast out spirits in the name of Jesus Christ (Mark 16:17). Demons submitted to the followers of Christ by the power and authority He gave them. When non-believers attempted to use the name of Christ in driving out demons, they met with dismal failure (Acts 19:13-16). Actually, the word "exorcists" appears only once in Scripture, Acts 19:13 KJV. W.E. Vine defines *exorkistes* as "one who employs a formula of conjuration for the expulsion of demons" (*Vine's Expository Dictionary of Old and New Testament Words*, Vol. II, p. 61). Again, Biblical expulsion of demons did not include such pagan rites.

A lot is heard today about exorcism. The practice has

been exploited in such novels and movies as *The Exorcist* and *The Omen*. The Roman Catholic Church claims its priests can exorcise people of demons. So do many charismatic teachers. They urge us to "claim the authority of the believer" and cast out demons, just like Jesus and the apostles did. If our faith is great enough, according to them, we can heal the sick, drive out demons and even raise the dead! Obviously, we do not subscribe to such teachings.

Proper distinction must be made between exorcism and casting out demons. Both are spoken of in the Bible (although exorcism is mentioned but once) but they are not one and the same. Jesus drove out demons but he never practiced exorcism (casting out spirits by use of magical incantations or spells). He did so by the Spirit of God (Matt. 12:28). Just a word was all it took – "Go" or "Leave" or "Depart." No laying on of hands, no jumping around, no waving a crucifix, nothing like that. Just the word. It was simple and the results were instantaneous and complete. Compare this with the complicated, drawn-out and ineffective efforts of men.

By the same token, those Jesus empowered to cast out demons simply spoke the word. The Twelve were given authority to drive out demons in the blessed name of their Lord. Only once are we told that they failed because that particular kind of demon took more faith, prayer and fasting.

The Seventy were also sent out with the power and authority to cast out demons (Luke 10:1). They returned from their mission with great joy, saying, "Lord, even the demons submit to us *in your name*" (Luke 10:17). That, we believe, is the key to understanding the difference between exorcism and casting out demons. One depends on the use of magic; the other on divine power. Driving out demons by merely involving the name of Jesus, like any other magical formula, is not what God wanted (or wants) men to do. The seven sons of Sceva, professional traveling exorcists, tried to do that and instead of driving out demons were themselves driven out of a house by the demon! Also to be remembered are those at the judgment who will try to convince Jesus that they drove out demons in his name (Matt. 7:22). Jesus will tell these "exorcists" that He never knew them. The name of Jesus is too precious for unbelievers or fast-buck artists to drag around in the muck of modern-day exorcism.

Could exorcists in Biblical times actually cast out demons, even if it was by some other means than the power of God? Perhaps. The magicians of Pharaoh were able to duplicate several of Moses' miracles (Exod. 7:11, 22; 8:7). The devil is God's ape. The power he gives evil men is not as great as God's power but it is powerful enough to deceive men (2 Thess. 2:9-11).

One exception to this rule would be the unknown man who was driving out demons in the name of Jesus and yet was not one of the Twelve (Mark 9:38, 39; Luke 9:49, 50). John and the other apostles thought he should terminate his work because he was not one of them. Jesus said the man was not against them, therefore, he was for them – even if he was not with them in their travels. It appears the man was a believer in Christ, even if he was not a traveller with Him. Whoever the man was, he was both sincere and successful.

CAN CHRISTIANS DRIVE OUT DEMONS?

Are Christians today invested with power to drive out demons? Are we supposed to? Are we remiss in failing to do so? Does God want us to be involved in a "deliverance" ministry? We think not. For one thing, Christians have never been ordered to cast out demons. Those who would argue with this and go to Mark 16:17 for "the authority of the believer" need to read the entire context. Jesus had just rebuked the eleven for their lack of faith (Mark 16:14). When they would begin to really believe that He was the risen Christ, they would be able to drive out demons. It would be a sign that would follow them in their ministry.

Did it? Of course. "Then the disciples went out and preached everywhere, and the Lord worked with them and confirmed his word by the signs that accompanied it" (Mark 16:20). What signs? Driving out demons. And speaking in tongues. And not being harmed by deadly snakes or poisons. And by healing the sick. Why don't the modern exorcists and charismatics claim the power to handle vipers or sip strychnine? Some poor people actually do and pay the ultimate price for their folly.

Should Christians get involved in "deliverance" ministries? Hear Ben Alexander:

> The New Testament not only commands us to preach Christ, but also warns us about the enemies of our souls – demons. They are not to be taken lightly. However, Christians can be sidetracked into making demon exorcism a ministry. They become obsessed with trying to cast out demons. This practice is inconsistent with God's Word. Over the past several years I have listened to exorcists calling every sin and sickness a demon. These so-called deliverance ministers go into churches and tell Christians that if they have certain characteristics they are demon possessed. They call them to the front of the church and begin to cast out demons of cancer, demons of stomach ulcers, demons of diabetes, etc. They start attacking the demons of sins: lust, greed, gossip, lying, homosexuality. The list is endless. Not content with demons of sins and sickness they begin to cast out demons of loneliness, poverty, depression. By the time the exorcist is finished almost every Christian in the church believes he has a demon.
>
> The problem with this type of thinking is that the guilt of sin is removed from the person involved and the blame is placed on the demon. God holds us accountable and personally responsible for our sins (Matthew 15:19). Nowhere does the New Testament say that demon possession is the cause of sin. Neither is all sickness related to demon possession. Most illnesses have no relationship to demons whatsoever. We must avoid two extremes of thinking:
>
> (1) disbelieving that demons exist,
>
> (2) blaming demons for all sins and sicknesses.
>
> . . . The casting out of demons from Christians is not

only unscriptural but very dangerous. Many Christians today are suffering from psychological problems because some zealous person believed he had power to cast out a demon. A man in England, Michael Taylor, was told he had a demon of murder and that he would murder his wife. This he promptly did.

One hears of deliverance ministers working for hours to cast out a demon. Their victim ends up emotionally and physically exhausted. In Acts 16, when Paul commanded a demon to leave, "it came out that very hour." In my ministry almost every week I counsel people who have been told by ministers of the deliverance ministry that they are possessed. It is sad and this foolishness brings Christianity into disrespect. Rather than spend time seeking demons, these people should seek to evangelize the lost. Instead of filling people's minds with demons, they would do far better to fill their minds with the love of Jesus (*Exposing Satan's Power Newsletter*, Vol. XIV, No. 1, Jan.-Feb., 1985).

To the testimony of Ben Alexander we would add the probing questions of a great Bible student, Don DeWelt:

There are four questions we must ask and answer in the present day problem of demon possession: (1) *How do we identify the presence of demons in people?* Are we to define their presence by mere physical observation? If so we could go into the mental institutions and find many who would closely fit the descriptions in the gospels. Are we to then to conclude that all mental sickness is in reality demon possession? This would be a dangerous assumption. Without the ability to "discern spirits" we have no sure way to pinpoint the presence of demons. "Discerning of spirits" is tantamount to mind reading. Can you claim such ability? Our blessed Lord did it. "He needed not that any man should bear witness concerning man for *he himself knew what was in man"* (John 2:25). . . .

(2) *Who gave you the authority to cast out demons?* Our Lord gave such authority to the twelve and to the seventy. Did He give you such power? Please indicate in the New Testament where such prerogatives are available for me. I would *indeed* like power first to *know* (not to guess) demons were present and then get the authority to cast them out . . . .

(3) *Where in the New Testament* (or Old Testament) *do*

we have demons referred to us as "The demon of lying" or "The demon of lust"? This identification runs *down the whole catalog of human failures.* Sickness, not sin, is associated with demons. In the New Testament, man himself is consistently blamed for his sin – not demons. We agree with those who teach that Satan is not omnipresent and therefore must work through evil spirits, or demons. But, demon attack is vastly different from demon possession . . . .

(4) Can you please show me an example (a clear cut, unequivocal example) of one Christian possessed by one demon? Most exorcism today is done by unauthorized persons (at least I do not know who gave them such authority) upon suppositional evil spirits. These evil spirits (?) are identified with sins. Such never appears in the New Testament. The suppositional demons inhabit persons who already have the Holy Spirit living in them, of whom John plainly says – "greater is He (the Holy Spirit) who is in you than he (Satan) who is in the world" (1 John 4:4) . . . (*The Power of the Holy Spirit*, Vol. 4, pp. 463, 464).

HOW ARE PEOPLE TO BE DELIVERED OF DEMONS TODAY?

The former spiritualist Ben Alexander answers this question as follows:

I do not believe that we can cast out demons today. However, there is an exorcist and that is the person of the Holy Spirit . . . . I believe there is a sure cure for demon possession and/or demon obsession. That is: (1) We must pray for that person, (2) we must teach them the Word of God, (3) it is imperative that we give them the Agape love of Christ, and (4) it then depends entirely on the person himself – he has to take the next step that is according to Acts 2:38. Peter said, "Repent, and let each of you be baptized in the name of Jesus Christ for the forgiveness of your sins; and you shall receive the gift of the Holy Spirit."

Deliverance from demon possession is not as complicated as many people make out. The answer to not only demon possession but to all sins is found in obedience to Christ. When one becomes a Christian he receives the gift

> of the Holy Spirit. The Bible tells us in 1 John 4:4 that greater is He (the Holy Spirit) that is you, than he (Satan) that is in the world! (*Demon Possession*, pp. 3, 4).

If any should be found to be possessed by spirits, they can be delivered from demons at the same time – and in the same way – that they are delivered from their sins. We refer not to exorcism but conversion. Mankind is under the curse of sin. All have sinned and continue to fall short of God's perfect standard (Rom 3:23). Sin is what separates us from God (Isa. 59:1, 2). To break God's law is sin (1 John 3:4). All acts of unrighteousness are sin (1 John 5:17). Whoever sins is of the devil who, himself, sinned from the beginning (1 John 3:8). It was for this very purpose that the Son of God was manifested – to destroy the works of the devil (1 John 3:8). When Christ comes in, Satan and his demons must exit!

Our dear Lord promised full and free forgiveness to all who will put their faith and trust in Himself as the Son of God (John 3:16; 3:36; 8:24; 20:31), publicly declare their new-found faith in Christ (Matt. 10:32; Acts 8:37; Rom. 10:9, 10), repent, or turn away from their sins (Luke 13:3, 5; Acts 17:30, 31), and be baptized for the forgiveness of sins (Mark 16:16; Acts 2:38; 22:16). When the Holy Spirit comes into a person's life, the unholy spirits are forced to flee. Jesus taught that whoever sins is a slave to sin but when He sets a man free, the man is free indeed (John 8:34, 36). All those whom Christ freed are free from sin, condemnation and death (Rom. 8:1, 2). Those who have been freed by Christ should take their stand in the liberty that they have been given (Gal. 5:1). Never again should they go back to the sins of the past. Never again should they dabble or traffic in the spirit world. They are now new creatures in Christ, the old life is gone, all things are new (2 Cor. 5:17). By putting on the full armor of God, they can withstand the onslaughts of the devil (Eph. 6:10-18).

To those who may be ruled by sin, self, Satan, the spirits, we say: believe on the Lord Jesus Christ; repent (turn away) from sin; confess with your mouth what you believe in your heart about Jesus; be baptized for the forgiveness of your sins and the gift of the Holy Spirit. And remember, "Everyone who confesses the name of the Lord must turn away from wickedness" (2 Tim. 2:19). Get rid of any and every thing that in any way, shape or form is connected with the spirit world. Those in Ephesus even burned valuable books (Acts 19:19). What shall a man give in exchange for his soul? The devices *of* Satan that once ensnared you must be given up forever.

When Jesus comes, the tempter's power is broken . . . .
for all is changed, when Jesus comes to stay!

43 ATTITUDES TOWARD THE SPIRIT WORLD

We begin to bring this book to a close where we began – by appealing to the authority of the Word of God. What does the Bible say about the kind of attitude we should have toward the spirit world? This is the only safe ground on which to take our stand and we take it without shame or reservation. Everything we believe and practice must be established by a "thus saith the Lord." The Bible is our only rule of faith and practice.

SEVEN ATTITUDES TO DEVELOP

There are at least seven sound attitudes that God wants us to develop toward the spirit world.

1. First, we cannot help but be impressed by the number of times that solemn warnings are sounded in Scripture concerning contact with the spirit world. *In a word, contact with the spirit world is absolutely forbidden.* It is true that the people to whom the commands and warnings were given have long since perished (some, like King Saul, as a direct result of disobeying God's command, 1 Chron. 10:13). But the Old Testament was written so that we might learn and profit from the mistakes and errors others have made (Rom. 15:4; 1 Cor. 10:11). Will we be wise enough to learn or not?

Not only should we fear the God who gave the divine prohibitions, we should also fear the evil powers of darkness that He warns men about. Those who scoff at the idea of demons are, in effect, jeering at the God who inspired the Bible. Would God give such strict warnings about something that was harmless, silly or even non-existent?

2. Not only should we fear to disobey God's warnings about contact with the spirit world, we should avoid the very appearance of evil (1 Thess. 5:22). Anything that is even remotely connected with the world of demons should be avoided at all costs. Some will argue that such things as seances, Ouija boards, "Dungeons and Dragons," certain rock songs and the like are not really connected with demonism. For the sake of argument, let us say they are correct. Nonetheless, we would argue that they certainly have the appearance of evil and therefore should be shunned. A person can take this argument too far and apply it to things that may be ridiculous but it is better to be safe than to be sorry. Are there things that have the overtones of the spirit world, things that smack of Satan? This Biblical principle urges us to avoid those questionable things.

3. At the same time, God's Word cautions us about being too inquisitive of the spirit world. Someone has estimated that 80% of research specialists who study diseases eventually take on the symptoms of that particular disease. This could certainly be true of demonology. That is why we have tried to limit ourselves in this book to Biblical demonology. We should not feel constrained to know every word on the subject of demons but we should know the Word – what the Bible says about demons. There are some things that God would have us remain somewhat ignorant on and this may be one of them. Paul advises, "Have nothing to do with the fruitless deeds of darkness . . ." (Eph. 5:11).

4. Yet, God does not want us to be ignorant of Satan's devices (2 Cor. 2:11). God wants us to know something about what demons are and how they operate. The demons are some of Satan's most effective tools in attacking the work of Christ. The Bible tells us about their nature, characteristics, evil objectives, wicked ways and means. The things we need to know about demons can be found in God's Word. By putting on the helmet of salvation and

taking up the shield of faith, we can be protected against the fiery darts of the wicked (Eph. 6:16,17). By arming ourselves with the sword of the Spirit, the Word of God, we can take the offensive against Satan and his hordes (Eph. 6:17). On one hand God seems to be saying, "Don't be too interested in the spirit world" and on the other hand, "Don't be ignorant of how the devil operates."

5. Certainly God would have us to "try" or "test" the spirits to see whether they are from God or not (1 John 4:1-6). There are many false prophets and false teachers in the world today. How are we to know if their teaching is from God or Satan? The only way we can know for sure is to measure their teachings by the only reliable measuring stick we have – the Word of God. The noble Bereans give us a good example of evaluating what we hear: "They received the message with great eagerness and examined the Scriptures every day to see if what Paul said was true" (Acts 17:11). If people who weren't even Christians yet would investigate the teachings of an *apostle*, shouldn't we who are Christians investigate the teachings of *apostates*?

6. Not only are we to examine the teachings of those who may be inspired by spirits; we are to expose them for what they are when they are found to be "ministers of Satan." Does Satan have his ministers today? Hear Paul: "For such men are false apostles, deceitful workmen, masquerading as apostles of Christ. And no wonder, for Satan himself masquerades as an angel of light. It is not surprising, then, if his servants masquerade as servants of righteousness. Their end will be what their actions deserve" (2 Cor. 11:13-15). Paul further adds that the church is to "expose" them (Eph. 5:11). If the church fails to expose false teachers, the unwary and unknowing are ripe victims for the devil. Without opposition from the church, the kingdom of Satan will continue to grow, even making inroads into the unprotesting church. The church needs to take the offensive in examining and exposing teaching that is nothing more than "doctrines of demons." "Everything exposed by the light becomes visible, for it is

light that makes everything visible" (Eph. 5:14, 15). How far the modern church has strayed from this concept! When Polycarp, the venerable bishop of the church in Smyrna, encountered the Gnostic leader Marcion on the streets of Rome, he was going to pass on without speaking. Marcion stopped him and said, "Don't you know me anymore, Polycarp?" "Yes," answered Polycarp. "I know who you are. You are the first born of Satan!"

7. Last, we need to understand that demons are not content to just oppress us; they, like their master, are out to devour us (1 Pet. 5:8). If we do not develop a militant attitude and posture against our unseen foe, all is lost. We are involved in a last-ditch, aggressive, no-holds-barred battle with the unseen forces of darkness (Eph. 6:12). Now, more than ever, we need to see the importance of being fully equipped to stand our ground.

The devil and his demons know their time is short (Rev. 12:12). They know their fate is fixed (Matt. 25:41). Every day that passes by is a day closer to their doom. Satan has launched a final offensive against God, Christ, the holy angels, the church, you and me. He has pulled out all the stops and is pouring on the coal. What are you and I doing about it? How are we facing this deadly onslaught?

SEVEN PIECES OF ARMOR TO PUT ON

God wants us to be strong through His mighty power (Eph. 6:10). He tells us to put on the "full armor of God" so that we can successfully take our stand against the devil's schemes (Eph. 6:11). Above all, He wants us to understand that our struggle is not human in origin – it is not against "flesh and blood." Wicked people are not our enemy; the world is not our enemy. Our foes are the rulers, authorities, powers of the dark world, spiritual forces of evil in heavenly places – in other words, wicked angels and unclean spirits (Eph. 6:12)! We are involved in "The Invisible War."

So what are we to do? Turn tail and run? Throw in the towel? Wave the white flag of surrender? No! God, in essence, says, "Put on my armor so you can take your stand and win the war!"

First, there is the "belt of truth" to buckle around our waist. This belt (truth) will hold our sheath which, in turn, holds our sword (the Word of God). "Thy word is truth"(John 17:17). The truth will assure us of victory: "the truth shall make you free" (John 8:32).

Second, there is the "breastplate of righteousness" (Eph. 6:14). Note that we are not just to have it but to have it on, or in place. What good does righteousness do if we leave it on the shelf? It must be worn, it must be seen. The breastplate covers a vital area – our heart. Without the righteousness of Christ covering our life, we are nothing, we are vulnerable to the arrows of Satan. We live for Christ because Christ died for us, God imputing His righteousness to us for His sake (2 Cor. 5:21).

Third, our feet are to be fitted with "the readiness that comes from the gospel of peace" (Eph. 6:15). The first Christians were ready to give an answer or defense to any man – even if that man was a burly Roman soldier with a sharp Roman sword held to their throats! Are we ready to share the gospel of peace with those in a sin-sick, war-torn world? We are not just to maintain the church, we are to grow the church as well. New recruits are needed. We are not just to hold the fort; we are to advance the cause!

Fourth, we are to take up the "shield of faith" (Eph. 6:16). With faith as our shield, we can be spared many spiritual wounds from the fiery darts of Satan and his demons. Faith in our dear Lord keeps us from being wounded by the fiery darts of the devil. Faith is the victory that will overcome the world (1 John 5:4). It will also overcome the powers of darkness.

Fifth, we are to take the "helmet of salvation" (Eph. 6:17) and place it on our heads. The head, representing the mind, is another vital spot. One good blow to the head and we are goners. We need to know that we are saved (1 John

5:13), not just "hope so" or "think so." Let us have the assurance of salvation. There is a great battle for the minds and souls of men. Let us have the mind of Christ (Phil. 2:5).

Sixth, we are to unsheathe the "sword of the Spirit," which is the Word of God (Eph. 6:17). So far, all the pieces of armor mentioned are *defensive* in nature. Now we have an *offensive* weapon in our hands – the sword of the Spirit! The devil will flee before the Word of God! Jesus routed Satan with His effective use of Scripture. Three times He said, "It is written" (Matt. 4:4, 6, 10). "Then the devil left him . . . ." (Matt. 4:11). The more you have of God's Word in your heart, the more you will be victorious over Satan. Take the blade to the devil. Slash away the bonds of Satan that hold men in sin. *Use* your sword – don't just polish it and admire it.

Seventh, we are admonished to "pray in the Spirit on all occasions" (Eph. 6:18). How do we think we can win the battle without prayer – the weapon against which there is no defense? Jesus was a man of prayer. The apostles were men of prayer. The early church was a praying church. All the great men and women of God have been people of prayer. Where do we get off thinking that we can have power with men and power with God without fervent seasons of prayer? The devil trembles when he sees the weakest saint on his knees. Think how we could rout the forces of evil if every Christian was a praying Christian!

May God help us to do what He commands in order to win "The Invisible War." *"Put on the whole armor of God so that you can take your stand against the devil's schemes . . . . so that when the day of evil comes, you may stand your ground, and after you have done everything, to stand"* (Eph. 6:11, 13).

44 THE FATE OF DEMONS

The awful fate of the demons is not a pleasant thing to think about but the Bible describes it in vivid detail. Let's look at this matter in closer detail in this final chapter.

DÉJÀ VU

Demons appear to be the unclean spirits of the wicked dead. God, in His sovereign purpose and design, has permitted them to escape the Hadean realm. God can do anything He pleases to fulfill His purpose (Isa. 46:10, 11). One reason the demons fear their future so much is they *have been there before*! The torment of hell will be déjà vu for them.

When a person dies, two things happen. First, the body is buried and goes back to its original element, dust. God told Adam, "Dust you are and to dust you will return" (Gen. 3:19). But man also possesses a spirit. What happens to the spirit when a person dies? Hear wise Solomon: "The dust returns to the ground it came from, and the spirit returns to God who gave it" (Eccl. 12:7).

When the beggar Lazarus died, no mention is made of his burial. His body may have been callously thrown on the garbage heap. Many homeless beggars were treated in such fashion. But his spirit, the real Lazarus, was "carried by the angels" into the presence of Abraham (Luke 16:22). There he was "comforted" (Luke 16:25).

But the rich man was not in comfort. He was in "agony" (Luke 16:25). He, too, had died. Without a doubt his burial was the finest money could buy. But his departed spirit had been consigned to a place of torment – hell (Luke 16:23). This is more properly translated "Hades." Hades was the unseen abode of the dead. It consisted of two places separated by a great chasm (Luke 16:26). The place of comfort was known as Paradise. This is where Jesus told the penitent thief he would be when he died (Luke 23:43).

The other compartment of Hades is Tartarus. It is an awful place where the spirits of the unrighteous dead go at death to await the Judgment and the "real thing" – everlasting hell. Here in this place of torment, the rich man was separated from God, was tormented in flames and suffered unbearable thirst (Luke 16:24).

Peter says that the angels that sinned were sent to Tartarus to be held for the final Judgment (2 Pet. 2:4). Jude adds a similar thought (Jude 6). If demons are actually fallen angels, as some surmise, this would be evidence that the demons know what their fate will be like. They have been in a place very much like hell already. Their future is not bright. How dreadful will be their eternal place of suffering after the Judgment. Little wonder that demons quaked at the sight of Jesus and cried out, "Have you come here to torture us before the appointed time?" (Matt. 8:29). Many of them have "done time" already in the hell-like but pre-hell place, Tartarus. They know its horror, grief and pain. They do not look forward to their "homecoming." In Jesus' day, they even preferred animal embodiment over returning to their former estate. The demons possessing poor Legion cried, "What do you want with me, Jesus, Son of the Most High God? Swear to God that you won't torture me . . . . Send us among the pigs" (Mark 5:8, 12).

WHAT IS HELL LIKE?

Demons greatly fear their future home. And rightly so! The Bible describes the eternal place of suffering where Satan, his angels and the demons shall dwell.

1. *Hell is.* Over 100 times the Bible affirms the existence

of hell. Our Lord said more about hell than any other person in the Bible (see Matt. 5:22,29,30; 10:28; 23:15, 33; 25:41, 46 et al.). Demons do not deny the reality of hell. Why should man be so foolish as to question the existence of hell?

2. *Hell is a place.* Hell is more than a condition or a swear word. Judas, the son of perdition, went "to his own place" (Acts 1:25). That place was not heaven. Heaven is a real place. Jesus said, "I am going there to prepare a place for you, and if I go and prepare a place for you, I will come back and take you to be with me that you also may be where I am. You know the way to the place where I am going" (John 14:2-4). Heaven is a real place. So is hell.

3. *Hell is a place "prepared for the devil and his angels"* (Matt. 25:41). The demons under Satan's control also know that this place of torment awaits them (Matt. 8:29). Satan and his evil helpers will suffer forever in the lake of fire (Rev. 20:10). If fallen man could only realize that God has not appointed them to suffer wrath but to obtain salvation through our Lord Jesus Christ (1 Thess. 5:9). Hell was not prepared with people in mind. This does not mean that some people will not go there (see 1 Cor. 6:9, 10; Gal. 5:19-21; Rev. 21:8; 22:15).

4. *Hell is a place of fire.* Some dispute this arguing that the Bible's references to fire are only symbolic. But this gives little comfort. If fire is symbolic, what does it symbolize? Something much worse than fire? That is even more horrible to think about. Notice these references to the fire of hell in Scripture:

"Everlasting fire" (Matt. 18:8)
"Blazing fire" (1 Thess. 1:7)
"Eternal fire" (Jude 7)
"Fiery furnace" (Matt. 13:42, 50)
"Fiery lake of burning sulphur" (Rev. 21:8)
"The fire is not quenched" (Mark 9:48)

5. *Hell is a place of darkness.* Those who are now in Tartarus dwell in darkness (Jude 6). Darkness can be a terrible thing. The plague of darkness in Egypt was so thick

that it could actually be felt. "The Lord said to Moses, 'Stretch out your hand toward the sky so that darkness will spread over Egypt – darkness that can be felt'" (Exod. 10:21). How much more frightening must be the stygian dungeons of darkness in Tartarus. But worse yet is hell for it is called a place of "outer darkness" (Matt. 25:30). It is a place of "blackest darkness" (Jude 13). Men who cringe at the thought of entering a dark cave where bats fly about should think twice before living in sin so as to be cast into a place of "felt darkness" where demons dwell!

6. *Hell is a place of unearthly sounds.* Jesus said the rich man cried out in agony (Luke 16:24). He also warned that there would be "weeping and gnashing of teeth" (Matt. 25:30). Those who have worked with the wounded and dying (like medics, doctors and nurses) testify to the ghastly sounds that such make. If hell were only eternal screaming, that would be enough to set your nerves on end. If demons "shrieked" before their torment at the sight of Jesus, imagine how dreadful their cries will be in hell.

7. *Hell is a place devoid of rest.* Revelation 14:11 says, "And the smoke of their torment rises for ever and ever. There is no rest day or night for those who worship the beast and his image, or for anyone who receives the mark of his name." Think of it. No rest. Day or night. Forever! The need for rest is all-consuming. Imagine what it would be like to never be able to rest. On top of that is torment. Revelation 20:10 says that the devil will be tormented day and night for ever and ever. This is the ugly fate of Satan, his angels, demons and all who choose to live for the devil instead of God.

8. *Hell is a place of burning thirst.* The rich man, who undoubtedly had quaffed copious amounts of the finest wines in his day, is now reduced to begging a single drop of water from the beggar he had ignored at his gate. "Father Abraham, have pity on me and send Lazarus to dip the tip of his finger in water and cool my tongue, because I am in agony in this fire" (Luke 16:24). Again, if hell were only eternal thirst it would be bad enough.

9. *Hell is eternal.* Dante said a sign should be erected over the door of hell: "Thou who enter this door; leave all hope behind." Why? Because the Bible says that hell is eternal. Jesus called it "eternal punishment" (Matt. 25:46). His brother, Jude, described the "eternal fire" (Jude 7). The devil and his evil agents will be tormented for ever and ever (Rev. 20:10). Never again will they be "loosed" to roam the earth and afflict mankind. Their fate is sealed. Hell is forever. A poet has written:

There is a dreadful hell,
And everlasting pains,
Where sinners must with demons dwell
In darkness, fire and chains.

A WORD TO THE UNSAVED OR UNSURE

There is absolutely no hope for the demons and fallen angels. But this book is not being written *for* demons and fallen angels – it is written *about* them. These words are for people. There are two kinds of people: the saved and the lost. You are in one class or the other. If you are not saved, or do not have the assurance of salvation, the following words are directed to you.

Hell was not prepared with people in mind. It was created for the devil and his angels. Jesus said so (Matt. 25:41). God has not appointed men to suffer wrath but to obtain salvation through the Lord Jesus Christ (1 Thess. 5:9). How is it possible for a person to escape hell and enter heaven? A loving and merciful God has placed a huge roadblock on the road to hell. That roadblock is called the cross. He allowed wicked men to nail His only Son to the cross. A person has to go around the cross to go to hell. Who in his right mind would ever do such a foolish thing?

Christ died for all on the cross for "all have sinned" (Rom 3:23). The wages of sin is death and Jesus paid the supreme sacrifice when He took our place on the cross. The gift that

God offers you and me is eternal life through Jesus Christ (Rom. 6:23).

Here is how eternal life can be obtained:

1. Place your heart-trust in Jesus as the Son of God and the Savior from your sins (John 3:16; 8:24). It is not enough to mentally assent to the facts we find in Scripture about Jesus. The demons believe that Jesus is the Son of God and even confess that He is such. But there is no surrender of their hearts to Jesus. They have sworn allegiance to Satan and will pay the awful price. Believing in Jesus is much more than mentally agreeing with the testimony in Scripture about Jesus. "For it is with your heart that you believe and are justified . . ." (Rom. 10:10). Faith in Jesus is a matter of the heart, not the head.

2. Publicly declare your allegiance to Jesus Christ. Faith in Jesus must not remain in your heart. That is where it starts but not where it should end. "If you confess with your mouth, 'Jesus is Lord,' and believe in your heart that God raised him from the dead, you will be saved. For it is with your heart that you believe and are justified, and with your mouth that you confess and are saved" (Rom. 10:9, 10). Whoever confesses Christ before men will be personally confessed by Jesus before the Father (Matt. 10:32). In the Bible, men made this "Good Confession" before being baptized (Acts 8:37).

3. Turn away from the practice of sin. The Bible calls this "repentance." To repent means to change: to change your mind and, as a result, to change your way of living. The reason Christ died on the cross was because of man's sins. Shall we continue in sin that grace may abound? God forbid (Rom. 6:1, 2). Jesus demands repentance (Luke 13:3, 5). God "commands all people everywhere to repent" (Acts 17:30). Be sorry for your sins. More than that, demonstrate your sorrow by turning away from everything you know to be sin. God demands changed lives.

4. Be immersed in water in the name of Jesus Christ in order to obtain the forgiveness of your sins. What God has commanded, no man has the right to forbid or forbear.

Jesus said, "Whoever believes and is baptized will be saved, but whoever does not believe will be condemned" (Mark 16:16). Is baptism essential to salvation? Jesus said so. So did the apostles. Listen to Peter: "Repent and be baptized, every one of you, in the name of Jesus Christ so that your sins may be forgiven. And you will receive the gift of the Holy Spirit" (Acts 2:38). When a penitent sinner who has confessed the faith he has in his heart about Jesus enters the waters of baptism, he is trusting Jesus to forgive him of all his sins. In baptism, his sins are washed away (Acts 22:16). This is why Peter wrote that baptism saves (1 Pet. 3:21). Not baptism *per se* but the baptism of a penitent believer.

5. Live a life of faithfulness to Jesus. Let us live for Him who died for us. We should serve Christ all the days of our lives out of gratitude for what He did for us on the cross. The early Christians were admonished, "Be faithful, even to the point of death, and I will give you the crown of life" (Rev. 2:10). Those first Christians devoted themselves to a life of worship and service (Acts 2:42). Can you and I do less?

The fate of demons is simply awful to think about. Surely no one in his right mind would choose to spend eternity in hell with them. There is not one good reason why anyone should ever experience the fate of demons. God is not willing that a single soul perish. He wants all to be saved (2 Pet. 3:9; 2 Tim. 2:4). He has made salvation available through Jesus Christ. Believe Him, accept Him, obey Him and be saved. Today!

BIBLIOGRAPHY

Alexander, Ben. *Demon Possession.* Exposing Satan's Power Newsletter, Vol. XIV, No. 1.

———. *Demon Possession.* Joplin: Exposing Satan's Power Ministries, Inc.

———. *Out From Darkness.* St. Petersburg, FL: Miranda Press, 1993.

———. *Ouija Boards.* Joplin: Exposing Satan's Power Ministries, Inc.

———. "Spiritualism: Satan's Tool." *The Lookout*, Jan. 20, 1980.

———. *The Seance.* Joplin: Exposing Satan's Power Ministries, Inc.

Applebury, T. R. *Studies in First and Second Corinthians.* Joplin: College Press, 1971.

Baldwin, Stanley C. *What Did Jesus Say About That?* Wheaton, IL: Victor Books, 1977.

Barber, Burton W. *The Mortality of Man's Body – The Immortality of Man's Spirit.* Ottumwa, IA: Voice of Evangelism.

———. *The Ruin and Redemption of Man.* San Juan, Puerto Rico: P/R Publications.

Barclay, William. *The Daily Study Bible Series* (17 Volumes). Philadelphia: Westminster Press, 1975.

Barker, William P. *Everyone in the Bible*. Westwood, NJ: Revell, 1966.

Barnes, Albert. *Barnes' Notes on the New Testament* (One Volume). Grand Rapids: Kregel Publications, 1962.

Barnhouse, Donald Grey. *The Invisible War*. Grand Rapids: Zondervan, 1982.

Berry, George Ricker. *The Interlinear Literal Translation of the Greek New Testament*. Grand Rapids: Zondervan, 1961.

Boatman, Russell. *What the Bible Says About the End Time*. Joplin: College Press, 1980.

Boles, Kenny. *Thirteen Lessons on Ephesians*. Joplin: College Press, 1980.

______. *Thirteen Lessons on Philippians, Colossians and Philemon*. Joplin: College Press, 1979.

Breese, Dave. *Know the Marks of Cults*. Wheaton, IL: Victor Books, 1978.

Cairns, Earle E. *Christianity Through The Centuries*. Grand Rapids: Zondervan, 1966.

Campbell, Alexander. *Popular Lectures and Addresses*.

Chromey, Rick. *The Ten Most Dangerous Rock Groups in America Today*. Privately published in Norfolk, Nebraska, 1985.

Clarke, Adam. *Clarke's Commentary* (6 Volumes). New York/Nashville: Abingdon Press.

Communicator's Commentary (12 Volumes). Waco: Word Books, 1982.

Cottrell, Jack. *What the Bible Says About God the Creator.* Joplin: College Press, 1983.

Crawford, C. C. *Survey Course in Christian Doctrine*, Vol. I. Joplin: College Press, 1962.

Cruden, Alexander. *Cruden's Complete Concordance*. Grand Rapids: Zondervan, 1964.

Davidson, Stibbs & Kevan. *The New Bible Commentary*. Grand Rapids: Eerdmans, 1968.

Davis, John J. *The Birth of a Kingdom*. Grand Rapids: Baker Book House.

DeHaan, M. R. *The Angels of God*. Grand Rapids: Radio Bible Class, 1967.

Delaney, Terryl. "How Far Is It To Heaven?" *The Chosen People*, April, 1983.

DeWelt, Don. *Acts Made Actual*. San Jose: Old Paths Book Club, 1954.

______. *Paul's Letters to Timothy and Titus*. Joplin: College Press, 1961.

______. *The Power of the Holy Spirit*, Vol. IV. Joplin: College Press,1982.

DeWelt, Don and Johnson, B. W. *The Gospel of Mark*. Joplin: College Press, 1984.

Dickason, C. Fred. *Angels: Elect and Evil*. Chicago: Moody Press, 1979.

Dickinson, Curtis, "The Witch Cult." *The Witness*, Vol. X. No. 8. August, 1970.

Dinwiddie, Richard D. "Two Brothers Who Changed the Course of Church Singing." *Christianity Today*, Sept. 21, 1984.

Dowling, Enos. "With a Song in Their Hearts." *Christian Standard*, May 3, 1981.

Edersheim, Alfred. *The Life and Times of Jesus the Messiah* (2 Volumes). New York: Longmans, Green and Co., 1901.

Eerdmans Handbook to the Bible. Carmel, NY: Guideposts, 1973.

Eerdman, Charles R. *The Epistle to the Hebrews*: An Exposition. Philadelphia: Westminster Press, 1934.

Evans, William.*Great Doctrines of the Bible*. Chicago: Moody Bible Institute, 1939.

Fields, Wilbur. *Thinking Through Thessalonians*. Joplin: College Press, 1971.

Flom, Gary J. *A Biblical Study of Life After Death*. Torrington, WY: Privately published.

Foster, R. C. *Studies in the Life of Christ*. Joplin: College Press, 1995 reprint.

Fudge, Edward. *Our Man in Heaven*. Grand Rapids: Baker Book House, 1974.

Garman, Joe R. *Fifty Fascinating Facts About Angels*. Joplin: American Rehabilitation Ministries.

Garrett, Ouida. "The Ministry of Angels." *Restoration Review,* Dec. 1992.

Graham, Billy. *Angels: God's Secret Agents*. New York: Pocket Books, 1977.

______. *Approaching Hoofbeats*. Waco: Word Books, 1983.

Gray, James Camper and Adams, George M. *Gray & Adams Bible Commentary*. Vol. IV, Matt.-Acts. Grand Rapids: Zondervan.

Gundry, Robert H. *A Survey of the New Testament*. Grand Rapids: Zondervan, 1970.

Halley, Homer H. *Halley's Bible Handbook*. Grand Rapids: Zondervan, 1965.

Hammond, Al. "A Christian Looks at Demons and Psychic Phenomena." *The Lookout*, March, 1968.

Henry, Matthew. *Matthew Henry's Commentary on the New Testament* (10 Volumes). Grand Rapids: Baker Book House, 1983.

Heibert, D. Edmond. *First Timothy*. Chicago: Moody Press, 1957.

Hoven, Victor E. *Outlines of Biblical Doctrine*. Eugene, OR: Northwest Christian College Press, 1948.

Hunt, Donald G. *Simple, Stimulating Studies in the Great Book of Acts*. Ottumwa, IA: Voice of Evangelism, 1984.

Hutson, Dr. Curtis. *Heaven: Bible Answers to Questions Most Often Asked About Heaven*. Murfreesboro, TN: Sword of the Lord Publishers, 1981.

International Standard Bible Encyclopedia (5 Volumes). Chicago: The Howard-Severan Co., 1930.

Irvine, Wm. C. *Heresies Exposed*. New York: Loizeaux Brothers, Inc., 1951.

Jackson, Wayne. "*Demons* - What Do You Know About Them?" *The Christian Courier*, Vol. XX, No. 2. June 1984.

Jennings, Alvin. *Exorcism*. Ft. Worth: Star Publications.

Johnson, B. W. *A Vision of the Ages: Lectures on the Apocalypse*. Hollywood: Old Paths Book Club.

———. *The People's New Testament With Notes*. Nashville: Gospel Advocate Company.

Joppie, A. S. *The Ministry of Angels*. Grand Rapids: Baker Book House, 1954.

Josephus, Flavius. *Josephus: Complete Works*. Grand Rapids: Kregel Publications, 1966.

Knowles, Victor. *Of Glory and Shame: An Exposition of I Cor. 11:3-16*. Oskaloosa, IA: Vanguard Publications, 1978.

______. "Angels and Demons: The Cosmic Conflict." Joplin: One Body Ministries, 1994.

______. "Rage for Angels." *Image*, Vol. XI, No. 1, Jan.-Feb. 1995.

______. "The Unpardonable Sin." *Vanguard*, Vol. IV, No. 4, April 1976.

______. *Thirteen Lessons on 1 & 2 Peter*. Joplin: College Press, 1985.

Koffarnus, Richard. "Things That Go Bump in the Dark." *The Restoration Herald*, Vol. LVII, No. 8. September 1983.

Kuiper, B. K. *The Church in History*. Grand Rapids: Eerdmans, 1966.

Lambert, O. C. *Catholicism Against Itself*, Vol. I. Winfield, AL: Fair Haven Publishers, 1963.

Lard, Moses. "Hades, or the Unseen." *Lard's Quarterly*, Vol. II, April 1865.

Lockyer, Herbert. *All the Miracles of the Bible*. Grand Rapids: Zondervan, 1965.

______. *Everything Jesus Taught*. New York: Harper & Row, 1984.

Little, Paul E. *Know What You Believe*. Wheaton, IL: Victor Books, 1979.

Matthew, Paul. *Basic Errors of Catholicism*. Murfreesboro, TN: DeHoff Publications, 1952.

McGarvey, J. W. *New Commentary on Acts of Apostles*. Cincinnati: Standard Publishing.

______. *The New Testament Commentary*. Vol. 1 - Matthew & Mark. Des Moines: Eugene S. Smith.

McGarvey. J. W. and Pendleton, Philip Y. *Commentary on Thessalonians, Corinthians, Galatians and Romans*. Cincinnati: Standard Publishing.

______. *The Fourfold Gospel: A Harmony of the Four Gospels*. Cincinnati: Standard Publishing.

McGee, J. Vernon. *The Unpardonable Sin*. Pasadena, CA: Thru The Bible Books, 1978.

Mead, Frank S. *The Encyclopedia of Religious Quotations*. Westwood, NJ: Revell, 1965.

Miethe, Terry. *A Compact Dictionary of Doctrinal Words*. Minneapolis: Bethany, 1988.

Milligan, Robert. *Commentary on Hebrews*. Nashville: Gospel Advocate Company, 1968.

______. *The Scheme of Redemption*. St. Louis: Christian Board of Publication.

Morgan, G. Campbell. *The Teaching of Christ*. Old Tappan, NJ: Revell.

Nave, Orville. *Nave's Topical Bible*. Byron Center, MI: Associated Publishers and Authors, Inc., 1970.

Needham, Mrs. Geo. C. *Angels and Demons*. Chicago: Moody Press.

Oberst, Bruce. *Letters From Peter*. Joplin: College Press:1962.

Orr, William W. *All About Angels*. Wheaton, IL: Scripture Press.

Penn-Lewis, Jessie (with Evan Roberts). *War on the Saints.* Parkstone, Poole Dorset, England: The Overcomer Literature Trust.

Peretti, Frank. *This Present Darkness.* Wheaton, IL: Crossway Books, 1986.

———. *Piercing the Darkness.* Westchester, IL: Crossway, 1989.

Pulpit Commentary (51 Volumes). New York/London: Funk & Wagnalls.

Reese, Gareth L. *New Testament History: Acts.* Joplin: College Press, 1976.

Shuster, William G. "Critics Link a Fantasy Game to 29 Deaths." *Christianity Today*, May 17, 1985.

Smith, William. *Smith's Bible Dictionary.* Grand Rapids: Zondervan, 1965.

Strong, Augustus Hopkins. *Systematic Theology* (3 Volumes). Chicago/Los Angeles: The Judson Press, 1961.

Strong, James. *Strong's Exhaustive Concordance of the Bible.* New York/ Nashville: Abingdon Press, 1967.

Swindoll, Charles R. *Satan . . . The Occult.* Fullerton: Insight for Living, 1972.

Tyndall, John W. *Why We Have a Devil.* St. Louis, MI: Metropolitan Correspondence Bible College, 1930.

Unger, Merrill F. *Biblical Demonology.* Wheaton, IL: Scripture Press, 1970.

Van Baalen, Jan Karel. *The Chaos of Cults.* Grand Rapids: Eerdmans, 1952.

Vincent, M. R. *Word Studies in the New Testament* (2 Volumes). MacDill AFB, FL: MacDonald Publishing Company.

Vine, W. E. *Expository Dictionary of Old and New Testament Words*. Old Tappan, NJ: Revell, 1981.

Wand, Bernard. *Angels: They're All Around, and They're Watching Over Us*. Boca Raton, FL: Globe Communications Corp., 1994.

Walvoord, John. *The Revelation of Jesus Christ*. Chicago: Moody Press, 1966.

Wilkes, L. B. "Unclean Spirits and Demons." *Lard's Quarterly*, Vol. II, 1865.

Wilson, Dr. Clifford. *Crash Goes The Exorcist*. Melbourne, Australia: Word of Truth Productions, 1974.

Wilson, Seth. *Learning From Jesus*. Joplin: College: Press: 1979.

Zondervan Pictorial Bible Dictionary. Grand Rapids: Zondervan, 1964.

INDEX OF SCRIPTURES: ANGELS

Old Testament
Genesis

Exodus

Leviticus

Numbers

Deuteronomy

Joshua

Judges

2 Samuel

1 Kings

2 Kings

1 Chronicles

Nehemiah

Job

Psalms

Ecclesiastes

Isaiah

Ezekiel

Daniel

Hosea

Micah

Haggai

Zechariah

New Testament
Matthew

(Matthew)

Mark

Luke

(Luke)

John

Acts

Romans

(Romans)

1 Corinthians

2 Corinthians

Galatians

Ephesians

Philippians

Colossians

(Colossians)

1 Thessalonians

2 Thessalonians

1 Timothy

2 Timothy

Titus

Hebrews

(Hebrews)

James

1 Peter

2 Peter

1 John

Jude

Revelation

(Revelation)

(Revelation)

INDEX OF SCRIPTURES: DEMONS

2 Chronicles

Nehemiah

Job

Psalms

Proverbs

Ecclesiastes

Isaiah

(Isaiah)

Jeremiah

Ezekiel

Daniel

Micah

Nahum

Zechariah

Malachi

New Testament
Matthew

(Matthew)

Mark

(Mark)

Luke

(Luke)

John

(John)

Acts

(Acts)

Romans

1 Corinthians

2 Corinthians

Galatians

Ephesians

(Ephesians)

Philippians

Colossians

1 Thessalonians

2 Thessalonians

1 Timothy

2 Timothy

(2 Timothy)

Titus

Hebrews

James

1 Peter

2 Peter

1 John

(1 John)

2 John

Jude

Revelation